The World Book of
hope.

edited by
Leo Bormans

The World Book of
hope.

*The
source of
happiness,
success&
strength*

⊿⊿ | LANNOO

www.theworldbookofhope.com

www.lannoo.com

© 2016 Lannoo Publishers (Tielt, Belgium), Leo Bormans and authors

9789401431354

D/2015/45/440

NUR 740

Editor-in-chief: Leo Bormans

Design: Kris Demey

Photography: Getty Images & Corbis (selection by Kris Demey)

(except for the hopeful projects: own collection)

© Photo Leo Bormans & Kofi Annan: Amrah Schotanus

Editing coordination: Annemiek Seeuws / Lannoo

Text editing: Katie Sherman

Translation English – Dutch: Fred Hendrickx

Translation English – French: Evelyne Codazzi

Translation Bloem, Stalpers, Geldof, De Wachter, Walburg, Krumm: Irene Schaudis

Contents

Welcome to The World Book of Hope

"What do you know about hope?" I asked a friend. He thought for a moment and answered: "I'm afraid of it. I hope I never have to rely on 'hope' as the only thing I've got left." His answer surprised me. But what did I actually know about hope? Little or nothing. I vaguely associated the concept with the **future, desires, and expectations**. With a view in the distance of an unattainable heaven filled with love and happiness. I thought of fear, doubt, and uncertainty, but also of a liberating, positive force. The more people I asked about the meaning of hope, the clearer it became that we all realize how important hope is in our lives, but that we otherwise have few words for it and little insight into what it actually is.

I have already spent several years immersed in the study of happiness and love. For *The World Book of Happiness* and again for *The World Book of Love*, I asked one hundred researchers from around the world to let us in on the secrets of these universal concepts **in a scientific manner**. It was an educational quest that many readers in dozens of countries shared with us. I travel the world in order to talk about these issues and in this way help people and society make progress. Former president of the European Council Herman Van Rompuy even offered *The World Book of Happiness* to all world leaders. Moreover, we have shown on the basis of large-scale university research that small, positive changes can indeed influence our happiness. I thought my work was done. But something kept gnawing at me.

Happiness is the ultimate motive for what we do. If you ask people anywhere in the world why they do the things they do, the answer is often "I want to be happy and contribute to the happiness of my family and friends." We allow ourselves to be guided by many positive emotions, such as gratitude and joy. The highest emotion, however, is *love*. We want to be in love, to love and to be loved. **But what is the motor of our actions?** That turns out to be *hope*. Unhappy people are not the only ones looking for happiness. Lonely people are not the only ones looking for love. It is one of humanity's permanent and universal quests, driven by the power of hope and imagination. But what kind of fuel does that motor need to run?

Once again I traveled the world in search of the best researchers that could provide me with more insights. The **psychology of hope** turns out to be a young, dynamic branch of research. Can we find a universal framework for better understanding and learning to use this powerful human instrument? In this book, one hundred scientists from around the world share what we know about hope. Not fuzzy thoughts, but facts, knowledge based on research gathered from recent experiments or life-long study. They do this in a language that everybody understands.

In this way, they unveil the secret power of hope in study and work, love and relationships, sickness and health, education and health care, prison and freedom, management and leadership, therapy and economy, with young and old... They even show how pessimism can have a positive influence and how, in spite of everything, we can gain from mistakes, traumas, or negative experiences. **Sometimes one door opens only when another has closed.**

Hopeful people are happier, healthier, and more successful. They use their own *will-power* and *way-power*, feel connected and supported. They try not only to survive but also to master—and remain the master of—their actions, their lives, and their futures. This goes much further than optimism, wishing, daydreaming, or self-fulfilling prophecy. Hope is a powerful action, a concrete form of positive anticipation. It is striving with its "sleeves rolled up," a powerful instrument that helps optimists and pessimists alike to become proactive persons who achieve their own goals and have an impact on the world around them. Hope is not just about the future—more than anything, it is about building our resilience in the present.

People differ and people change. But **no one can live without hope.** This book confronts us with the many forms and characteristics of hope. It also teaches us that we can always, more or less, take control of our lives. In that sense, scientific research into the essence of hope is a hopeful experiment in itself.

I would like to thank all the researchers who share their knowledge with us in this book, from the bottom of my heart. A special word of thanks goes to Nobel Prizewinner Kofi Annan, who wrote the first chapter, and to Martha Nussbaum, who finishes the book with a universal and hopeful message.

We live in times of immense and ongoing change. That frightens people. Fear, however, is the worst advisor in all that we do. The best is hope, even in the most difficult circumstances. May this book reinforce your personal source of success, resilience, and happiness, so that you can continue to support, encourage, and inspire others.

Leo Bormans
Author and coordinator of *The World Book of Hope*
www.leobormans.be

P.S.
We have also included **ten hopeful projects** in this book—initiatives that connect and strengthen people through hope. For this reason we have also established the "Hope Prize." If you've had hopeful experiences or developed hopeful initiatives, we invite you to share them at **www.theworldbookofhope.com**.

*I dedicate this book to all the people
in the world who will never read it.*

With special thanks to my parents, Riet, Ine, Kasper,
my family and friends, the many people who support and inspire me,
and all those who work on this hopeful project.

The Power of Hope

"I used to think hope was just a warm, vague feeling. It was that sense of excitement I got before Christmas when I was a child. It lingered a while and then disappeared. Today I have a different perspective. Hope is like oxygen. We can't live without it. It leads to better performances, more success and greater happiness overall. Hope is both the belief in a better future and the action to make it happen. It gives us the power to effect change. We create the future we want for ourselves and others."

Prof. Shane J. Lopez
Gallup senior scientist and one of the world's leading researchers on hope, author of *Making Hope Happen*. University of Kansas.

Learning Hope

Positive emotions about the future include faith, trust, confidence, hope, and optimism. Optimism and hope are quite well-understood. They have been the objects of thousands of empirical studies. And best of all: they can be built. Optimism and hope cause better resistance to depression when bad events strike, better performance at work, particularly in challenging jobs, and better physical health. I have even found that teaching ten-year-old children the skills of optimistic thinking and action cuts their rate of depression in half when they go through puberty.

"How can I be happy?" is the wrong question, because without the distinction between pleasure and gratification it leads all too easily to a total reliance on shortcuts, to a life of snatching up as many easy pleasures as possible.

I am not against the pleasures. But there are strategies under your voluntary control that are likely to move your level of positive emotion into the upper part of your set range of happiness: gratitude, forgiveness, and escaping the tyranny of determinism to increase positive emotions about the past; breaking habituation, savoring, and mindfulness to increase the pleasures of the present; learning hope and optimism through disputing to increase positive emotions about the future.

Prof. Martin Seligman
Director of the Positive Psychology Center of the University of Pennsylvania (USA), one of the founding fathers of positive psychology. Author of *Authentic Happiness* and many other publications in the field.

Your personal hope scale

Yes, you can measure your personal level of hope. A good start might be
the test at www.gainhope.com. The following are the kind of questions
you can expect in the first section, dealing with your current and recent thoughts
and feelings. That is, how you feel today and over the past two weeks.
Answer from 1 (none), 2 (little), 3 (weak), 4 (strong), to 5 (very strong).
Is your result higher or lower than average (25)?

1. I feel hopeful about achieving a major life goal.

2. I feel loved by someone.

3. My emotions are in control.

4. I draw inspiration from my spiritual beliefs.

5. I can turn to a good friend or family member to help me relax.

6. I am able to rely on outside help to achieve my goals.

7. I feel part of a group.

8. I feel that I matter to someone.

9. There are people in my life that are inspiring me to do my best work.

10. Spiritual guidance is contributing to my success in life.

This is hope

Hope is complex. The diversity of ideas and perspectives in this volume is a testament to the breadth and depth that is the world of hope.

Many readers are familiar with the Indian fable in which several blind men encounter an elephant. As each grasps one part of the mammoth, they are certain to have in their possession a spear, a rope, or a pillar. In a Sufi rendition, Rumi adds the following observation: "The sensual eye is just like the palm of the hand. The palm has not the means of covering the whole of the beast."

Psychologists approach hope as a mindset of probabilities attached to specific goals. One might compare this to the spear in the hand of the blind man, our thoughts cast forward, aiming towards a specified future. In nursing and medicine, hope is a coping resource, a buffer against illness and calamity. Hope is a lifeline, akin to the rope offered to a drowning individual. Philosophers and theologians prefer to view hope as a foundation that is rooted in relationships or faith. Hope is a pillar.

In truth, hope is all of the above, a tool for envisioning definable goals, a coping resource, an expression of trust and openness as well as a spiritual gift earned by faith, prayer, or ritual. In the course of a lifetime every individual is apt to experience these different shades of hope.

As social creatures, our greatest need is attachment. The first and most basic experience of hope is the awareness that one is not alone. This begins in infancy with the presence of reliable caregivers. Rumi agreed, suggesting that the ultimate "portal of hope" was found in the mystical path and not privatized goal-setting.

In times of peace and good health our hopes may be to achieve and to acquire; to march confidently towards tomorrow. One of the greatest myths of antiquity is the story of Prometheus who angered the gods by bringing fire to humankind. In Shelly's immortal words, Prometheus "wakened the legioned hopes which sleep within folded Elysian flowers...he tamed fire...and tortured to his will iron and gold, the slaves and signs of power."

If our welfare is threatened, hope can be transformed into a tool for coping. Our hopes may lie in restoring what has been lost or simply holding our ground. In the Oxford English Dictionary, hope is traced back to 1000 AD and refers to an island in the middle of a waste-land, a protected area, and a safe resting place near a mountain or other point of ascent.

When we believe that the concrete and ordinary will not suffice to meet our needs for presence, control, or safety, we turn to some form of spirituality. Hope now rests on faith, or what psychologist James Fowler called deep "centers of value." This experience of hope may be compared to a form of light or heat. In my own research, I have found that at least seven different kinds of hope can be extracted from the world's major religions.

In summary, I believe that the most profound expressions of the human spirit derive from hope. The greatest works of art and the best books, as well as the most enduring wonders of the ancient world, as well as the Olympics, Baseball, and Soccer—all of these human achievements share a common denominator: they bring more hope into the world.

May this book offer you a better understanding of hope that is empowering, engaging, liberating, and true.

Dr. Anthony Scioli

Anthony Scioli is one of the world's leading authorities on the psychology of hope. He is currently involved in several large-scale hope projects, including the development of interventions to foster hope in youth as well as those confronting serious illness. He has also developed a comprehensive measure of hope that you can try out at www.gainhope.com. Further on in this volume he offers a basic framework for understanding hope ("The network of hope").

Dream big

"To live is to choose. But to choose well, you must know
who you are and what you stand for, where you want to go
and why you want to get there." This is the message of hope
from Nobel Prize winner **Kofi Annan**.

As I travel around the world, I have often been asked, usually by young people: "What do
you do to become a good global citizen?" I always tell them: "It begins in your community,
in your university, in your school." When you see something going wrong, don't just walk
on; stop, pay attention, and sometimes even intervene. **Intervening doesn't mean you
have to go and hit somebody.** Sometimes it is enough to see somebody being bullied and
two people fighting and for a third party, a bystander, to say: "Stop. This is wrong."
That can make a real difference for the victim. It encourages him or her to fight back,
to stand up. It gives them courage to defend themselves.

We have to remember that we don't have to take on the big challenges. Whatever little
we can do in our own little corner makes a difference and collectively we make a giant step
forward. We should remember that **even the big events start with one small thing.**
Even genocides start with the humiliation of one individual. So, if we can do something
at the individual level and protect someone, we are moving ahead.

I grew up in Ghana. When I was a teenager we were going through the struggle for
independence. It was a very exciting period. The talk about a new country, a country that
is going to take charge of its own destiny, develop its economy and social and political
norms. **As young people we were so excited.** I was in a boarding school and we used to
play roles, pretending we were politicians, arguing one side of the case or the other.

And then we achieved independence and lots of changes followed. Suddenly the police
commissioner was an African, the head of the army, the head of government. So I grew up
with the feeling that change is possible, **even dramatic change is possible.** This has helped
me go through life trying to change things and challenge things.

Kofi Annan and Leo Bormans, author of this book, first met at the great conference Hope XXL (2012, Leiden, The Netherlands) where they both addressed more than 800 young people from all over the world.

I'm sure some of you will join groups, bureaucracies, companies… Sometimes the greatest impediment to change and reform is the restraint that people, whether they are bureaucrats or workers, put on themselves. When you throw out an idea ("Can we do this? Can we try this?"), they say: "No, it has never been done, it will never work." Or: "The boss will not accept it, the government will not accept it." That's not good enough. You have to test it, you have to try it. **Don't put unnecessary restraints on yourself** within the system you should be able to challenge.

Anyway, that's where it started for me, in Ghana. And then I went to study in the United States and in Europe and then started my international career in my twenties with the World Health Organization in Geneva. And at that point I thought I would work for them for two years and then go back home. But one thing led to another, I became Secretary General of the United Nations, and here I am. But let me assure you, I am not one of those who will pretend that at the age of ten I knew exactly what I was going to do and that all that I wanted to be was Secretary General. Nothing could be further away from my mind, but one thing led to another and it happened. **Never give up dreaming. And your dreams can be big.**

Kofi Annan (1938) has served as the seventh Secretary General of the United Nations (1997–2006). Kofi Annan and the United Nations were the co-recipients of the 2001 Nobel Peace Prize "for their work for a better organized and more peaceful world." He is the founder and the Chairman of the Kofi Annan Foundation, as well as the chairman of The Elders, a group founded by Nelson Mandela. Kofi Annan is widely recognized as an icon of hope. This text is taken from Kofi Annan's speech at the Hope XXL Conference (Leiden, december 2012) and is published with his kind approval.

"Optimism is at the root of human functioning in an uncertain world."

Hope and green frogs

At conferences all over the world he is widely known as the "Indiana Jones of positive psychology" because his research on emotions has taken him to such far-flung places as India, Greenland, Kenya, and Israel. Dr. Robert Biswas-Diener takes us to the jungle of emotions, inhabited by apes and frogs, to unveil the strength of hope.

In a recent study, researchers tested the ability of great apes, such as orangutans and chimpanzees, to make predictions about behavior. To do so they had the apes watch as a hand reached toward and grabbed one of two toys: a green rubber frog or a yellow rubber duck. The apes became familiar with the hand choosing and grabbing the green frog. Then, the researchers swapped the position of the toys and showed the hand reach out halfway and stop before moving toward either toy. The apes were affixed with sophisticated eye tracking gear and the scientists could study where the apes' gaze went. Interestingly, the apes were more likely to look at the green frog. That is, the apes made visual predictions about where the hand would go and which toy it (and the person it belonged to!) would prefer. This ability to predict the goals and behaviors of others is similar to that found in human infants.

This extraordinary finding is suggestive that mental predictions about the future are both a natural phenomenon and one associated with intelligence. Optimism is simply a version of future prediction. It is the hopeful notion that the future will unfold favorably.

Interestingly, as a form of thinking about the future, optimism is also closely associated with the development of intelligence in animals. The same mechanisms that allow us to set long-term professional goals, to plan for a holiday next summer, and to take life-long wedding vows are also those that are implicated in optimism.

Without a dash of hope people would not be able to open businesses, take new jobs, or move to new cities. Optimism is at the root of human functioning in an uncertain world. And, as the ape study suggests, we are hard-wired for it. We have a deep need to believe that the future might be better—not necessarily that it will be better.

The trick, to the extent that there is a trick involved with hope, is to balance wishful thinking with hard reality. This is no easy task, of course. My recommendation is to take, to the extent possible, a flexible approach to hope. On the one hand it is good to be realistic about risks and failure. On the other hand, it can be helpful to believe that despite these hardships a better life is possible, although not guaranteed. In the end, I believe that this is the great human narrative: that there is always the possibility to rise up, to learn, to grow, to overcome, and to succeed. All of us, everywhere, are looking ahead to that next instant when the hand grabs the green frog.

The keys

- → **Optimism is simply a version of future prediction. It is the hopeful notion that the future will unfold favorably.**
- → **We have a deep need to believe that the future might be better—not necessarily that it will be better.**
- → **The trick is to balance wishful thinking with hard reality. To the extent possible, take a flexible approach to hope.**

Robert Biswas-Diener, PhD, is a leading authority on positive psychology coaching and is widely recognized as a major pioneering voice in this field. He is both a researcher as well as a practitioner. Two of his successful books are *The Upside of Your Dark Side* and *The Courage Quotient*. What does hope mean for him? "For me, hope is to be found in wishing for a positive future. I am amazed by people— their capacity for good and their ingenuity—so I am hopeful that conditions will improve for everyone. For myself, I know that I can handle hardship, so when things sometimes go wrong I know I will be able to withstand it, and that also improves my capacity for hope."

The network of hope

He is the author of two successful books on hope: Dr. **Anthony Scioli** has been studying hope for nearly three decades. He has developed a general theory of hope that combines the insights of scientists and philosophers, as well as poets and writers, and weaves them into one large tapestry: the network of hope. This offers a basic framework for understanding what hope really is about.

My understanding of hope guides my professional work on this topic and also shapes how I look at many life events both past and present, near and far. It is an integrative approach fashioned by extracting the best of hope from psychology, philosophy, theology, and medicine. It is a large net, wide enough to cover the myriad faces of hope represented in this volume; and with enough perspective to offer a bird's eye view of hope.

I believe that hope is best viewed as a four-channel emotional network built from biological, psychological, social, and spiritual resources. **A well-built hope network provides feelings of adequate empowerment and presence as well as protection and liberation whenever an individual's needs for mastery, attachment, or survival are challenged.** The hope network is geared for growth (feed-forward processes) as well as repair and maintenance (feed-back processes). The four hope sub networks (control, social, safety, and spiritual networks) operate in a semiautonomous fashion, sometimes working independently, sometimes together.

The hope network might also be compared to a five-story building with three connected wings (see Figure 1). From left to right, the three wings represent the mastery, attachment, and survival channels. The five stories, in ascending order, represent the developmental building blocks of each sub network, ranging from genetic endowments and infant needs to social and spiritual resources. Notice that I have folded spirituality within the other three channels. Spirituality can be viewed as a fourth channel that emerges from, and functions in support of, mastery, attachment, or survival needs. Depending on the individual, the belief system, and the demands of a particular situation, the spiritual aspects of hope may supply a greater dose of empowerment, connection, or assurance.

	MASTERY BUILDING BLOCKS	ATTACHMENT BUILDING BLOCKS	SURVIVAL BUILDING BLOCKS
5th LEVEL: BELIEFS & BEHAVIORS			
Recurrent Hope Beliefs Recurrent Hope Feelings Recurrent Hope Behaviors	I am Empowered Supported Collaboration	The Universe is Kind Connected Openness	Protection is Available Safe Self-regulation
4th LEVEL: THE FAITH SYSTEM			
Elements of Faith	Centers of Value	Centers of Value	Centers of Value
3rd LEVEL: THE HOPEFUL CORE			
Mastery-Oriented Traits	Goal-Oriented Trust Mediated (Assisted) Control Sanctioned Aims		
Attachment-Oriented Traits		Relationship-Trust Self—Other Bonds Openness	
Survival-Oriented Traits		Survival-Oriented Trust & Care Recruitment Terror Management & Liberation Beliefs Symbolic Immortality	
2nd LEVEL: NATURE & NURTURE			
Psychological Endowments Social-Cultural Endowments Spiritual Endowments	Talent & Goal-Directness Support & Guidance Purpose	Trust & Openness Care and Love Presence	Defense Mechanisms & Coping Skills Cultural Terror-Management Lessons Salvation Promises
1st LEVEL: HOPE BLUEPRINTS			
Biological Endowments	Mastery Needs & Related Motives	Attachment Needs & Related Motives	Survival Needs & Related Motives
FIVE LAYERS OF THE NETWORK	**MASTERY BUILDING BLOCKS**	**ATTACHMENT BUILDING BLOCKS**	**SURVIVAL BUILDING BLOCKS**

The Hope Network

LEVEL 1: *Hope-Related Motives*

The first level consists of hardwired needs and motives relating to mastery, attachment, and survival. It is inherent in human nature to strive for mastery and control; to seek close bonds and grieve after separation or loss, to resist obliteration, and escape from danger. There is strong evidence that certain brain areas have evolved to support each of these specific functions.

LEVEL 2: *Endowments and Supports*

Family, culture, and spiritual beliefs all play a role in the development of hope. Mastery requires determination and a guiding hand. In the West the need for coaching, mentoring, and spiritual direction are receiving increasing attention. In contrast, Hindus as well as the West African Ifa, to cite just two examples, have long relied on gurus and shaman along with elaborate rites of passage to ensure individual and group success.

Hope-related attachments derive from the intertwined resources of trust and openness. Without openness, trust is stymied. A lack of trust precludes openness. Gabriel Marcel, the existentialist philosopher, dubbed openness the "fruit and pledge" of fundamental hope. In humans, the quality of care and attention received early in life is a major factor in the full development of these capacities.

Rudimentary survival skills are present at birth. Newborns express delight when sweetness touches their lips and disgust in the presence of foul odors. Intensely social, humans derive added layers of protection from countless group memberships. Beyond self and society, humanity has sought assurance via religious and spiritual beliefs. Hindus access the inner Atman. The Navaho and Lakota turn to ancient tribal customs. Buddhists find salvation in the promise of an afterlife devoid of want and suffering.

LEVEL 3: *Hope Traits (The "Hopeful Core")*

Mastery and attachment resources generate the "will to hope", the capacity for finding purpose and meaning through goal-setting. Hope derives from a mastery "middle ground," a feeling of empowerment derived via a perceived relationship with a force or presence. Sophocles wrote, "Heaven helps not the men who will not act." In the Christian Bible, Paul declares, "I can do all things through Christ which strengtheneth me." The Tibetan monks believe "Men… by depending upon the great may prosper; a drop of water is a little thing, but when will it dry away if united to a lake?" A Koran prayer implores, "Add to my strength through him and make him share my task." William James wrote of the "the more" in religious experiences, a felt union with a power that is experienced as simultaneously "out there" and partly "in here." Hope-centered mastery is further strengthened by the perception that goal commitments are sanctioned by one's family, community, or a higher power.

A second cluster of traits is derived from attachment. **Relational trust is based on openness and disclosure towards a valued person or transcendent presence.** Whether it is a loved one, a Christian shepherd, a Hindu inner god, or a Native American guiding spirit, the character of hope includes a strong sense of continued presence.

The third set of traits is for self-protection and includes survival-oriented trust, terror-management capacity, and a sense of symbolic immortality. Survival trust requires a perceived external resource strong enough to deliver one from evil. A capacity for terror management implies adequate buffers to remain calm despite threats of harm or loss. Symbolic immortality is acquired by investing parts of oneself in one's family, community, or culture, resulting in a sense of self that is enlarged and enduring.

LEVEL 4: *The Faith System*

Faith is a prerequisite for hope. Such beliefs may be religious or non-religious, but they must be grounded in transcendent centers of value that relate to mastery, attachment, or survival. One or more sources of faith may underlie hope. For one individual, faith may be invested in a higher power or the self, whereas for another it may be family and community. Faith can be realized through mastery and attachment, via attachment and survival, or by embracing all three motives.

LEVEL5: *Hope Feelings and Behaviors*

Hope is more than a cold, static set of expectations. It involves discernible feelings and a commitment to action. Erik Erikson alluded to its "surface and depth." Emily Dickinson paid homage to the "tune without the words." Sholomo Breznitz described the "work of hope" in managing stress. Hope-based mastery includes feelings of empowerment and the pursuit of transcendent goals. Hope-based attachments spawn a sense of continued presence and trust along with displays of openness. Hope-based survival may include the belief in a benign universe but also emotional self-regulation and acts of care recruitment.

Anthony Scioli is a leading authority on hope. He is a professor of psychology at Keene State College and on the graduate faculty at the University of Rhode Island (USA). He maintains a part-time private practice. Dr. Scioli received his PhD. from the University of Rhode Island and completed Harvard fellowships in human motivation and behavioral medicine. Dr. Scioli has written two books on hope, developed a variety of hope assessment tools, and has studied the role of hope in cancer survivorship and non-progression of HIV. He coauthored the chapter on theories of emotion for the *Encyclopedia of Mental Health*. Dr. Scioli serves on the editorial board of *The Psychology of Religion and Spirituality* and *The Journal of Positive Psychology*. His hobbies include wine-making, following the Boston sports teams, and trying (sometimes successfully) to replicate his mother's Italian cooking. "Hope is a torch we can pass onto others."

"We should be optimistic and strive for a growing and agile mindset."

Interventions of hope

"By having the willingness to learn and un-learn, young people don't only become more hopeful themselves. They can also enhance hope in their communities, which is the need of the hour," says **Raza Abbas**, who is the facilitator of hope-centered workshops for students in Karachi, Pakistan. "To thrive in the 21st century, hope is the new prerequisite and way of life. It is a healthy lifestyle to enjoy the countless blessings that we currently do possess."

While we have the greatest population of youth in Pakistan's history, we are presented with the challenge of tapping the potential of young people for the country's socio and economic development. This aspiration cannot be achieved without understanding the fundamental problems young people experience today and pondering over solutions to these problems. Some of the challenges toward youth development include high anxiety levels, unemployment, inadequate career counseling, and career guidance.

The Hope-Centered Workshop is an integrative, evidenced-based approach to conceptualizing, assessing, and building hope that can be used across cultures and spiritual belief systems. It is based on the work of Anthony Scioli (whose approach is also presented elsewhere in this book). **The workshop is a "whole-brain" approach**, combining cognitive-behavioral exercises with philosophical reflections and meditative-hypnotic exercises. Five modules are included in this intervention: two attachment modules and one each for mastery, survival, and spiritual hope.

A comprehensive self-report hope scale is administered before and after the workshop.

Positive mindset

In our pilot research, hope scores increased significantly, with an effect size of 1.07. The qualitative feedback was equally encouraging. An exit interview was conducted after the intervention with all participants. Themes of empowerment (mastery), greater openness (attachment), hope for improved self-regulation, coping (survival), and heightened awareness to spiritual needs were commonly reported. Some participants found the more meditative components of the intervention difficult.

"I started off the workshop with a very demoralizing mindset. Currently my mindset is really very different and positive than what I initiated with. I will give credit to hope workshops for diverting me towards positivity," says student Anushay Hussain. "The workshops are **an extremely inspiring effort for those who want to save themselves from the darkness of hopelessness,"** adds student Verda Butt. "The idea of carrying out a research on such a rarely studied topic in this country was not only unique but zealous at the same time. It has been a great learning experience. I feel more hopeful towards my life and profession now. I hope there are more similar researches carried out in future in Pakistan and this region," says Senior Lecturer Ifrah Shah.

Torch bearers

The pilot of the research was to strengthen the supply side of youth character building and employability by facilitating hope-centered, institutionalized training for teachers at educational institutions. These trainings improve the demand side by instilling hope in students at all levels in making educated and informed career decisions. The implication of the study is a source for socio-economic think tanks to re-strategize educational policy.

Based on the pilot study program, hope should be introduced as an elective in the school curriculum worldwide for a sustainable impact leading to optimistic graduates facing the work challenges of the 21st century. **Imparting hope in youth leads to social justice**

for a safer global world. Establishment of a hope-centered foundation is the need of the hour that inspires humanity irrespective of race, gender, age, religion, and disability.

People from all walks of life should be optimistic and should strive for a growing and agile mindset. They should have self-confidence and believe in themselves and the future, especially during times of adversity. Therefore they should collaborate with professionals that are hope torch bearers around the globe. The knowledge is available, let's use it.

The keys

- → **The Hope-Centered Workshop is an integrative, evidence-based approach to conceptualizing, assessing, and building hope that can be used across cultures and spiritual belief systems.**
- → **Establishment of a hope-centered foundation is the need of the hour that inspires humanity irrespective of race, gender, age, religion, and disability.**
- → **People should have self-confidence and believe in themselves and the future, especially at times of adversity.**

Raza Abbas is Chief Executive Officer of the Pathway Global Career Institute, Pakistan. He earned his dual degrees from The University of Arizona in Business Administration and Communication (USA). Amongst speaking at numerous premier international and national forums, he is honored to have presented his research at the Inaugural UNESCO Chair on Lifelong Guidance and Counseling Conference at the University of Wroclaw, Poland, in 2013. He focuses on hope-centered interventions teacher training, career guidance, youth capacity building, and social entrepreneurship.

After the earthquake: Gap Filler

The 2011 earthquake in Christchurch, New Zealand's second largest city, left 185 dead and led to the loss of 80% of the central city's buildings and abandonment of entire suburbs due to land damage. Apart from the official rebuilding program, some volunteers stood up to turn the scar into a source of hope for the city. Gap Filler is one of the most creative and hopeful answers to the disaster. A team of seven people and 1,700 volunteers create hope by sound gardens, moving dance floors, a cycle-powered cinema, murals, and a Pallet Pavilion in deserted places. How does it work?

Gap Filler is an urban regeneration initiative operating in Christchurch, New Zealand. A charitable trust, it was created by three people from backgrounds that include visual arts, event management, architecture, film, and theater.

Transitional movement

Since September 2010, Gap Filler has created and facilitated more than 45 projects around the city and enabled 40 more. The initiative has had a large role to play in putting Christchurch on the map in terms of its creative, community-led response to the disaster. Thanks to the help from Gap Filler and some other groups, Christchurch now has what is called a Transitional movement, which is used to refer to those creating projects, interventions, and responses to the largely vacant central city. There is even a festival

every year in October, the only one of its kind in the world, called the Festival of Transitional Architecture. Gap Filler has been bringing life to the city through its most raw, traumatic stages, and gaining an international profile while doing so.

Every Gap Filler project is different and almost all of them involve volunteers. The organization is values driven believing in experimentation and learning from the findings, leadership, creativity, community engagement, and resourcefulness. Gap Filler sees its role as to lead by example; to treat the city as a laboratory for experiments by a range of people and communities. **Short-term, low-risk experiments in the temporary or transitional space can provide learning that can feed into the long-term rebuild and fabric of the city.**

Test ideas

Gap Filler projects after the earthquake have included:

1. **The Dance-O-Mat**—a coin operated dance floor on a vacant site. Plug it in, put in $2 courtesy of an old washing machine from a Laundromat, and you get 30 minutes to boogie.

2. **The Think Differently Book Exchange**—books chillin' in a commercial fridge.

3. **Sound Garden**—musical instruments made of recycled materials situated in a Greening the Rubble garden for people to jam with others.

4. **RAD Bikes**—a community bike workshop. Learn how to fix your own bike or fix up old, unloved bikes to then gift on to those who need them.

5. **The Pallet Pavilion**—a community venue made from 3,000 CHEP wooden pallets. Built by volunteers across 6 weeks, this incredible project hosted more than 200 events such as live music, markets, cinema, lectures, and more.

6. **A Cycle-Powered Cinema**

7. **An ongoing Education and Community Outreach program** sharing our learning with the wider community to inspire action and social change.

A natural disaster is a traumatic, deeply disempowering experience. There are times of great optimism when everyone is full of hope to rebuild the city better than ever. And then there are the lows—the fatigue, the despondency, the disillusionment, and anger from those poor souls still battling with insurance companies and living in leaky, damaged houses even now, after all these years. Gap Filler's temporary projects do a range of things in the city. They beautify the broken landscape with injections of creativity and quirkiness. They **provide opportunities for people to participate in shaping their city and feel empowered through doing so.** They provoke, critique, and question and allow people to feel involved. All of this is very important for the health and well-being of Christchurch's people.

Coralie Winn, Director and Co-Founder of Gap Filler, Christchurch (New Zealand)

More information:
www.gapfiller.org.nz

"We prefer to be with others who make us feel more optimistic."

Making pessimism work

"The effects of positive states of mind such as optimism have often been discussed as able to produce both positive and negative outcomes for people and society," says Prof. **Miguel Pereira Lopes**. But his research has shown that we are also able to make pessimism work. How?

It seems true that feeling optimistic sometimes makes people more proactive and able to achieve their goals. However, it also seems to be the case that being optimistic sometimes makes people confident that things will become better without any action on their own. The truth is that **we will probably keep feeling both optimistic and pessimistic throughout our lifetime** and, the better we can learn how to take out the best of each situation, the better we can manage to be happy. What may thus be the "click" that makes optimism and pessimism work instead of turning people into passive human beings? I have learned from my research that hope has such a powerful effect!

Hope is a powerful tool for turning both optimistic and pessimistic individuals who become passive into proactive people who set and achieve their own goals and make an impact in the world. In a research published in *The Journal of Positive Psychology* in 2008 my fellow researchers and I have found that when people feel higher levels of optimism and hope they become more proactive in their life. However, what is more interesting is the role hope plays when people are feeling pessimistic. **When people feel pessimistic, hope reduces their levels of passive behavior and turns them into more active individuals in their work and life.** Hope reveals itself as the way of taking out the best of optimism as well as making people act more proactively when they feel pessimistic. As such, one should help others and oneself to increase their levels of hope as an antidote to pessimistic beliefs that lead to passive behavior.

Alternative ways

My research has also focused on how we can use hope to promote more proactive coping, particularly when people are feeling pessimistic. When separating the two faces of hope— the will and the ways—we found that it was the "ways" side of hope that made the difference in putting pessimism to work favorably. Put into practical wording, hope can leverage proactive recovery and behavior when people are in a pessimistic mood through the outlining of possible alternative ways to achieve their goals. As such, **you can become a proactive agent of change simply by thinking about alternative pathways to achieve your goals and dreams.** This is particularly effective when you start feeling pessimistic about the possibility that things will run fine.

Good vibrations

But how about if you could help make the world more proactive too? How can you become an agent of hope and proactivity in your world? In a book I have recently published named *Good Vibrations: Three Studies on Optimism, Social Networks and Resource-Attraction Capability* you'll find scientific research showing that people prefer to be with others who make them feel more optimistic. I termed that effect as "alter-optimism" to accentuate the fact that it is not how much you feel optimistic that matters, but how much you make those around you feel optimistic, i.e., sending them "good vibrations." A similar reasoning can apply to hope. **Despite the levels of hope you feel yourself, you are always able to create higher levels of hope in others.** In other words, it is in your hand to become an "alter-hopeful agent"! And now you know: What do alter-hopeful agents do? They help others find new and alternative ways to achieve their goals and dreams. They open up possibilities instead of shutting down their dreams and aspirations. So do not waste your time anymore, and go make your peers increase their levels of hope and proactivity.

Strong engine

Hope is a strong recovery engine for socio-economic development as well. In a recent scientific paper published in the *Journal of Socio-Economics* about the psycho-sociology of business and economic cycles, I outlined a socio-economic model that considers unrealistic optimism as a cause for economic downturns and **hopeful pessimism as a cause for economic recovery and development.** This means that the benefits of acting based on the scientific principles of hope theory can go beyond the local effects among people and can have a societal impact. This evidences our responsibility for spreading hope throughout our social relations and outlines the ethical demand of assuming that responsibility. For if it is true that collective hope can have such a socio-economic power, it is also true that it all starts with the simple micro action that an "alter-hopeful agent" undertakes.

The keys

→ **Hope reveals itself as the way of taking out the best of optimism as well as making people act more proactively when they feel pessimistic.**

→ **Hope can leverage proactive recovery and behavior when people are in a pessimistic mood through the outlining of possible alternative ways to achieve their goals.**

→ **It is not how much you feel optimistic that matters, but how much you make those around you feel optimistic. Collective hope is a strong socio-economic power.**

Miguel Pereira Lopes is an Assistant Professor at the School of Social and Political Sciences, Lisbon University (Portugal). He is the President of the Board of INTEC - Behavioral Technology Institute, a not-for-profit organization he founded to run applied quality of life research. Miguel holds a PhD in Applied Psychology and a Post-Doc in Economics. His work has been published in numerous international peer-reviewed journals and he is the (co)author of several books on talent management, leadership, and positive organization studies. Miguel is ethically committed with his own research and tries to live according to it, including attempting to seize each interactional opportunity to act as an "alter-hopeful agent" and help others to enlarge their horizons and dreams.

Making hope happen

"Hope is created moment by moment through our deliberate choices. It happens when we use our thoughts and feelings to temper our aversion to loss and actively pursue what is possible. When we choose hope, we define what matters to us most," says **Dr. Shane J. Lopez**, one of the world-leading authorities on the psychology of hope and author of the successful book *Making Hope Happen*. His message is clear: Hope matters. Hope is a choice. Hope can be learned. Hope is contagious.

To attain hope, you need to create momentum. It's helpful to name the core beliefs that support the how of hope, but it's even more important to know how they work together. So I'd like to offer another way, first proposed by Rick Snyder, to understand hope in action. It combines the beliefs into a three-part process that carries us to a better future. It also describes each element of the process as a set of learnable skills. Here are the three parts:

1. Goals. We seek out and identify an idea of where we want to go, what we want to accomplish, who we want to be—whether tomorrow or over a lifetime. Some goals are vague or fleeting, and quickly forgotten. Others are actively shaped and modified over time. Hope is built from the goals that matter most to us, that we come back to again and again, and that fill our minds with pictures of the future.

2. Agency. The word *agency* is shorthand for our perceived ability to shape our lives day to day. As "agents" we know we can make things happen (or stop them from happening), and we take responsibility for moving toward our goals. Over time, we develop our ability to motivate ourselves; we build our capacity for persistence and long-term effort. Agency makes us the authors of our lives.

3. Pathways. We seek out and identify multiple pathways to our goals, pick the most appropriate routes for our situation, and monitor our progress over time. These are the plans that carry us forward, but we're aware that obstacles can arise at any time. So we remain curious and open to finding better paths to our desired future.

For now, I just want to visualize these elements as a continuous feedback loop. Each element can set the others in motion. Each interacts with the others in ways that can reinforce, modify, or diminish them. When each is strong, together they form a cycle that enhances hope. When even one is weak, hope diminishes until we intervene to strengthen the element that is undeveloped or faltering.

This simple model works whatever your goals, age, or circumstances, whether you're most concerned about your family, your business, your community, or your personal development. But life is anything but simple. Hope has many faces and it flourishes in unexpected places. One of the most striking qualities of hope, however, is that hopeful people spread hope to almost everyone they meet.

Shane J. Lopez, PhD., is a Gallup Senior Scientist living in Lawrence, Kansas (USA). He is one of the world's leading authorities on the psychology of hope. He has published seven professional books, including the *Encyclopedia of Positive Psychology*. His research on "Making Hope Happen" is dedicated to all people who believe that the future can be better than the past or present and who are looking for a way to make it so.

"We are our best selves

in the context of important others."

High hopes

She completed her doctoral degree at the University of Kansas
under the guidance of C. R. Snyder, the originator of the hope theory.
While in graduate school she developed and tested an intervention
to increase hope and decrease symptoms of depression and anxiety.
Now Prof. **Jennifer Cheavens** teaches students and cares
for patients, singing the popular song "High Hopes."

Each year when I get to the section of my positive psychology course where we focus on hope,
I ask the students if they know the song about the ant and high hopes. You know the ant.
The one with "high, apple pie, in the sky" hopes? My students never admit to knowing
this song (popularized by Frank Sinatra), which I think is a shame because it is a really
beautiful depiction of the most empirically supported definition of hope. In C. R. Snyder's
conceptualization, hope is identifying what you want, mapping out the routes or ways
to get what you want, and then keeping yourself motivated to use those routes to get to your
goals, even when others might not think you can do it. The ant wants to move the rubber
tree plant, decides the best way to do so, and keeps on that path until he succeeds.

Benefits

There is tremendous research support for this model of hope. Those with high hope
succeed in goal pursuits in many different domains, including academic, athletic,

and interpersonal relationships. People with higher hope set goals that are more difficult and take longer to achieve than people with lower levels of hope. Challenging goals likely serve to maintain the interest, attention, and enthusiasm of the goal-setter, in turn increasing the likelihood of maintaining a goal pursuit, and eventual success. Hope is also associated with setting goals that both involve and benefit other people. Much of the positive psychology literature suggests that we are our best selves in the context of important others. **Individuals with high hope generate goals that support and nurture others** in a way that seems to result in many benefits for the goal-setter.

When I first started studying hope in graduate school, I was inspired by the high hopers around me but couldn't help but wonder whether hope was for the few or for the many. The exemplars of hopeful thought bounced back from adversity, overcame obstacles, and persevered toward their well-explicated goals. **But what about those of us who struggled to believe that we could reach our goals?** What about those who saw obstacles and set-backs as blockages and dead-ends? Identifying the myriad ways in which those with high hope were better off than those with low hope was informative but did not answer the question that really was most of interest to me.

Hope for the many

Over the years, I have become convinced that hopeful thought is a skill that can be acquired or learned. Our research suggests that most of us can take the lessons from high hope people and apply them to our own lives. We can become more practiced at thinking about the things we want in our lives in ways that increase the likelihood of accomplishing those things. **Thinking about the specifics of what we want and developing a number of ways to get to the goal seems to increase hope.** Additionally, perceiving goal obstacles as challenges instead of barriers to what we want can help us maintain motivation over time. Finally, generating goals that fit with our values and are connected to others is consistent with being a more hopeful person. We can harness the power of hope to make our own lives and the lives of others better. Hope is for the many.

Oops, there goes another rubber tree plant.

The keys

→ **Those with high hope succeed in goal pursuits in many different domains.**

→ **Most of us can take the lessons from high hope people and apply them to our own lives.**

→ **Generating goals that fit with our values and are connected to others is consistent with being a more hopeful person**

Jennifer Cheavens is an Associate Professor of Psychology at the Ohio State University (USA). She continues to conduct research aimed at understanding the construct of hope and incorporating hope into treatments for individuals with mood and personality disorders. She is lucky to be surrounded by examples of hopeful thought every day, including students striving to understand the world in new ways and patients developing plans to make their lives better.

"Adults serve as important models of hopeful thinking for children."

Models of hope

Hopeful individuals are more likely to have higher levels of determination and demonstrate more flexible thinking in identifying different paths to reach a goal. Is this an attitude we can teach ourselves and our children? Prof. **Kimberly Hills** firmly says yes. We should all aspire to be models of hope for others.

We generally define hope as a feeling of expectation and a desire for certain things to happen. The general person's understanding of hope involves the belief/feeling that a specific outcome can somehow be obtained. We see hope manifest even in situations where people are against all odds. Does hope matter? Research and clinical practice both suggest that yes, it does matter. When people are hopeful that a certain outcome is possible, they are more likely to have the courage and strength to put forth the necessary effort to work toward those outcomes. Hope can be an important factor in accomplishing one's dreams and goals for the future.

Will or way?

We know we both need the "will" (agency) and the "ways" (pathways). Does one matter more than the other? This aspect of the hope theory continues to be debated in research and practice. What we are finding is that agency often plays a larger role. For what about the situations where there is no strong, objective evidence to suggest that a successful pathway exists? **Does hope still matter even if a person is told that the only medical treatments available to them have only a 10% chance of success?** The research suggests that yes, hope can still be an important influence in situations where objective evidence of a pathway is small to none. So perhaps in some situations; it is the combination of will and simply the strong belief that a pathway will manifest *somehow* (e.g. you will be in that 10%), that is so essential to hope.

The hope strategy: 11 do's

How can we encourage hope for ourselves and for others? Here are 11 tools.

Goal Setting

1. Goal setting is important. **Develop and set realistic goals, including goals that are "stretch goals."** "Stretch goals" are goals that push you slightly higher than your original goal. These kind of goals can be energizing and push you to work harder.

Pathways

2. **Flexible thinking.** Thinking more flexibly about your goals and adjusting them when warranted not only provides more pathways toward your long-term goals but also reciprocally effects our motivation to put effort toward those goals.

3. **Changing the way you perceive setbacks** by thinking more flexibly is critical to building both the will and the way toward your goals.

4. **Break long-term goals into steps** or short-term aims.

5. **Develop strategies to overcome barriers** and help you cope with obstacles toward your goals.

6. **Relationships matter.** Develop relationships with others where you can help each other work toward goals.

Agency

7. **Learn self-talk strategies** that positively promote behaviors toward your goals.

8. **Recalling previously successful pursuits** can be important when faced with adversity.

9. **Limit self-pity** when things don't go your way. Don't allow yourself to be surprised repeatedly when things don't go your way.

10. **Let go of goals or modify them** when the goal is unrealistic or blocked.

11. **Be patient** with yourself as you learn strategies to improve your agency thinking.

Develop skills

Our environment and upbringing influences our perceptions and beliefs that contribute to hopeful thinking and attitudes. Adults serve as important models of hopeful thinking for children and children acquire hope through both subtle and obvious interactions with their environment. **We can promote both agency and pathway thinking in ourselves and others.** Hopeful thinking and attitudes can improve when individuals develop skills in the areas of goal setting, agency thinking, and pathway thinking. This means that although our upbringing may influence our current levels of hope, our current environment also plays an important part and we all can develop a more hopeful attitude.

In both my research and my clinical work with children and families, I have learned that understanding others' perceptions and skills related to hope can be critical in guiding them through challenging situations. We should all aspire to be models of hope for others. In the face of adversity, one should always begin and end with hope.

The keys

> → **Hope matters. It can still be an important influence in situations where objective evidence of a pathway is small to none.**
> → **Our environment and upbringing influences our perceptions and beliefs that contribute to hopeful thinking and attitudes.**
> → **Hopeful thinking and attitudes can improve when individuals develop skills in the areas of goal setting, agency thinking, and pathway thinking.**

Kimberly Hills is an Associate Professor of Psychology at the University of South Carolina (USA). Born in one of the last generations to remember what life was like before technology, she is intrigued by her students' and clients' new preferences for communication and enjoys the challenge of learning about current youth culture. She codirects the Positive Psychology Research Lab at USC with Scott Huebner where their work focuses on understanding child well-being and why well-being matters. Their lab has published extensively on the state of well-being in children and adolescents. As a clinical professor, she spends significant time providing clinical services and training graduate students.

"Genuine hope can occur
no matter what the circumstances."

The inner choice of hope

People hope for a better future, and it's hard to avoid doing that. But there are many matters that we cannot affect. We cannot choose some of the circumstances that befall us. "Real hope," say **Maja Djikic** and **Keith Oatley**, "is about making inner choices, about matters we can affect."

Is hope a dream? Is it a fantasy of a better future? If hope depended on imagining a future, what should we say about the quiet despair of refugee camps, nursing homes, crushing poverty, or the processions of days of physical, emotional, intellectual, or spiritual imprisonment. The more imaginative the victim, the worse would be the hopelessness, because of the thought of forfeiting the future.

But it is not any inability to imagine a better life that brings about hopelessness. It is the reality of circumstances of the world that prevents the despairing from making choices that allow them to live their lives as they would wish. Hope is an ability to make choices that allow the self to keep moving forward despite circumstances. As Maya Angelou put it: "You may not control all the events that happen to you, but you can decide not to be reduced by them."

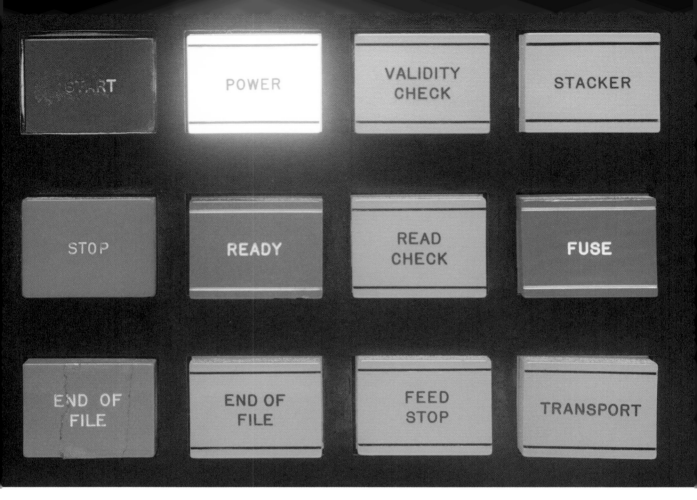

Blind hope

Every kind of suffering seems to contain within itself a glimmer of hope. One may believe that this is because hope is tied to a future goal—that things may get better. But what about a cancer patient who knows he will die, and then does die? Is not his situation hopeless? Would not any hope he may have be an illusion? Is this the meaning of "blind hope," that humans may hope no matter how irrational the circumstance, to protect themselves from unbearable truths? It depends. If a patient's hope is for future survival, the hope is not so much blind as false. The blindness of hope has more to do with the fact that genuine hope can occur no matter what the circumstances. **Even the most constraining circumstance can allow choice as how to experience it**: with despair and fear, or with courage and dignity.

An early writer on this issue was the Stoic philosopher Epictetus, who argued that we should not identify ourselves with our bodies because we cannot affect what they are,

and sometimes cannot affect what happens to them. We should identify ourselves
with what is up to us. Epictetus was born a slave around the year 55, and was crippled.
One commentator said his leg was deliberately broken by his master. But as Epictetus later
wrote: "You can fetter my leg, but not me." His hope depended on learning to cultivate
an attitude within himself, because what he thought and felt was not up to circumstance.
It was up to him.

Internal decision

In reflections on his time in concentration camps, Viktor Frankl said "everything can be
taken from a man but one thing: the last of the human freedoms—to choose one's attitude
in any given set of circumstances, to choose one's own way." According to Frankl and other
existentialists, there is always choice, but sometimes it cannot be seen. The choice is not
in doing something externally to pursue one's goals, but an internal decision of how
to experience what happens, and possibly maintain one's growth as a human being.

Like Viktor Frankl, Nelson Mandela suffered imprisonment, yet he made an inner choice,
which he set at the center of his experience: he chose not to hate his jailors, but to become
compassionate towards them. **Concentrating on inwardness does not mean neglecting
the world of others.** At a healing and reconciliation service in December 2000, dedicated
to HIV/AIDS sufferers and for the healing of South Africa, Mandela said: "Our human
compassion binds us one to the other... as human beings who have learnt how to turn our
common suffering into hope for the future."

Existential state

Hope may seem to be just another emotion, like fear or anger. It waxes and wanes,
as emotions do, and appears triggered by circumstance. We may think of others as more
or less hopeful or hopeless, as if hope were a personality trait. Hope, though, unlike
the emotion of anger or the personality trait of introversion, may be thought of as an existential
state, cultivated by increasing awareness and the opportunity for choice. Whatever our
circumstances—illness, disability, imprisonment, or a desolate state of the world—we are
one insight away from hope, an ever-present if not always perceived gift of choice.

The keys

→ **Hope seems to be about wishing for a better future, but really it's about cultivating an inner attitude. Hope is an ability to make choices that allow the self to keep moving forward despite circumstances.**

→ **Some things we cannot choose. The choice is not in doing something externally to pursue one's goals, but an internal decision of how to experience what happens.**

→ **Hope, unlike the emotion of anger or the personality trait of introversion, may be thought of as an existential state, cultivated by increasing awareness and the opportunity for choice.**

Maja Djikic is Director of the Self-Development Laboratory in the Rotman School of Management at the University of Toronto (Canada). At the age of 16 she fled with her family from Bosnia as rocket-shells and tanks destroyed communities. After, she worked with a team documenting the genocide in that country. She is a personality psychologist, fascinated by the process of personality development. **Keith Oatley** is professor emeritus at the University of Toronto (Canada). He was born in London six months before the start of World War II, lived there throughout the war, and remembers his early school years amid rationing and bombsites. He is a cognitive psychologist and novelist. His most recent books are *Therefore choose*, an existentialist novel, and *The passionate muse: Exploring emotions in stories*. In their work, Maja and Keith strive to do what they love and to love what they do.

"Is hope another trap set by the gods or a final gift?"

Pandora: hope in a jar

When in the Greek myth all the evils had left Pandora's jar, the only remaining thing at the bottom of the jar was "hope." "There is no final answer as to whether hope is another trap set by the gods or a final gift," says Prof. **Evangelos C. Karademas**, who lives and works on the Greek island Crete.

According to Greek mythology, when Prometheus stole fire from the gods and delivered it to humans, Zeus decided to punish not only him but also humans for using the stolen gift. Thus, he asked Hephaestus to create from clay a woman who would be similar to a goddess but speak and behave like a human. It was Pandora, who was given by the gods as a bride to Epimetheus, Prometheus's brother. Zeus also gave to the couple a wedding gift: a big jar. Although he warned Pandora not to open the jar, Zeus never told her what it was filled with. He already knew that **Pandora was curious enough.** So, eventually, she lost her self-control and opened the jar and then all forms of evil, plague, and suffering were released into the world. At the very last moment, Pandora managed, with the permission of Zeus and the help of some gods, to close the jar, keeping inside only hope. Ever since, hope is a major agent of human behavior. Also, a most interesting one; even for science.

Optimism

Several terms have been used in the scientific psychological research to refer to hope. One of the most representative is optimism, which reflects the general tendency to expect positive outcomes in the future even in the face of obstacles. A great number of studies have shown that optimism is a protective factor for well-being and health against a diversity of stressful conditions. It is associated with better physical and psychological health, better adaptation to chronic illness, and also the use of more adaptive coping strategies and health-promoting behaviors. Moreover, research has shown that optimists have better social connections, are more able to prioritize their needs and goals, persist more in their efforts, and, therefore, are more likely to finally achieve their aims.

Health

At the University of Crete, Greece, we have focused on the relation of optimism to the experience of illness. We have found that optimism can protect chronic patients from despair and helplessness even in the face of significant health problems. Also, our research has shown that optimism serves as one of the links between other personal characteristics and health. We have found, for instance, that social support and life satisfaction are related to optimism and, through this, to better health. Also, some of our findings suggest that optimism is associated with greater attention paid to positive (e.g. well-being related) than negative (e.g. threat related) stimuli. Overall, there is ample evidence that the original plan of the gods works: hope can make life more tolerable. But, is this always true?

Persistence

As the myth goes, hope was the only thing kept inside Pandora's jar. It is a question, however, whether Zeus permitted that as a token of goodwill toward humans or as a final act of vengeance, in the sense that even hope cannot really help people. In fact, there is some evidence, although rare, that optimism may indeed have a negative impact. For example, research has shown that optimists sometimes fail to recognize that a specific goal is lost and they persist in their efforts even after several negative outcomes. Also, the findings of one or two studies suggest that optimists, at least under certain circumstances, tend to ignore threats and see only the bright side of things. In addition, in a study of ours, we found that at the higher levels of optimism, there was almost no connection between cardiac patients' current health condition and their understanding of this condition. In other words, the very optimistic patients tended to rely more on their generalized positive expectations about the future than on specific information about their health, which could be an unsafe practice, at least under certain circumstances.

Although it is not clear under which conditions high optimism may prove to be harmful, this issue is definitely very interesting for future research. Even so, however, most studies indicate that hope/optimism is a positive human asset.

Combination

In the Greek myth, there is no final answer as to whether hope is another trap set by the gods or a final gift. It seems that it lies with us to use hope in a constructive way, mainly by combining it with other positive personal characteristics. When it is paired with self-control and the awareness of personal strengths and weaknesses as well as reality, then hope may become a powerful means to endure the inevitable fear and pain in our lives.

The keys

→ **Hope is closely linked to optimism. It can protect chronic patients from despair and helplessness and is a general protective factor for well-being and health.**
→ **High optimism may prove to be harmful. You may fail to recognize that a specific goal is lost or ignore certain threats.**
→ **We should use hope in a constructive way, mainly by combining it with other positive personal characteristics (e.g. self-control and the awareness of strengths and weaknesses).**

Evangelos C. Karademas is an associate professor of clinical health psychology at the University of Crete (Greece). His research interests include the role of stress in behavior and health, adaptation to chronic illness, and the self-regulation process. He has authored a book and several articles and chapters in scientific journals and editions on these topics. To him, the key to a good life is to try to combine hope with a sound understanding of circumstances and life as it is, and with a steady effort to achieve personal goals.

Rowena A. Pecchenino

"To live, even the economically rational live in hope."

Economics of hope

"Hope is all but absent from the discipline of economics, the so called dismal science," says professor of economics **Rowena A. Pecchenino**, who explores hope and despair in economic thought. "This absence is notable since hope is fundamentally at the center of choice, and economics is fundamentally about choice."

From whichever disciplinary perspective I examine hope, I find that hope, however it is defined—and it is defined in myriad ways—gives life meaning while its absence makes life unbearable. I, as an economist, first found this absence troubling, but then realized hope wasn't absent, rather it was in hiding. When speaking to economists about hope in an economic context, especially young economists still steeping themselves in economics qua economics and proving themselves as economists, they generally dismiss hope as being the domain of cock-eyed optimists, dreamers, and the irrational. Economic man is, if nothing else, rational rather than hopeful. And this is their mistake. Hope is not optimism; hope is not unfounded dreams divorced from reality; hope is not irrational. Hope does not undermine rationality.

Rationally hopeful

So how can hope be brought out of hiding and into the light of economic analysis? As hope is manifested in many ways, there is no simple fix. However, once characterized, the rationally hopeful and the choices they make can take their place alongside their more narrowly rational colleagues. So what characterizes the rationally hopeful? They can be goal oriented, with the future—their personal future and the future more generally—being the focus of their plans. Rather than seeking instant gratification, they look ahead and plan how to get from where they are to where they want, individually or collectively, to be. They can be single-minded in pursuit of their goal, shutting out contrary information which may suggest they are on a fool's errand. They do not, in general, characterize their goal as having a specific probability of success: heads the goal is achieved, tails it isn't. Instead goal attainment depends on their desire and ability to transform what is into what should be or at least to move toward what should be even if they know that their goal is unattainable in their lifetimes or through human effort alone. Alternatively, they may see their lives as being a journey on which they have embarked and where their hopefulness provides a means of understanding or accepting fortune and misfortune with equanimity even when life is close to its end. The rationally hopeful are, however reluctantly, "economic men".

Taking decisions

If what characterizes the rationally hopeful still remains unclear, looking at what characterizes the despairing, those who have given up hope, may prove helpful. Those without hope are outside of and alienated from society. Their social relationships are stunted or impossible.

Life itself has little or no meaning or value. They are trapped in the present without a future. Thus, it is the hopeless rather than the hopeful whose rationality could be called into question.

Hope or its absence permeates human existence and informs all aspects of human behavior from the individual to the social. That we can function and indeed flourish depends on our ability to choose, to make decisions, and this ability often depends on whether we have or have lost hope, on whether we can perceive and plan for and believe in a future, endure in that belief as we work toward that goal no matter the set backs, the longness of the odds, the haziness of the goal, or its obvious unachievability. It depends as well on whether we believe that the journey we're on is worth taking even when the journey is near its end. Our ability to do and to be better, to transform ourselves and our societies, to be satisfied with what we have while still working to make things better, to choose our life paths all depend on hope. To live, even the economically rational live in hope.

The keys

→ **Hope does not undermine rationality. Hope is fundamentally at the center of choice, and economics is fundamentally about choice.**

→ **Rather than seeking instant gratification, the rationally hopeful look ahead and plan how to get from where they are to where they want, individually or collectively, to be.**

→ **Our ability to do and to be better, to transform ourselves and our societies, to be satisfied with what we have while still working to make things better, to choose our life paths all depend on hope.**

Rowena A. Pecchenino (BA Cornell, MSc LSE, PhD Wisconsin) was born in Berkeley, California. In 1985 she was appointed assistant professor at Michigan State University, and was promoted to professor in 1997. She is now Professor and Head, Department of Economics, Finance & Accounting and Dean, Faculty of Social Sciences at the National University of Ireland Maynooth (Ireland). She has held various visiting posts in the US, UK, Italy, Australia, and Ireland. She conducts research in a number of distinct fields in economics from macroeconomics and banking to the philosophy of economics. Her recent work explores hope and despair in economic thought. She is an avid cook, a lover of music, art, the built and the natural worlds. What does give her hope? "That people strive to make the impossible possible."

*"Sometimes positive thinking
has become an obligation."*

*The tyranny
of positive thinking*

There are an estimated 14 million cancer cases around the world.
According to the World Cancer Research Fund International,
this number is expected to increase to 24 million by 2035.
Thrown between hope and despair, patients probably meet
someone who encourages them to think positive. It might help.
But Prof. **Miles Little** states it is not as easy as that.

Hope is a positive state of mind that is focused on some end that is perceived to be desirable.
It may be hope for wealth, happiness, revenge, health, and many other things that would
secure one's survival, security, or flourishing in some way. **The positive thought
movement urges an instrumental approach to hope.** By banishing despair or a recognition
of the threats inherent in illness or disaster, it claims, your outlook will be improved
in measurable terms. That is to say, if you have cancer and get your thinking right, you will
conquer your illness, live longer, feel better. You will win over the physical threat that will
overcome your less optimistic fellow sufferer.

Shame

This pins hope to cure. Cure is the end to which you must direct your whole being,
even when there is evidence that the disease is beyond curative treatment. Think positive
and you will overcome. This burden has been examined by a number of authors and there
is conflicting evidence about measurable effects on survival.

When I looked after patients with advanced cancer, one of the saddest issues that I faced came when trying to help **patients whose disease had progressed despite their earnest and trusting participation** in positive psychology programs. They expressed their own shame at having failed their mentors, who had assured them that they would be able to control their cancers if they "got their thinking right." Their burdens were increased by their "failure."

Miracle

I know well that meditation and support help people with cancer to enjoy a better quality of life, and I encourage that route for anyone for whom it seems helpful. But this is not the same as the obligation to think positive that has become an "oppression" or a "tyranny." Hope for cure is not the only hope that patients should be allowed or encouraged to accept. **Hope for a meaningful death may also be a legitimate ambition when the time comes.** There is always hope for a miracle, but it must not be the only hope that a man or woman should be permitted to have toward their end of days.

The keys

→ **Meditation and support help people with cancer enjoy a better quality of life. That route should be encouraged for anyone for whom it seems helpful.**

→ **But this is not the same as the obligation to think positive that has become an "oppression" or a "tyranny."**

→ **Hope for cure is not the only hope that patients should be allowed or encouraged to accept.**

Miles Little is Emeritus Professor of Surgery at the University of Sydney (Australia). He is the Founding Director of the Centre for Values, Ethics and the Law in Medicine in the Department of Surgery at the University of Sydney.

"You can live some weeks without food,
only days without water,
but not a second without hope."

The clash of pathways

Once known as "The Switzerland" and "The Paris" of the Middle East, now Lebanon is permanently in the news with bomb explosions, refugees, and conflicts. Prof. **Shahe S. Kazarian** lives and teaches in Beirut. Talking on hope, he is caught in the clash of divergent pathways.

Hope is a mosaic assembly of positive emotion; character strength (optimism, future-mindedness, and future-orientation); religious virtue along with love and faith; sense of purpose in life; and cognition with the twin beliefs that people are motivated to pursue desired goals in life, and that they find ways to attain these goals. The individualist and horizontal Western worldview of hope socializes youth to a culture of *personal* agency in which people choose their own goal maps and pathways and rely on their own character strengths to attain their desired outcomes. Similarly, the collectivist and hierarchical worldview of hope (amal and rajaa in Arabic) in the Arab world socializes youth to a culture of *collective* agency in which people establish and pursue goals and pathways informed primarily by institutions external to the self, such as family and political or sectarian in-groups. In both cultures, the personal agency and the collective agency may be informed by the fear and hope duality of religion that inspires people's faith in and dependence on the ultimate love, wisdom, benevolence, compassion, and mercy of the Almighty and invocation of His will (Inshallah, in Arabic) for desired outcomes within this lifetime and/or in the post-mortem life. An unintended consequence of the culture of personal agency is empowerment of a narcissistic "I" at the expense of the collective goodness of the "we", whereas an unintended consequence of the culture of collective agency is empowerment of the "we" at the expense of a marginalized and sacrificial if not martyred "I."

The first take home message: Socialization of youth in both the culture of personal agency that nourishes confidence, competence, achievement, and self-actualization, and the culture of collective agency that nurtures social connectedness, warmth, and caring is more likely to invoke greater individual and collective love, happiness, and hope in the global village.

Passionate dreams

The culture of hope in Lebanon is a rainbow challenged by the clash of emotions (fear in the Western world and humiliation in the Islamic world) and the clash of civilizations (Western vs. Islamic domination of the world) globally, ethnic and sectarian struggles regionally, and the clash of social and religious intergroup identities fueled by the politically splitting media personalities locally. **The turbulent and disharmonious collective memory of the people of Lebanon is manifest**, for example, by one in-group dreaming of an independent secular nation-state, another in-group being passionate about a Lebanon as an appendage to a larger Arab collective, a third in-group aspiring for a religiously informed space, and so on.

Culture of war

On the wings of adversity and uncertainty invoked by the clash of intergroup identities, the culture of war has been a dominant pathway in the worldview of hope in Lebanon supplemented by peripheral pathways such as individual and media trade with horoscopes, psychics, fortune tellers, and cup-readers (all external agents to the collective agency), humoring of political turmoil (e.g., making fun of car explosions), and the face-saving-humiliation-avoidant adage, "neither victor, nor vanquished." The consequence of the culture of war pathway for the people of Lebanon has been regression **from a "mission of love" to a "mission of despair"**: destruction of living space; tragic loss or disappearance of more than 150,000 human lives; fragility in health (including mental health) and cultural and economic livelihood; and collective hopelessness of a hemorrhaging and brain-drained youth.

People killing people

The limited success of the "people killing people" pathway has invoked **a clash between the "culture of war and martyrdom" pathway and the "culture of peace and life" pathway** to social justice and happiness. As an illustration, the local implementation of "culture of life, hope, and optimism" initiatives such as "I Love Life" by proponents of the culture of peace pathway is met with cynicism if not hostility by opposing in-groups that construe such collective hope inspiring programs as Crusader Hopes or "foreign imported solutions" by colonized colonizers. What is significant is that the lead actors of the human drama involving the clash of in-group identities and their divergent hope pathways are equally convinced in their roles as the oxytocin of optimism, perhaps best captured in the Arabic proverb, "You can live some weeks without food, only days without water, but not a second without hope."

The second take-home message: We need to empower youth embedded in conflicted pathways because of the clash of in-group identities to a culture of dialogue informed by trust, empathy, and forgiveness to enable a future mosaic assembly of peace, social justice, gratitude, love, and happiness locally and globally.

The keys

→ **Socialization of youth in both the culture of personal and collective agency is more likely to invoke greater happiness and hope.**

→ **The lead actors of the human drama are equally convinced of their divergent hope pathways.**

→ **We need to empower youth embedded in conflicted pathways because of the clash of in-group identities.**

Shahe S. Kazarian is Professor in the Department of Psychology at the American University of Beirut (Lebanon). He has been Past President of the London Regional Psychological Association and a founding member of the Lebanese Psychological Association. Kazarian enjoys classical music, international travel, and quality time with family and friends. He believes that the heroic life narrative of people of the world is not a tragic landscape of martyrdom but a triumphant journey of human flourishing.

Sara Michli is a graduate student in the Department of Psychology at the American University of Beirut. Her research interests are focused on the interface between positive psychology and cultural psychology.

Peer to peer

Last year, he co-published the book *To save the world, with P2P to a post-capitalist society*. This definitely sounds like an overambitious title, yet Michel Bauwens really meant it. Why would the peer-to-peer dynamic be such a powerful reason for hope?

The concept of "peer to peer" was first used to indicate technological structures whereby computers and their users could talk directly to each other, without having to pass through an intermediary. It was used, for example, in the context of "P2P filesharing," i.e. people sharing music and videos without asking for payment. So what is important here is not the technological, but the human relationship that it enables. We can now very easily connect with each other on a global scale. So **peer to peer is the ability that many of us now have to freely contribute to huge and complex projects.** Again, why is this a sign of hope?

Fake abundance

To understand this, we have to look at what is so **fundamentally wrong with the organization of our world**, that we are actually in the process of severely harming our planet and climate.

1. Our economic system is based on the belief that we can have infinite growth. We could call this belief system "pseudo-abundance," or fake abundance.

2. We believe that the things that are easily and freely shareable such as knowledge, culture, innovation, technology, and science, should be made artificially scarce.

We create huge problems through our unsustainable economic practices and make it very difficult for people to work together on the solutions, by privatizing knowledge. **Peer-to-peer technologies and human dynamics allow for the free and easy sharing of the world's knowledge at very low cost.** Hence it makes it increasingly difficult, if not impossible, to truly privatize knowledge. Those who favor the privatization of human knowledge basically have to either increase legal repression or actually sabotage technological instruments, and this is increasingly untenable and losing legitimacy.

Open source

Millions of people in the world are now creating shared knowledge (think Wikipedia), shared code (think Linux), and shared design (think the WikiSpeed open-source car). Though these may seem

like "immaterial" activities, they have a huge influence on our material economy.

Indeed, when private corporations design products and services, they always have to do so for the market, hence they design to maintain scarcity, otherwise the necessary tension between supply and demand would be lacking. As we know, **planned obsolescence is not a bug, but a feature in our current system.** But communities who design open-source cars or distribute energy solutions have no such motive. Thus, global open-design communities design for sustainability. Entrepreneurs who then make and sell these products on the market start producing sustainable products and services.

There is another reason why P2P offers hope: when people peer-produce together freely, they do so because they are passionate. And passionate people are happy and hyper-productive! Unlike workers who are either coerced or have to accept jobs they don't like just to survive. Hence we see **a new economy emerging that is based on contributory commons, where people contribute, paid or unpaid, because they really want to.** And around these contributions, a vibrant entrepreneurial economy can be created, which creates livelihoods. These communities are

strong enough to create their own democratic organizations, which create and defend their infrastructures of cooperation.

Save the world

Now think for a minute what this could mean for the future. Our civil society would become productive, with citizens contributing to common pools of knowledge, software, and design.

This society would consist of voluntary and happy contributors, it would be sustainable, and would have to be socially just to function properly. This is why P2P is indeed a source of hope and can indeed "save the world."

Michel Bauwens, founder of
the Foundation for Peer-to-Peer Alternatives
More information: **www.p2pfoundation.net**

*"Devoid of any positive prospect
makes the suffering unbearable."*

The essence of Hell

Active hope is a strong motivational force. According to **Cristiano Castelfranchi**, it is the power of wish and possibility. But hope may have some dangerous drawbacks. And why exactly is the word mentioned in the inscription at the entrance of Hell?

Hope is distinct from other anticipatory representations. Comparing hope with positive expectation proper, we notice different reactions, either when disappointed or when fulfilled. Unlike hope, positive expectation implies a normative component according to which the expected outcome is viewed as "bound" to happen. That is why disappointed positive expectations are typically associated with a sense of injustice, as if one were suffering something unfair, whereas disappointed hopes just elicit discomfort, sadness, and the like. Fulfilled positive expectations may be accompanied by relief in that the risk of disappointment is definitively over. However, the stronger a positive expectation, the weaker the associated satisfaction, because what "should" happen just happened. By contrast, the fulfilment of one's hopes is very far from being perceived as one's due— quite the reverse. Therefore, full joy, rather than mere relief, is the most likely reaction. The distinctions provided also allow us to explain the possible coexistence of some anticipatory representations, but not others. For instance, whereas positive and negative expectations about the same event cannot coexist, **hope can coexist with a negative expectation**, as well as with fear, accounting for anxiety. Moreover, the comparison between positive expectation and hope allows us to distinguish hope from a sense of personal mastery, optimism, trust, and faith.

Active hope

Hope is a strong motivational force. Typical of active hope are attitudes of persistence, patience, and readiness to take advantage of favoring conditions. These motivational implications can be considered responsible for the crucial role hope seems to play in fostering an individual's well-being. For instance, hope has been found to be a precondition for agreeing to attend therapy and remain in treatment, and it also seems to dramatically impact the success of the treatment.

The importance of hope not only for psychological well-being, but also for physical health, is increasingly supported by a variety of studies. **Hope seems to be a painkiller**, in that it relieves physical pain, strengthening the organism and favoring recovery. This exemplifies the well-known route from mind to body: the body reacts in accordance with the anticipation of a possible pleasurable (or less painful) state, by producing its own painkillers (like endorphins). The other way around is also worth considering: an actual improvement in physical health, even if small, may favor the patient's hope in recovery. In turn, hope will set off the production of the body's painkillers, thus further fostering recovery.

Passive hope

Despite all of those positive implications, hope may have some drawbacks. To start with, when hope is maintained despite a negative expectation, there might be some cost implied: the possible (albeit cautious) waste of resources. Second, hope might favor a self-deceiving attitude or inaccurate perception of reality. However, accuracy is compatible with a hopeful attitude. **Hope represents a sort of shield** against the negative consequences implied by uncertainty about the future—premature discouragement and disengagement from pursuit—by favoring a view of success as plausible, and motivating us to strive for it. But "plausible" can still be distinguished from either "probable" or "certain." Third, there is a passive facet of hope, which may have detrimental implications.

Hope does not always foster one's motivation to strive for the hoped-for outcome. It may even restrain motivation, and this risk is intrinsic to its very nature. In fact, hope might favor a passive waiting for the desired outcome to "spontaneously" happen. We view a couple of conditions that are likely to orient such passive waiting.

To start with, the hoped-for outcome may be deemed to depend to some extent on forces that are beyond one's control. Now, in some cases (or for some people), such a confrontation with the limitations of one's agency may lead to the conclusion that, as far as one's agency is concerned, X is impossible, and that X is possible only through the intervention of external agents or forces. This exclusive reliance on external factors will orient the individual to passively wait for the desired outcome.

Positive fantasies

Moreover, hope may happen to focus on the desired result, with no consideration of the possible conditions or plans for obtaining it. In such instances, the hopeful mind-set merely consists of positive fantasies about X, figuring it as already realized. **Dwelling on positive fantasies about the desired outcome is likely to reduce motivation,** for at least two reasons: first, focusing on the final result, one tends to disregard any possible planning in view of it; second, having virtually experienced the satisfaction conveyed by such result, one may feel little need to act in order to realize one's fantasy. That is why hope may be devoid of any propulsive role, and even be detrimental, because it remains confined to the status of a dream.

Hope remains a resource of invaluable importance. Suffice to consider that as long as there is hope, unfulfillment and actual frustration are relatively easy to endure. Conversely, hopelessness can be conceived of as the worst human condition. If there is no possible anticipation of a better future, there is no meaningful future, and little reason to live as well. Not surprisingly, the inscription at the entrance to Hell, according to Dante Aligheiri, is "Abandon hope, all ye who enter here." Dante provides another phrase that is even more representative of the suffering of hopelessness: the sorrow of those who "still desiring, live without hope." That is, the wish component is still there, but devoid of any positive prospect, and this makes the suffering unbearable. This is precisely the psychological essence of hell.

The keys

→ **Active hope is a strong motivational force. It is a painkiller.**
→ **Hope may have some drawbacks. Passive hope may even restrain motivation.**
→ **Still desiring but living without hope is the psychological essence of hell.**

Maria Miceli is coauthor of this text.

Cristiano Castelfranchi is professor of Economical Psychology at LUISS University in Rome (Italy), and of Social Psychology at Uninettuno telematic university; retired full professor of General Psychology, University of Siena; and ex-director of the Institute of Cognitive Sciences and Technologies of the Italian National Research Council (ISTC-CNR) in Rome, where he is presently coordinator of the Goal-Oriented Lab. He is active in the antipsychiatric movement; loves modern and baroque architecture; and secretly writes poems and produces ready-made art. "My hope is that science will not only be useful for producing technology, goods, money, and so on; but also for building knowledge and diffusing it, in order to change our collective understanding and behaviors, improve our critical attitude toward dominant powers, provide tools for governance, and favor political participation."

"Hope is your motivation and inspiration
if you're standing at the bottom of the ladder."

To each
his own ladder

"Hope has to do with our perspective, with accepting our situation as it is and experiencing control over it," say **Sjaak Bloem** and **Joost Stalpers**. As economic psychologists, they study the behavior of patients in the health-care system. "In health care, hope is an important motivation. It can help you improve your 'experienced health'." But in hopeful health care, peace, grip, and pride also play a role.

A ladder is a good way to show how people experience their health. The highest rung on the ladder is a person's best day in a given period, and the lowest rung their worst day. The higher up the ladder, the healthier a person feels. Because everybody's opportunities and limitations are different, each individual has his or her own ladder. How a person experiences his or her health (read: his or her physical and mental functions) can be described by choosing the rung that best fits.

The premise that each person has his or her own ladder also means that standing at the bottom or the top of the ladder is different for everyone. An individual can stand at the top of the ladder in spite of the fact that he or she cannot walk because of paraplegia, while another individual might stand at the bottom of the ladder because he or she cannot walk because of a sprained ankle. Studies have identified the most important factors that determine a person's position on the ladder: **control and acceptance**. Control has to do with the feeling that you can influence your situation, while acceptance relates to the degree to which the state of your health is part of your life. Standing at the top of the ladder means having a feeling of control over how you experience your health and being able to give it a place in your life. Standing at the bottom of the ladder means the opposite: the feeling that you have no control and cannot accept your health situation. The way people experience their health is not static but continually changing.

High or low

To help people climb higher up the ladder or to stay high on the ladder, we can employ different strategies. If people are standing high on their ladder, they are best rewarded with **pride**. They do not need long-term coaching, only affirmation. This can be "a pat on the back" from friends and family or health-care professionals, but also because they find affirmation in information intended for them. People can stand lower on the ladder because they experience little control, but also because they have difficulty accepting their health situation. For the first group, people with little control, it is important for them to get a **grip** on their situation. This can be accomplished by helping them give structure to their lives. Paper or electronic diaries can be useful in this approach, but so can apps that help regulate medication. People who have a problem with acceptance mostly need **peace**. One way of finding it is through contact with others in the same situation.

Low acceptance and little control ensure that people end up standing at the bottom of the ladder. For them, **hope** is a central mechanism for climbing higher up. Personal counseling and attention—for example, through coaching—are the best medicine.

Rung by rung

Hope is necessary for recognizing the importance of your own behavior. This is essential for convincing people to (help) build the things they want to achieve. What each individual wants to achieve is not a fixed, ready-made end result. **Hope is the trigger, the basic** condition for getting into action. There is something "somewhere," "further away," that might become a reality by working on it. Hope has an active meaning. It doesn't mean looking back at what was—what you as an individual were able to do. It means that people, alone or with others, have to learn how to deal with the available possibilities for making progress in the here and now, higher up the ladder, rung by rung, until other mechanisms become more functional.

Hope is dealing with the situation in which you find yourself. With baby steps, giant steps, one rung at a time, you rise up the ladder within the possibilities open to you. Every rung is a goal in itself. Small, large—it doesn't matter—as long as it fits you. Hope is your motivation and inspiration if you're standing at the bottom of the ladder.

The keys

→ **The way people experience their health changes all the time. Our position on the ladder is determined by our feeling of more or less acceptance and control.**

→ **High on the ladder of acceptance and control, we are best rewarded with pride (affirmation). In the middle, by grip (structure) and peace (for example, contact with others in the same situation).**

→ **For those at the bottom of the ladder, hope is the central mechanism for rising higher. Coaching and counseling can help immensely.**

Sjaak Bloem is a professor at Neyenrode Business University (the Netherlands). He has studied economic psychology at the University of Tilburg and has worked there as an assistant professor. He is an expert in health consumer behavior, methodology, and health innovations.
Joost Stalpers, PhD, is an economic psychologist and conducts research into the influence of psychological factors on the experience of health.

"Hope is the last to die."

Hope despite low happiness

"International surveys on happiness and well-being show that Serbia consistently ranks among countries lowest in well-being and that Serbs are among the unhappiest people on earth," say **Veljko Jovanović** and **Vesna Gavrilov-Jerković**. "However, our research reveals a paradox exemplified in the Serbian version of the proverb: *Where there's life, there's hope*."

Although Serbia has faced adversity over the past few decades (two wars, political instability, economic depression, moral breakdown—with the consequent fall in well-being), the levels of hope in Serbian youth do not significantly lag behind those of their peers in developed and more stable countries. Hope is indeed the last to die. In other words, studies show that the vast majority of Serbian adolescents report feeling hopeful "much of the time"

or "most of the time." Questions emerge from this paradox: How is it possible to find reasons to hope even in a country with unfavorable living conditions, and why are relatively high levels of hope accompanied by low levels of overall happiness?

Control

We argue that hope is a resource that operates and plays a prominent role in adverse circumstances, especially those beyond one's control. Hope encompasses a positive stance toward the future and the belief that things will get better, thus helping individuals to manage stress and crises, ameliorate problems, and navigate through life—even in such disadvantageous conditions. Our research in Serbia shows that the function of hope under conditions of existential deprivation is to develop and maintain positive emotions, rather than to motivate concrete action. In other words, hope helps young people face difficult existential problems beyond their control by relying on traditional expectations ("I hope things will get better" or "I hope this will be over soon"), thereby preserving positive emotions despite unfavorable circumstances, while also safeguarding their own self-respect and sense of self-efficacy.

In turn, such a stance leads them to persist in hoping, even when no real improvement occurs in living conditions, and to expend additional effort in adapting to opportunities. This situation is further complicated by features of Serbian culture (such as an underdeveloped sense of personal accountability for well-being, with the corresponding expectation that a collective authority such as the state should step in and somehow make things better), which underscores the importance of not losing hope amid already reduced well-being.

Risk

Hope leads to greater well-being. If we are able to maintain hope in difficult circumstances, we have a chance of greater happiness, health, and positive adaptation. Our results show that high levels of hope contribute in a stable, long-term manner to greater life satisfaction, reduced distress, and a greater number of positive emotions—but only when combined with emotional flexibility and the disposition to adapt actively to various challenges.

Paradoxically, high levels of hope in certain situations show unexpectedly negative effects, especially in subjects who express hope in a better tomorrow yet react to increased stress by passively avoiding problems. Results show that such subjects are at an increased risk of symptoms of emotional distress.

Hope requires more than waiting for a better tomorrow to appear as if by magic. Unless you take action, you expose yourself to disappointment and stress. Use the positivity and excitement of hope to accept what you cannot control while taking steps to change what you can. By doing so, you increase the chance of achieving your goals, of loving yourself and others, and of living a life that makes sense. Hope is a good friend who stays by your side.

The keys

→ **Even under conditions of great existential uncertainty and risk, young people succeed in showing as much hope as their peers in economically and politically stable countries.**

→ **Hope's adaptive function varies according to culture and context: in collectivist settings with many existential challenges, hope serves more to increase positive emotions and maintain self-esteem, rather than for achieving life goals.**

→ **Hope is not always positive. If we hope for improvement yet avoid facing the problem, merely waiting passively for things to sort themselves out, we are at greater risk of emotional distress.**

Veljko Jovanović is Assistant Professor of the Department of Psychology, University of Novi Sad (Serbia). He is a pioneer in the research of well-being in Serbia. He hopes that his work will raise awareness about well-being as the ultimate goal of community and public policy in his country. He is grateful to his parents, sister, and friends for making his life meaningful and hopeful.
Vesna Gavrilov-Jerković is Professor at the Department of Psychology, University of Novi Sad (Serbia). Her research interests are positive clinical psychology, psychological protective factors, behavioral change mechanisms and processes in psychotherapy, and models of health-related behavioral change. She is married and the mother of a happy, optimistic teenager. She enjoys traveling, teaching, conducting research, and laughing with friends.

Optimism and decision-making

"While this book focuses on hope, I'd like to focus on the related term optimism," says Prof. **Walter Schaeken**. "Optimism and hope are both psychological constructs revealing positive outlooks about one's future, whereby optimism is a more general belief in a successful future and hope is more related to one's own capabilities to secure this successful future." These constructs play an important role in the daily decisions we make.

Let's be honest: if you think about it, making decisions is easy. Suppose I am thirsty and wonder what I should drink. The first thing you might do when making decisions is look for relevant information and consider the likelihood of various possible alternative actions or choices available to you. So I might think there is a small chance that there is beer in the fridge (e.g. .30), but that there is a much larger chance that there is sparkling water in the cellar (e.g. .70). The following aspect of your decision-making might be coming up with the benefits and costs that you will receive when you choose a particular alternative and to assign utilities. That is, you establish the strength of your like or dislike of these outcomes. In the example this might mean I think through the ideas that I definitely like beer, but that I still have to work and I know that alcohol does not increase my work efficiency. On the other hand, sparkling water is an excellent thirst quencher for me, but I don't like going down the stairs to the cold cellar.

So putting numbers to these considerations, the utilities for beer might be +60 for the taste and –20 for the negative effect on my work; the utilities for the sparkling water might be +60 for the thirst quenching and –40 for the stairs. **The penultimate step is to do some math; that is, you multiply the utilities with the likelihoods, which gives you the expected utility of the possible outcomes.** This leads in the example to .30 × (60 – 20), which is 12, for the beer, and to .70 × (60 – 40), which is 14, for the sparkling water. The final step is to choose the best decision, and that is the option with the highest expected utility. In this example, this would mean I shouldn't be lazy but should go down the stairs to the cold cellar to pick up the bottle of healthy sparkling water.

Weighting

However, research shows that this rational account of decision-making is unrealistic. Humans are often not doing this. Our decision process is characterized by heuristic processing. According to Shah & Oppenheimer (2008), these heuristics rely on, for instance, examining fewer cues, reducing the difficulty associated with retrieving and storing cue values, simplifying the weighting principles for cues, integrating less information, and examining fewer alternatives.

Why do human beings opt so often for heuristic processing? Some scientists argue that we use these heuristics because we save effort by using them. However, the dark side of its use is that this happens at the cost of accuracy (Shah & Oppenheimer, 2008). The danger of such an account of heuristics is that they become too much associated with errors. Other scientists, like Gigerenzer, therefore, claim that some heuristics are ecologically rational to the degree that they are adapted to the structure of the environment. In other words, it's sometimes a better idea to use a heuristic instead of rational thinking: heuristics can be more accurate than normative thought.

Failure

One famous heuristic in the domain of decision-making has to do with considering the likelihood of different outcomes. Research found evidence for an optimism bias, which, by the way, sounds better than "unrealistic optimism," as it is also referred to. The optimism bias is the tendency to underestimate the likelihood that we will experience negative events compared to others. The classical study of Weinstein (1980) shows, for instance, that students believe they are more likely to own their own home and that they believe they are less likely to have a drinking problem than their peers. There is much evidence for this effect, although recently Harris and Hahn (2011) claim that quite a lot of the studies showing the optimism bias have statistical problems, so that evidence for unrealistic optimism may be overstated. However, Shepperd, Klein, Waters, and Weinstein (2013) convincingly show that these statistical problems are not nearly as problematic as they might seem and that the evidence for the optimism bias in cases where people make comparative judgments is clear and consistent.

Why then would we have this specific bias? Exciting research of Marshall and Brown (2006) shows that there is an interesting link between expectancies of success and people's emotional reactions to outcomes. People with high expectations in general feel good, and those with low expectations tend to feel bad in general. Moreover, people who expect success evaluate their outcome more positively than those who expect a failure, even in cases where they didn't reach their goals. Especially fascinating was their finding with respect to the attributions people made. The optimists took responsibility for their successes, but their failures were, according to them, due to the circumstances. The pessimists did the opposite: their success was largely caused by the circumstances (e.g., "the test was really easy"), and their failure was attributed to their own trait (e.g., "I'm not clever enough"). These observations might also be linked with the line of research showing that individuals with depressive symptoms show decision-making deficits (see, for instance, Gradin, Kumar, Waiter, Ahearn, Stickle, Midelers et al, 2011). Important to add is that people truly believe their optimistic predictions. Simmons and Massey (2012), for instance, showed that optimistic predictions persisted, even when participants were paid $50 for an accurate prediction.

Flexible

Are people always optimistic? No, they are not. The work of Sweeny, Carroll, and Shepperd (2006) shows that **we do not embrace optimism all the time. The closer we are to moments where we will receive feedback, the more people decrease their optimism.** One clear illustration of this was the observation that students were pessimistic about the outcome of their exams just before they would receive feedback. One plausible reason for this effect is that this mechanism of a downward shift in optimism prepares us better to respond to bad news that might occur.

In other words, it looks as if our optimism bias has strong advantages, but also that people are able to show or use it flexibly. This is, of course, important, because we do not want people to underestimate their own chances for skin cancer and therefore not take the right precautions. This human flexibility, although clearly still not good enough, is a good starting point to investigate this optimism bias from an ecological rationality viewpoint: In what environment or circumstances during decision-making is optimism successful? Once we know these conditions better, it will become easier to use the benefits from the optimism bias, without having the drawbacks of it. I'm optimistic about our chances of succeeding in this task. And therefore, I decided, it's time for that beer.

The keys

→ **The optimism bias is the tendency to underestimate the likelihood that we will experience negative events compared to others. Research found evidence for an optimism bias.**

→ **Optimists take responsibility for their successes, but their failures are, according to them, due to the circumstances. Pessimists do the opposite.**

→ **Our optimism bias has strong advantages, but people are also able to show or use it flexibly.**

Walter Schaeken is a full professor in experimental psychology at the University of Leuven (Belgium), specialized in deduction, decision-making, and experimental pragmatics. He has published many peer-reviewed papers in journals like *Psychological Review*, *Cognition*, and *Journal of Experimental Psychology* and chapters and contributions in peer-reviewed conference proceedings. He likes to tire his body with long runs, but also to feed it with good food and fine drink in the company of friends. And in the evening, good books turn out to be great company. "These enjoyable bodily and mental sensations are the best soil for my confidence in the fact that, despite encountering once in a while less than ideal circumstances and events, I will always come through."

"Psychotherapy is not about hope,
but instead about building and activating hope."

Hope in therapy

"One day, in a psychotherapeutic session, an adolescent girl,
15 years old, told me: 'By building my future life, in the present,
I am choosing my past life. I think this is my way of having hope
and feeling powerful in my present life. This is why I never give up,'"
Prof. **Teresa Freire** tells us. She has met children and adolescents
in psychotherapy for almost 30 years.

One of the most important things I have learnt in those 30 years, taught by the children
and adolescents I have met, is about hope and its role in our lives. Not because it is associated
with suffering, or psychological disorder or psychopathology, but instead because it is
intrinsically related to positive functioning, being a central resource in a human's repertoire.

Children and adolescents inspire us about hope. Not because they are always hopeful
(not at all!) but because as naïve persons (without the rationality of adults) they show
day-by-day, moment-to-moment how they manage the basic processes of hope. Sometimes
they feel hopeful because life is going well and they become even more hopeful. Sometimes
they are not capable of doing anything, but still they hope they will. Sometimes they know
how to do, how to attain, but uncontrolled or unexpected circumstances arrive (any kind of
adversity), and still they have that hope things will change; even when they seem hopeless.

Motivation

My clinical intervention is sustained in positive psychology interventions that evolved from the emergence of positive psychology. Within this new approach, the concept of psychotherapy has changed its focus from symptom and problems to well-being or happiness and skillfulness. It is an integrative movement, not a replacement of the former by the latter, which means moving children and adolescents from deficit to strengths, from problems to solutions, from passivity to involvement, from inaction to achievement, from disturbance to optimal functioning. This is the movement for worthwhile living, being in psychotherapy or in any other situation of daily life.

Positive psychology has developed several theories about positive functioning and its association with the good life. In this perspective, hope theories have been developed showing the importance of motivation, agency, thinking, goal attainment, meaning, and how this involves feelings, behaviors or cognitions. Their application to psychotherapy, or positive intervention in general, is well recognized and **several studies and interventions try to understand the role of hope in the efficacy of the treatment.** In fact, psychotherapy is one context where hope is necessary to initiate and maintain involvement, because we deal with change and motivation to change. At the same time intervention processes tend to show an increase in hope from the beginning to the end of the intervention, because we work for efficacy in this changing process. But we don't yet know about the causal relations (if they exist) between hope and the outcomes of positive intervention.

Optimal functioning

Looking to people *in* development (always my focus on children and adolescents), I would say that psychotherapy is not about hope, but instead about building and activating hope. And for this to happen other multiple areas and resources need to be built through psychotherapy into daily life. This is the main focus of positive interventions, and they create the optimal conditions for the development of hope. Positive interventions deal with the best and the worst, the positive and the negative, the good and bad, the expected and the unexpected, because **what is important is the integration of these aspects in life trajectories** (past, present, future) and, remember… this is about hope. Positive intervention is not only about what is good in life but about new capacities of thinking, feeling, and acting to achieve well-being and flourishing. And this process chain is the main source of hope.

It's true; we need to create conditions for the emergence of hope. Optimal functioning is needed for hope to exist, because hope is not a determinant but instead a result and a product. Hopelessness is not what makes hope an emergent need or desire for people, because hope is not about problems, despair, or unhappiness. Hope is about goals, achievement, realization, attainment, and balance. The more this happens, the more hope is developed and thus becomes an individual strength and a resource. Nevertheless, hope needs to be fed and activated under optimal life conditions. In fact, hope is about optimal functioning.

The keys

→ **Hope is crucial in therapy. Not because it is associated with suffering, psychological disorder, or psychopathology, but instead because it is intrinsically related to positive functioning, being a central resource in a human's repertoire.**

→ **Psychotherapy is one context where hope is necessary to initiate and maintain involvement, because we deal with change and motivation to change.**

→ **Positive intervention is not only about what is good in life but about new capacities of thinking, feeling, and acting to achieve well-being and flourishing. And this process chain is the main source of hope.**

Teresa Freire is Assistant Professor in the School of Psychology in the University of Minho (Portugal). She belongs to the Research Unit of Psychotherapy and Psychopathology, being the Coordinator of the Research Group on Optimal Functioning. Teresa is a member of the European Network for Positive Psychology as a country representative member for Portugal. For her, hope is an everyday tool to manage daily situations aimed at building developmental trajectories. "The best translation of hope is to respect each child as a source of a new and better world, and to feel the responsibility of giving them the right opportunities for a worthy life."

"Greater pessimism is not synonymous with lower hope."

Hope for pessimists

"Whether the glass is half full or half empty, our research suggests that it is not so much how optimistic (or pessimistic) we are, but rather it is how hopeful we are that may make the greater difference in our lives," say **Elizabeth A. Yu** and **Edward C. Chang**. "The ability to believe that goals are attainable and being hopeful is what truly matters." There is hope for pessimists as well.

Myriad fables, countless anecdotes, and decades of research have told us that imagining the glass half full, thinking positively, and being optimistic and hopeful is beneficial and adaptive. However, with problems like depression, anxiety, and suicide affecting a large portion of the world population, how do positive thoughts (i.e. positive cognitions) such as optimism and hope come into play? Our research has led us to question what potential value the confluence of two different positive cognitions may have in relation to depression.

Positive cognitions

Higher levels of positive cognitions such as optimism and hope have been associated with higher levels of positive outcomes such as life satisfaction and subjective well-being. Such positive cognitions have also been associated with lower levels of negative outcomes such as depression and suicide. As depression rates continue to rise, it is important to determine how changing an individual's belief of the future (i.e., positive future-oriented cognitions) may help to mitigate negative outcomes like depression. However, among all the possible positive cognitions that can and have been studied, why is hope important, and how does it differ from other positive future-oriented cognitions?

As defined by Rick Snyder and his colleagues, hope is a two-part construct consisting of the belief that one has the ability to achieve a goal and the belief that one has the ability to generate many pathways to reach that goal. Theoretically, hope can be differentiated from other positive cognitions such as optimism. While optimism is the general belief that the positive outcome will occur, hope is more specifically the belief that one can secure a positive future. Thus, with the understanding that hope is theoretically different from other positive cognitions such as optimism, and with the background knowledge that positive cognitions are related to lower levels of negative outcomes, our research sought to understand how optimism and hope may work together in predicting negative outcomes, such as depressive symptoms.

Depressive symptoms

In a recent study of depressive symptoms in community adults (Chang, Yu, & Hirsch, 2013), we found empirical support that although hope and optimism are related to each other, they are not redundant, therefore pointing to the value of studying both these positive cognitions. Additionally, we found that both hope and optimism were unique and significant predictors of depressive symptoms in this group of community adults. Finally, we found an interactive relationship between hope and optimism in predicting depressive symptoms. In other words, regardless of whether an individual is an optimist or a pessimist, having a high level of hope is more indicative of having lower levels of depressive symptoms. Therefore, even if one generally believes that the positive outcome will always occur (i.e. being optimistic), believing that one has both the ability and means to reach specific goals is also valuable in protecting individuals from experiencing high levels of depressive symptoms. Our most interesting finding, however, was in examining how hope operates for pessimists. While being pessimistic may be associated with having greater levels of negative outcomes (as was shown in our study), being pessimistic but also hopeful greatly lowered the levels of depressive symptoms. Now, although it may seem ironic that someone could be both pessimistic and hopeful, similar to what was discussed above, greater pessimism is not synonymous with lower hope even if they may be related to each other. One could generally expect the negative outcome to occur but still have the belief that one can reach one's personal goals.

Increase hope

Our study provided a greater understanding for how positive cognitions and psychological problems are related. However, more work is needed in developing tools to increase positive cognitions, especially hope, in individuals who are more susceptible to negative outcomes such as depression. Despite there being room for growth in this area of research, our study begins to lay the foundation of the importance of considering the confluence of positive cognitions to potentially mitigate negative outcomes and to potentially increase the experience of more positive outcomes.

The keys

→ **Optimism is the general belief that the positive outcome will occur; hope is more specifically the belief that one can secure a positive future.**

→ **Regardless of whether an individual is an optimist or a pessimist, having a high level of hope is more indicative of having lower levels of depressive symptoms.**

→ **Being pessimistic but also hopeful greatly lowers the levels of depressive symptoms. The ability to believe that goals are attainable and being hopeful is what truly matters.**

Edward C. Chang is Professor of Psychology and Social Work at the University of Michigan (USA). He is Associate Editor of the American Psychologist and Fellow of the Asian American Psychological Association.
Elizabeth A. Yu is focusing on her doctoral studies in clinical psychology at the University of Michigan. She is interested in how positive cognitions are related to adjustment outcomes. Coauthors are **Shao Wei Chia, Zunaira Jilani** and **Emma Kahle**.

"*Hope is nourished by a sense of a higher purpose.*"

Hopeful people illuminating your path

"I have three heroes: Nelson Mandela, Aung San Suu Kyi, and Abraham Lincoln," says Prof. **Arménio Rego**, who was born in a small village in the north of Portugal. "Like everyone, I experienced suffering and frustration in my personal, family, and professional life. For some time, I nourished those experiences with hate and rumination. Those three giants helped me to discover that constant whining is a toxic nutrient of life and a route to more despair." How can we find hope in hopeful people illuminating our path?

My three heroes experienced huge psychological and physical suffering, faced dangerous enemies, and lived for decades dealing with awful obstacles and failures. Often, they experienced senses of impotence and upheaval when confronted with betrayals. They were tempted by "walking partners" who recommended backing down. But these giants never gave up, even when their lives were at stake.

Mandela: meaningful purpose

Mandela, defending himself in his 1963–1964 trial on charges of sabotage (incurring the risk of death penalty), told the court: "During my lifetime I have dedicated myself to this struggle of the African people. I have fought against white domination and I have fought against black domination. I have cherished the ideal of a democratic and free society, in which all persons live together in harmony and with equal opportunities. It is an ideal that I hope to live for and achieve. But if need be, it is an ideal for which I am prepared to die."

In the subsequent years, it was hope, fueled by such meaningful purpose and supported by other components of psychological capital (i.e. self-efficacy, optimism, and resilience), that helped Mandela, together with other prisoners, to produce a metamorphosis on Robben Island and, this way, in South Africa. Such as researchers Cascio and Luthans (*Reflections on the metamorphosis at Robben Island, 2014*) argued, the political prisoners on the island began a journey at the psychological and political levels to turn this "hell hole" into a symbol of freedom, personal liberation, and hope for the future.

Suu Kyi: resilience

When we reflect upon Suu Kyi's life, a similar pattern emerges: a strong combination of willpower and waypower (i.e. hope), fueled by a meaningful purpose and supported by strong levels of self-efficacy, realistic optimism, and resilience. Suu Kyi told an interviewer about her "terrible days" when she was under house arrest, in complete isolation: "Sometimes I didn't have enough money to eat. I became so weak from malnourishment that my hair fell out, and I couldn't get out of bed. I was afraid that I had damaged my heart. (…) I thought to myself that I'd die of heart failure, not of starvation (…). But they never got me up here", she said while pointing a finger to her head.

Lincoln: self-efficacy

Abraham Lincoln ("Honest Abe"), who abolished slavery in the US, was praised by Charles Francis Adams not because he possessed "any superior genius," but because he, "from the beginning to the end, impressed upon the people the conviction of his honesty and fidelity to one great purpose." D.K. Goodwin (2005) wrote: "From that moment on, propelled by a renewed sense of purpose, Lincoln dedicated the major part of his energies to the antislavery movement. Conservative and contemplative by temperament, he embraced new positions warily. Once he committed himself, however, as he did in the mid-fifties to the antislavery cause, he demonstrated singular tenacity and authenticity of feeling. Ambition and conviction united, "as my two eyes make one in sight," as Robert Frost wrote, "to give Lincoln both a political future and a cause worthy of his era."

What we observe, again, is hope fueled by a very noble and significant purpose, and supported by self-efficacy ("despite the appalling pressures he had faced from his very first day in office, he never lost faith in himself"; *Goodwin, 2005*), resilience to bounce back and move on ("possessed a life-affirming humor and a profound resilience that lightened his despair and fortified his will"), and realistic optimism ("nurtured in angst when the Enlightened confidence in its own optimistic solutions proved illusory"; *Guelzo, 2003*). Lincoln, like the other two heroes, experienced despair and setbacks. He even had depression; but, "fueled by his resilience, conviction, and strength of will," he recovered (*Goodwin, 2005*).

Three lights

In short, what I discovered with my three heroes was that their hope was nourished by a sense of a higher purpose. This purpose was illuminated not only by the other components of psychological capital, but also by an extraordinary capacity to forgive, unspeakable humility to learn from mistakes, **prudence and wisdom to devise clear goals in the middle of darkness and confusion**, and an unquestionable honesty. I learned two kinds of lesson. The first is more personal: despite difficulties, I have a good life, I have no reasons to complain, and I have the duty to guide my life as a compass, in which the North is where higher purposes are placed. The second lesson relates to my job as a researcher: there is much to learn through studying how hope interacts with other psychological strengths, and how other virtues are necessary to lead individuals (including leaders) to putting hope in the service of individual, organizational, and social betterment.

The keys

→ **We can always find hope in strong and hopeful people illuminating our path.**
→ **The hope of Mandela, Suu Kyi, and Lincoln was nourished by a sense of higher purpose and illuminated by forgiveness, humility, honesty, and the wisdom to devise clear goals in the middle of darkness.**
→ **We have the duty to guide our lives as a compass, in which the North is where higher purposes are placed.**

Arménio Rego is Associate Professor at the Universidade de Aveiro and member of Business Research Unit (Instituto Universitario de Lisboa: ISCTE-IUL) in Portugal. He has a PhD in Management and has published in journals such as *Journal of Business Ethics* and *Journal of Happiness Studies*. His research deals with positive organizational scholarship, his topics of interest being, among others, meaningful work, authentic leadership, and organizational virtuousness. He is (co)author of more than 40 books, including *The Virtues of leadership: Contemporary challenges for global managers* (Oxford University Press, 2012; with Miguel Pina e Cunha, and Stewart Clegg). Does he have a personal guiding line? "In order to achieve happiness, you must be prepared to suffer" (Suu Kyi). What most fuels his hope? "Loving my children and respecting the wishes of my (deceased) wonderful parents.

"Don't only praise and reward achievements but also efforts."

Hope at school

"Over the last 20 years, researchers have gained a clearer understanding of the relationships between hope and important aspects of students' lives," say **Susana C. Marques** and **Shane J. Lopez**. "Put simply, research demonstrates that more hopeful students do better in school and life than less hopeful students, which appears to be true across the board."

Our recent studies show that hope is positively associated with self-worth, life satisfaction, mental health, and academic achievement in Portuguese school-age students. Further, extremely high-hope students (top 10% of the distribution) differ from students with average (middle 25%) and extremely low hope (bottom 10% of the distribution) with significant higher levels in self-worth, life satisfaction, school engagement, and academic achievement. In the same line, extremely high and average hope is associated with mental health benefits that are not found among adolescents reporting comparatively extremely low hope levels.

Transmission

Given that hope is malleable and that the hopeless can learn to be hopeful, our youth need a focused effort from people who care about them and their future. Parents are the first important agents to impact children's hope. They model hope by the way they communicate, set goals, view challenges, and cope with problems. In the same manner, teachers play an important role in children's perceptions about their competences to achieve goals and to cope with obstacles that can arise. For example, educators can help students develop the capacity to think about the future in a complex way, to improve a flexible thinking about how to attain future goals and how to renew motivation when willpower is depleted. Additionally, being a high-hope parent and teacher facilitates children's hopeful thinking, and school psychologists are well positioned to stimulate this hope transmission. Some examples are:

→ Let teachers and parents know that children build hope through learning to trust in the ordered predictability and consistency of children interactions with them.

→ Explain the importance of being firm, fair, and consistent in engendering hope among their children.

→ Explain the importance of creating an atmosphere of trust, where students are responsible for their actions and supported to establish growth-inducing stretch goals.

→ Emphasize that children should be praised and rewarded for both their efforts and achievements.

→ Encourage teachers and parents to set goals that are made concrete, understandable, and are broken down into sub-goals.

→ Work with them to focus on long-range as opposed to short-term goals.

→ Emphasize the importance of preparation and planning.

→ Develop an atmosphere where students are focused on expending effort and mastering the information rather than a sole focus on obtaining good outcomes (e.g. high grades or stellar athletic records).

→ Encourage an atmosphere through a give-and-take process between teachers/parents and students.

→ Teachers should be encouraged to remain engaged and invested in pursuing their own important interests and life goals outside of the classroom.

→ Let them know that being a hopeful adult has many benefits. For example, high-hope people perform better at work, have higher well-being, and live longer.

By integrating hope into the curriculum or doing separate and regular hope-enhancing group sessions, school is an ideal place to work in groups and include relevant influences. It probably is accurate to say that all students, independently of their culture and language, need support from parents, school, and community to build their energy and ideas for the future. Building hope in our schools may be a good start to getting students excited and prepared for the future.

The keys

→ **More hopeful students do better in school (engagement and achievement) and life (self-worth and life satisfaction) than less hopeful students.**

→ **Given that hope is malleable and that the hopeless can learn to be hopeful, our youth need a focused effort from people who care about them and their future.**

→ **Being a high-hope parent and teacher facilitates children's hopeful thinking. There are lots of specific means available to stimulate this hope transmission.**

Susana C. Marques is Professor of Positive Psychology and Researcher of the Faculty of Psychology and Educational Sciences at Porto University (Portugal). Dr. Marques has published numerous hope-related articles and chapters, and she is currently serving as coeditor of the 3rd Edition of the *Oxford Handbook of Positive Psychology* (with S. J. Lopez and Lisa Edwards). She also works as a consultant applying hope and other strengths in organizations and school institutions and serves as the principal investigator on several national and international projects, including studies funded by the European Commission. The energy and persistence of her three-year-old son to achieve his own "goals" make her realize that every kid can make it when hope is supported. Coauthor of this text is **Shane J. Lopez**, author of another text in this volume: "Making Hope Happen."

Foster strengths

One of the school programs to foster hope in children and youth is the "Building Hope for the Future: A Program to Foster Strengths in Students."

This brief program comprises 5 one-hour sessions with students and direct work with key stakeholders (parents, teachers, and school peers). It was designed and implemented with Portuguese students by *Susana C. Marques*, *Shane J. Lopez*, and *J. L. Pais-Ribeiro* to help students to (1) conceptualize clear goals; (2) produce numerous ranges of pathways to attainment; (3) summon the mental energy to maintain the goal pursuit; and (4) reframe seemingly insurmountable obstacles as challenges to be overcome. A first implementation and examination of this program revealed that students in the intervention group increased hope, life satisfaction, and self-worth for at least one year and six months after the program.

Students focusing on hope and purpose

One of the hopeful effects of positive psychology is the growing interest of schools and universities all over the world in focusing on positive education. The University Tecmilenio in Mexico is a striking example of this evolution. With 38,000 students involved, it is one of the most exciting positive education programs in the world, focusing on education for hope and purpose.

Universidad Tecmilenio in Mexico has 38,000 students (from high school through master's level) in 29 campuses all over the country. One of their goals is that, in addition to acquiring professional skills, students develop competencies to enhance their well-being and lead full, purposeful lives. To do this, the university created the *Instituto de Ciencias de la Felicidad* (Institute of Happiness Sciences). Dr. Margarita Tarragona is the director of this institute.

She is passionate about processes of transformation in education, coaching, consulting, and therapy. In her work she incorporates research findings about well-being with collaborative and narrative practices to generate dialogues that help people expand their life stories and flourish.

Four pillars

Margarita Tarragona: "Our mission is to promote well-being through education, scientific research, and evidence-based practices. We do this in four ways: teaching about well-being, living well-being, researching well-being, and sharing well-being."

1. **"Teaching Well-being"** refers to the academic programs on the topic. The flagship course is a college positive psychology class that all freshmen take. It is a hybrid course that integrates online content (readings, videos, and exercises) and 6 experiential workshops (4 hours long) during the semester. Over 1,500 students have taken this class this year.

Through the Adult Education division the university offers a certificate program on the foundations of positive psychology. Over 110 professionals from different fields, including education, management, medicine, coaching, psychology, and journalism, have graduated from this certificate and are applying positive psychology in their work.

Something very unique about Tecmilenio is that a large number of administrators and faculty members are getting training in positive psychology: the president of the university, all of the vice-presidents, directors, campus directors, mentors, over 200 people in leadership positions, and 120 teachers have taken the certificate program. They are eager to see the effect that this system-wide training will have on their university.

2. **"Living Well-being"**

is about walking the walk and not just talking the talk. They want to be a positive organization and construct an "ecosystem of well-being" for all the people who study and work at the university. This entails having a strengths focus in relationships, cultivating appreciation and gratitude in everyday life, and implementing evidence-based practices to promote happiness and good health. The co-curricular activities are designed to explicitly address different components of well-being and they have campaigns to learn about, explore, and experience these elements of well-being throughout the school year.

3. **"Researching well-being"**

is about doing research. The university is especially interested in assessing the effects of their academic and co-curricular programs on the well-being of students and employees and they are systematically gathering data about these.

4. **"Sharing well-being"**

is about taking scientific knowledge about happiness beyond their campuses and offering training and consultation to different kinds of organizations in the communities.

"If you've got one foot in the future, and one in the past, then you are pissing on today."

Hope and gratitude

"If you've got one foot in the future, and one in the past, then you are pissing on today." Such was the wisdom I was told by a (recovering) addict when I was considering how to write an entry on gratitude for a book on hope, given that within psychology the two are not commonly considered together," says Prof. **Alex Wood**, who is an expert in studies on gratitude.

Indeed, at first blush, gratitude and hope seem most *incompatible*, given that gratitude represents positive views of the *present*, and hope involves positive expectations of the *future*. Like Janus, one faces forward and the other back. However, as the blunt quote suggests, hope alone is not enough for a good life—nor, for the individual concerned, sufficient for him to find the strength to overcome his addiction on a day-to-day basis.

Tragic hope

As the entries in this book show, hope can be positive, and a hopeless life may be unbearable. However, **hope without gratitude can be equally dangerous.** A person could, for example, not enjoy or appreciate their life on a day-to-day basis, living always for a future that may not materialize or which materializes so that most of life has been wasted. Literature is peppered with examples of such tragic hope, such as the archetype of the person who waits all of their life for a love that will always be unrequited. Indeed, given that life is finite, *any* time spent not appreciating the present but gazing longingly into the future may be considered tragic.

The side of organized religion referred to by Marx as the "opium of the masses" could be seen as trying to maintain tragic hope; agents of social control encouraging people to put up with abusive conditions today for hope of an afterlife of everlasting bliss (that at best was out of the control of those promising it). Indeed, the issue of control is generally problematic for hope, in that most of the things people hope for are out of their (complete) control, so the more that one hopes, the more one lets one's well-being be determined by events out of one's control. Finally, in some ways, people are constantly in a state of change; the "you" of this instant will not exist as such a second later, as you will have been changed by the experiences of the instant. This isn't a purely academic point; our research shows that people's core personalities change massively over time (indeed, more so than other "changing" things such as income). Over about a decade, even every cell in our body will be different. Given this, the future one hopes for will, in a very real sense, be enjoyed by a different person.

Genuine help

I'll not stress the benefits of hope, as this is done elsewhere in this book, but to the extent that hope can have a negative side, this side can mitigate if gratitude is also present. Sometimes people think of gratitude as a purely transactional emotion—it is something that one feels after being given something. We find that people's experience of gratitude is nearly totally dependent on how they view the help that they receive; people always feel gratitude when they receive help that they perceive to be valuable to them, costly to their benefactor, and intended by their benefactor with altruistic intent (to genuinely help them, rather than serve an ulterior motive). We all know people who feel more or less gratitude than others when we help them; our research shows this is totally due to how people automatically interpret events, whether their default is to see the help they receive as costly, valuable, and altruistically intended, or cheap, useless, and given due to ulterior motives.

Our experiments with school children show that we can train ourselves to have a more charitable (and often accurate) interpretation on these domains, and if we do so we feel more gratitude as a result. But gratitude is about more than simply appreciating help. Gratitude is a wider sense of appreciation of *all* that is good in the world, including aspects of the world itself, possessions, relative status, and simple existence. Our research that people who tend to experience more of one form of gratitude tend to experience more of all of the others, and that people who experience more gratitude in general have much better lives. More grateful people are happier, less stressed, and happier with their relationships. They sleep better, they cope better with adversity, and they maintain their well-being more successfully during life transitions.

Fostering appreciation

This wider sense of appreciation can be readily fostered. Simply keeping a diary in which one lists three things one is grateful for each day has a dramatic effect on well-being. Incredibly, it seems as effective at helping people with clinical levels of worry, depression, and body dissatisfaction as quite hard core therapeutic techniques (although, of course, less so than full therapy). Anecdotally, this seems to be due to the activity encouraging people to notice things on a moment-by-moment basis that otherwise would have gone over their heads.

Gratitude overcomes many of the potential challenges with hope, in that it involves appreciation of the present and is totally within one's control. However, gratitude without hope could have its own problems. A person could give up on trying to improve the world if they were too satisfied with what they have now *and* didn't have any hope that things were changeable. Thus, one needs both gratitude and hope together, to neither piss on today *nor* tomorrow.

The keys

→ **Since our core personalities change massively over time, the future one hopes for will be enjoyed by a different person.**

→ **People's experience of gratitude is nearly totally dependent on how they view the help that they receive. A wider sense of appreciation can be readily fostered.**

→ **Hope without gratitude (and vice versa) can be dangerous. Gratitude involves appreciation of the present and is totally within one's control. We need hope and gratitude together.**

Alex Wood, PhD, is Professor and Director of the Behavioural Science Centre at Stirling Management School, University of Stirling (Scotland, UK), which integrates the behavioral sciences (that focus on the individual) with the social sciences (which focus on the structure of society). He is known internationally for his work on well-being which is the integrative approach he brings to this area. In the last six years he has authored over 85 academic papers and books and conducted some of the founding research into gratitude. He has received numerous awards including an Honorary Chair at the University of Manchester and the GSOEP award for best research paper.

"We can practice our optimistic world-view by positive interventions."

One door closes, another one opens

"There is broad evidence that optimistic people tend to be more satisfied with their lives and the question arises: What are their secrets? One might say that they see and expect the bright side of life. But there is more," says **Sara Wellenzohn**. Recently, she got a good lesson in the Swiss mountains.

Early in the morning, I was hiking in the mountains with a friend. Another friend sent me a text message saying that she would join us later that day. I wrote her that clouds are coming up and that it soon might start to rain. Additionally, the weather forecast for the day was rather bad. I emphasized that we were expecting a rainy afternoon and, since I wanted to warn her, that our mood was already worsening. Little did I know how optimistic my friend was. She replied: "Well, the weather might be better in the afternoon, who knows? And if not, we will just have a nice time in the shelter up in the mountain." I reacted by joking about her message and her being that optimistic. Luckily this had no effect on her attitude and she joined our hiking tour in good humor.

As you might expect, in the end, she was right and it turned out to be a great sunny afternoon. We were having a good time while enjoying the scenic view over the valleys. I am grateful to my friend for the lesson that it is better to expect something good to happen rather than spending time worrying about things that might not come true. Surely this optimistic view had a positive impact on my and the whole group's mood. It is an intriguing question whether this view can be trained and whether it has an effect on a person's well-being.

Strategy

In our research group we are testing the effectiveness of so-called positive psychology interventions, which can be administered in online settings. The aim of this specific type of intervention is to enhance people's well-being. Of course, optimism could be seen as a useful ingredient for such interventions. Different researchers were interested in testing the effectiveness of the so-called "one door closes, another door opens" exercise. The main focus of this intervention is to think about things that went wrong in the past (the closing doors), but, in a next step, to also think about what unforeseen positive consequences (the opening doors) developed out of this.

The strategy that should be learned while doing this exercise needs to be distinguished from looking at the world through rose-tinted glasses. This means that problems or negative outcomes should not be ignored or belittled, but people are encouraged to get a more balanced view of an event. **Of course, there might be events that do not allow for seeing "opening doors," but many events might also have a positive aspect.** In some cases, the negative side might still overweigh, but letting oneself see the positive side might be a first step in the direction of an optimistic world-view. In any case taking some time to think about such situations, stepping back, taking a deep breath, might help us to see new perspectives.

Practice

Moreover, optimism is also about seeing and being aware of positive aspects in things that are not in one's power to change (e.g. the weather in my example, or events that lay in one's past). For many people this requires some practice, and people are encouraged to also employ creativity and openness to new perspectives. To illustrate this argument, referring back to the story, one needs to have an idea for an alternative activity if the weather might be bad. This means that if one aims at following the practice of "one door closes, another door opens," **it would be good to have an idea what the opening door could be.** The intervention aims at fostering this ability on the basis of past situations. Continued practice frequently helps people use this approach not only for past, but also for present and future situations and, by doing so, adapting the optimistic world-view.

Three months

In a recent study, we wanted to empirically test whether the "one door closes, another door opens" intervention has the potential to increase happiness in a placebo-controlled

intervention study. We tracked changes in happiness in our participants for a period of up to six months. We compared two groups: One group wrote about situations in which one door closed, but another one opened for seven consecutive days. Their changes in levels of happiness were compared to a placebo exercise, where participants also completed a task that took the same time. Before the intervention (at baseline) as well as directly after completing their assignments, after one month, three months, and six months they completed standardized measures for happiness.

The results of our study indicated that one and three months after the intervention-week the "one door closes, another door opens" intervention group showed higher increases in happiness, compared to the placebo group. Overall, the research question can be answered with "yes"—a self-administered optimism-based intervention can help people enhance their happiness.

Summing up, it seems that practicing one's optimistic world-view has an impact on the well-being of participants in such studies. One might argue that this also has an impact on other people and, who knows, this could even contribute to enjoying a nice day in the mountains.

The keys

→ In the "one door closes, another door opens" exercise we think about things that went wrong in the past (closing doors) and their unforeseen positive consequences (opening doors).

→ Optimism is also about seeing and being aware of positive aspects in things that are not in one's power to change. For many people this requires some practice.

→ Stepping back, taking a deep breath, might help us to see new perspectives. Self-administered optimism-based interventions help people to enhance their long-term happiness.

Sara Wellenzohn is a research associate at the Department of Psychology at the University of Zurich (Switzerland). In her PhD thesis she studies positive psychology interventions. For her master-thesis, she was based in a lab focusing on personality and assessment. She is a founding member and engaged in the board of directors of the Swiss Positive Psychology Association (SWIPPA). Besides contributing to establishing Positive Psychology in Switzerland and doing research on these topics, she likes spending her time with friends and on activities like hiking in the mountains or swimming in the rivers—enjoying and appreciating nature, hoping for the future to be the same and moreover, discussing and planning how we can contribute to that.

"It takes ten years to grow trees
yet a hundred years to nurture people."

Conquering fate

"The Chinese belief in igniting sparks is not only related
to personal belief in your potential, but also to the traditional
Chinese cultural belief in making earnest efforts to stand on your
own feet (*Zi-qiang buxi*) and offspring bringing hope to the family,"
say Prof. **Patrick S. Y. Lau** and Dr. **Florence K. Y. Wu**.
"It is this cultural trait that demonstrates how Chinese people
hold on to hope."

When students with special education needs (SENs) were first interviewed about their
planning for the future in the research for implementing positive youth development programs
in school settings, one of the conversational partners mentioned: "I hope to use my special
sparks to light up my life and that of my family. Though these sparks are 'too special' to
others, I hope I could use them. Our parents have spent too much time, money, and energy
nurturing me." In their eyes, the "specialty" and challenges ahead of the students
with special needs are well-recognized. Despite possible difficulties they might face
in the future, the students still hold a firm belief in the future and hope to bring changes
to themselves and their families by using their *sparks*.

A better harvest

As an agricultural-oriented nation, the repetitive process of sowing, waiting (for the plants
to grow), and harvesting cultivates our hope. We understand well that Mother Nature has
her own cycle and pace. Farmers pray sincerely to have the blessing from Nature
to have nice weather and, hence, to have a good harvest year. Even if there are floods and
droughts that might cause them to live under difficulties and challenges, farmers never

lose hope and have a strong will wishing to have a better harvest for the coming year. This is not solely a thought of dreaming positive outcomes in the future. It is internal strong belief in conquering fate, even though it seems to be uncontrollable, which empowers us to strive for a hopeful future. Fate does play an important role in sustaining hope for our nation. **Accepting fate in our lives is not implying a passive response to adverse and uncontrollable situations.** Fate is regarded as a goal to fight for or fight against. We are ready and content to meet that fate. We will conquer and cope with fate proactively and creatively in which we perceive hope as a trait comprised of willpower, faith, and actions.

Inherited goodness

This endurance is also made explicit and obvious in our education. There is one famous saying related to our education belief, which is "it takes ten years to grow trees yet a hundred years to nurture people." Nurturing is for the whole nation of people, upholding the belief that goodness could be inherited from generation to generation. With such belief in inheriting goodness, hope for the person, the family, and even the nation is embedded in the nurturing of younger generations. In the view of Hong Kong nowadays, quite a number of local scholars agree that **the promotion of hope and optimism in school is a promising way of wellness enhancement.** The implementation of career planning in schools is one of the ways to inspire students to visualize their future with the discovery of sparks—through self-understanding and self-acceptance. One interesting point worth noting is that career planning for the younger generation is not limited to the personal level. They wish to bring changes to the family too.

Ladder to heaven

Though the Chinese are subtle in expressing love to others, the story of "Love Stairs" well-demonstrates the belief in hope too. "Love stairs" is a true story about a couple living in a high mountain in Chongqing where the husband wished to "create" a staircase along the slope for his wife, connecting their world and the other's. Despite the steepness of the mountain, the husband kept building the staircase step by step from day to day for his beloved wife. The staircase could not be successfully built as there were many unpredictable difficulties. With the simple belief of leading his wife back to the common world, the husband persisted in building the staircase and finally the two worlds were connected. The name of the staircase in Chinese is "The Ladder to Heaven," signifying the extreme difficulty in building it. This story echoes the traditional fable "Old Man Yu (*Yu* meaning foolish) moves the mountains" that although plans and actions might be seen as "foolish" and "impossible," some Chinese still believe that they can achieve the impossible. This capability is not solely derived from the power of fates. Diligence and persistence are the keys to bring us hope and possibilities. With the willpower to believe and persistence to act and react, hope is sustained not only for a person or a couple, but also for a family and the nation.

The keys

→ **As an agricultural-oriented nation, the repetitive process of sowing, waiting (for the plants to grow), and harvesting cultivates hope in China.**
→ **For Chinese people hope is related to a strong belief in conquering fate.**
→ **The belief in inheriting the goodness, the hope for the person, the family, and even the nation is embedded in the nurture and education of the younger Chinese generation.**

Patrick S. Y. Lau is Associate Dean (Professional Programs) of the Faculty of Education, and Associate Professor in the Department of Educational Psychology at The Chinese University of Hong Kong (China).
Florence K. Y. Wu is a Research Assistant Professor in the Hong Kong Polytechnic University (China). She has dedicated her early career to the educational field, being a frontline secondary school teacher for a decade. Loving others (family, friends, and students) and being loved empowers her "to conquer fate, to persist in times of difficulties, and to believe there is always hope in the future."

Old Man Yu

In the traditional Chinese fable "Old Man Yu moves the mountain," Yu wished to move two huge mountains in front of his house. Everybody condemned his foolishness in doing something impossible. Old Man Yu persisted in moving the stones of the mountain from day to day. The rationale that upheld his belief was that his offspring of many generations in the future could help, even though he might not be able to accomplish the task in his life. This belief and persistence impressed the gods and the gods helped remove the two huge mountains in one night. This is a traditional Chinese fable to teach children to persist in their dreams and maintain hope even if there are some difficulties.

"Hope is a vital buffer and a valuable key."

Boosting hope

"Hope is not a belief that everything will turn out fine. Hope is rather the certainty that something is meaningful—regardless of how it turns out at the end," said Václav Havel, former President of the Czech Republic. Prof. **Alena Slezáčková** now measures hope for the international Hope Barometer, trying to find out how we can boost it.

Hope, for me, is the key to a happier future. If we lose the key, the door remains closed. If we lose hope, we remain locked in adversity and helplessness. People usually understand hope in terms of hopeful thinking, emotional experience, or something that transcends us—something close to our ultimate goals and spirituality. Many studies have demonstrated that happier people differ from others in their approach to the world, the way they think about it.

In our research, we have investigated how hopeful thinking gets reflected in different kinds of life experience in children, students, adults, old people, but also homeless shelter workers and clients. We have found, for example, that hopeful 14-year-olds achieved better grades at school. In university students, hope was closely connected to subjective well-being. More hopeful students were also more grateful for the good things in their life, and were more forgiving when they got into conflict with others. Hope plays an important role in old age as well: in elderly people of around 75–80 years of age, hope appears to be one of the key factors of "healthy aging," closely related to better health and satisfaction with life.

Hope Barometer

Apart from that, we studied hope and flourishing in homeless people and their caregivers in homeless shelters. Interestingly, it turned out that the homeless did not differ too much in their level of hope from the caregivers; yet, their quality of life was significantly worse. The main source of hope for the homeless were their families, especially children. However, they often added that, **in the end, people primarily have to find hope in themselves.** Homeless shelter employees also drew hope from their families, but their faith and beliefs served as an additional source. In fact, the ability to maintain hope proved to be the strongest predictor of the caregivers' flourishing.

More recently, we studied hope on a much larger sample of 1,400 respondents from all of the Czech Republic, aged between 15 and 79. The goal of the international project "Hope Barometer 2014" was to look into people's actual objects of hope and personal wishes, what they did to have their hopes fulfilled and whom they expected to provide them with hope. As it turned out, most Czechs expressed personal wishes that regarded relationships with other people. The most important ones included happy romantic relationships and family, good health, harmonious life, good relationships with other people, and personal autonomy. And who is the one we expect will provide us with hope? Most Czechs responded that they viewed hope as something for which everyone is responsible by themselves—thus, they saw themselves as their own major hope providers. The runner-up source of hope cited by the respondents were their romantic partners or spouses; the third place was taken by friends. Another valuable source could be the example of other people who can find solutions in difficult life situations. People primarily have to find hope in themselves, but partners and friends might help, as well as other people who find solutions in difficult situations.

Inspiration

We also wanted to know what Czechs do to fulfill their hopes. We found that in most cases, they ponder and analyze circumstances, read widely and gather information, and take responsibility. Thus, in accordance with the cognitive theory of hope, Czech respondents show rather rational, active, and individualistic approaches in pursuit of their hope. In addition, we found that more hopeful people, as compared with the less hopeful ones, are more satisfied with life, maintain high-quality interpersonal relationships, perceive their lives as more meaningful, and are also healthier. **Hope not only helps promote positive aspects of life, but serves as an important factor in coping with difficult life situations.** Out of the people who went through some traumatic experience, those who had hope reported significantly less negative outcomes.

So the ultimate question is: If hope is so important, how can we maintain or develop a more hopeful attitude? Some inspiration can be found in our findings: People who not only strive to fulfill their own needs, but participate in volunteering activities, show significantly more hope than other people, have more optimistic expectations for the future, and experience greater meaningfulness and spirituality in their lives. Thus, it appears that some of the powerful keys to a more hopeful and happier life include an others-oriented mindset, genuine concern for the welfare of others, and altruism.

Finally, here are some of our specific recommendations for boosting hope:
1. **See the positive things in life.** Try to worry less about what you do not have or cannot change; instead, value and be thankful for all the good that comes to you.

2. **Set up your priorities.** Ask yourself what it is you truly want to achieve in life, identify your true values, priorities and things you find meaningful, and try to live your life in congruence with them.

3. **Determine your goals.** Set progressive, adequate, and attainable goals and consider different ways and paths to achieve them.

4. **Be flexible.** Keep in mind that the path to your goal does not have to be the shortest, most straightforward or only one.

5. **Be connected.** Maintain social relationships and do not reject support from other people.

6. **Give hope to others.** From time to time, move your eyes away from your own wishes and desires and take a look around you. Can you bring a little hope to someone else?

To sum up, for me, hope is what builds us a meaningful bridge to a better future in times of adversity, uncertainty, and personal, social, or economic crises. By showing a direction, suggesting a way, and strengthening one's belief in attaining meaningful goals, hope can become a vital buffer protecting people against negativity, resignation, and despair. Therefore, hope is a valuable key to the flourishing of both the individual and the whole of society. Giving hope means giving future.

The keys

→ **People primarily have to find hope in themselves, but partners and friends might help, as well as other people who find solutions in difficult situations.**

→ **We can boost hope by seeing the positive things in life, setting up our priorities, determining our goals, being flexible and connected, and giving hope to others.**

→ **Hope can be a vital buffer protecting people against negativity and a valuable key to the flourishing of both the individual and the whole of society.**

Alena Slezáčková, PhD., is an Associate Professor at the Department of Psychology, Faculty of Arts, Masaryk University in Brno (Czech Republic). Her scientific interests and research focus mainly on happiness, flourishing, hope, and posttraumatic growth. Alena is a founder of the Czech Positive Psychology Centre. She is also an author of the first comprehensive monograph on positive psychology in Czech and a number of scientific and popular publications in the fields of positive psychology, health psychology, and personal development. She loves nature, traveling and exploring foreign countries, getting to know different peoples and cultures. Alena believes in goodness in people all over the world. Her motto is: "Everything will be alright in the end. If it's not alright, then it's not the end."

> *"People who hold a positive view on aging*
> *live at least seven years longer*
> *than people whose view is negative."*

A positive view on aging

"Myths, folk-wisdom, and literature suggest that aging has always been considered very ambivalently. Aging has multiple faces of which some are more bright and positive and others dark and negative," says Dr. Martin J. Tomasik. Having a positive view on aging benefits older and younger people.

On the positive side there are notions of appreciation, political activity of senators (related to Latin *senectus* meaning *old age*), expertise, wisdom, and generativity. That "the young are listening thoughtfully to the words of the elderly," sometimes "at the fireplace" and sometimes not, is almost an archetypical motif that almost everybody has heard of. And especially today we have many reasons to be optimistic about aging. Many people get older and life expectancy is steadily increasing both for those who are currently born and for those in their eighth or ninth decade of life. This increasing life expectancy is accompanied by increasing health and fitness so that over the past 50 years or so, people in many countries have gained five to ten years of "good life." And scientific evidence suggests that there is still substantial potential for further improvement both on the physical and the cognitive level.

This optimistic view, however, needs an important qualification. Especially in the very old, people beyond age 80 or so, reserve capacities quickly reach their limits and sizeable losses in various domains of functioning tend to occur. A case in point is the sharply increasing prevalence of dementia in the very old segment of the population with rates around 40% in the ninth decade of life. All these losses are often associated with notions

of de-individualization, senility, dependence, return to childhood, debilitation, uselessness, and hardship.

Negative mechanisms

These negative dynamics of gains and losses in old and very old age are also represented in our subjective theories or views on aging. When asked to describe our views on aging, we all (on average) expect the decline of desirable characteristics and the increase of undesirable ones (although certainly there are few exceptions such as "being well-read" or "wise"). Why this is the case is heatedly disputed in various disciplines of psychology and sociology. Some argue that a negative view on aging serves the enhancement of self-esteem in the young at the expense of the older outgroup. Others would say that young people are afraid to be confronted with their own mortality and thus try to psychologically distance themselves from the old ones by making "the old" as dissimilar from themselves as possible. Whatever the mechanism is on which our negative view on aging is built, it seems to be a very strong one. This is probably because a negative view on aging is internalized very early in life (starting in preschool) and therefore tends to function on both a conscious and an automatic level of processing, and because a negative view on aging is perpetuated for decades in a more or less ageist social context and thus is reinforced very often and in very different situations that we encounter.

That the negative view on aging is quite stable if we do not explicitly counter it somehow is also reflected in the fact that we usually do not change this view when we turn old ourselves. Paradoxically then, at some point in time we become victims of our negative view on aging as we implicitly or explicitly begin to apply it to ourselves. This is the point in time when the negative view backfires and becomes a negative self-fulfilling prophecy. We stop exercising because we believe that old people ought not to engage in too strenuous physical activities and, hence, reduce our physical fitness. We avoid complex mental operations because we believe that it is normal that older people become more senile and, hence, limit our cognitive challenges. We stop buckling up ourselves in the car because we believe that there is not much left to lose and, hence, statistically more often become victims of fatal traffic accidents.

Positive interventions

On the other hand, there is a plethora of psychological studies very convincingly demonstrating that a positive view on aging in older people predicts a full range of very positive outcomes including better cognitive functioning, lower cardiovascular reactivity to stress, higher independence with regard to activities of daily living, decreased use of tobacco and alcohol, higher physical activity, better subjective and objective health including the number of medical diagnoses, and, finally, higher life expectancy. Indeed, results from at least two large high quality studies from the United States and Germany suggest that people who hold a positive view on aging live at least seven years longer than people whose view is negative. This is more than is known from any other factor contributing to life expectancy including vegetarian nutrition or the reduction of body weight.

Furthermore, experimental psychological research has convincingly shown that the view we hold with regard to aging is not set in stone but can be effectively changed by means of quite simple interventions such as offering a very short "attribution retraining" in senior centers (in which old people learn that many diseases are not inevitable with old age but rather a consequence of an unhealthy life style) or by increasing contact and cooperation between younger and older people (in which young people reduce their stereotypically negative view on aging). Such interventions have been shown to effectively shift the view we hold about aging toward the positive side, to see age as something that is worth investing into, and, as a consequence, to increase healthy behavior such as walking or hiking. The earlier such interventions are applied the stronger the positive effects are supposed to be.

There is now enough empirical evidence both for the detrimental effects of a negative view on aging as well as for the positive effects of intervention that would justify the launch of interventions in schools and kindergartens aimed at shifting our view towards the gains in old age or at least to prevent a stereotypical degradation of everything that is related to age and aging. As a positive side effect, such interventions could overall reduce age segregation and age discrimination in our societies. There is hope that relatively simple and inexpensive measures can have a big effect on how healthy and satisfied we will age in the future. But we have to start now to make this hope a reality for ourselves and our children.

The keys

→ **A negative view on aging is internalized very early in life and becomes a negative self-fulfilling prophecy.**

→ **A positive view on aging in older people predicts a full range of very positive outcomes including better cognitive functioning, lower cardiovascular reactivity to stress, higher independence, higher life expectancy, etc.**

→ **We can and should change the attitude of young and old people toward aging through specific positive interventions.**

Martin J. Tomasik is currently working at the University of Zurich (Switzerland) in a research group that investigates age differences in engagement with and disengagement from goals. He was born in Wrocław (Poland), went to school in Koblenz (Germany), studied psychology at the Free University of Berlin (Germany), and wrote his doctoral thesis on "Developmental Barriers and the Benefits of Disengagement" at the Friedrich Schiller University of Jena (Germany). His general research interests comprise social, emotional, and motivational development across the life span. He is married and the father of three school-aged boys. After moving to Switzerland, he decided to learn skiing in which he makes slow but steady progress. Martin hopes that his research will contribute at least a little to us aging better in the future.

"Draw a person in the rain and analyze your drawing."

Hope against the rain

Before reading this text, just try it yourself. Draw a person in the rain. No more, no less. Done that? Now you are ready to read the analysis of Prof. **Sage Rose** and her colleagues about feeling more or less hopeful, and how to deal with it.

Students face many obstacles throughout their educational careers. Though obstacles can vary in type and intensity, they can unfortunately block academic success. When obstacles multiply or seem insurmountable, students can sometimes experience burnout and academic exhaustion because of these high demands. One group of students that may suffer the most distress due to constant high academic demands are medical students. They are especially vulnerable to academic burnout, which could lead to emotional exhaustion and a reduced sense of accomplishment. According to research literature, hope is a strong buffer against anxiety, depression, and feelings of hopelessness. Facilitating hope in medical students could reduce their academic exhaustion and potential burnout and support overall academic success.

Umbrella

Research by myself and my colleagues D. Elkis-Abuhoff, R. Goldblatt, and E. Miller (2012) examined the hope levels of 103 first and second year medical students at a Northeastern United States medical school. These students experienced ongoing stress throughout

their programs due to attempts to continuously achieve at high levels. We were interested in measuring the objective levels of hope using the Dispositional Hope Scale (DHS) and secondly interested in determining whether a projective measure of hope would reflect similar results in the same sample. The art-based measure of hope introduced to the medical student sample was the Draw a Person in the Rain (D-A-P-R).

Unlike the self-report DHS, the D-A-P-R requires the individual to deal with an environmental element, rain, in an attempt to uncover information regarding one's self-image when faced with an unpleasant environmental stressor. The D-A-P-R procedure is designed to prompt emotional vulnerability by drawing a projection of the individual. **This technique assesses one's internal tension and how well their coping strategies are sustained when additional pressure is confronted.** In the D-A-P-R, the representation of protection against the rain like an umbrella, coat, or boots, can indicate the level of emotional defenses, coping, and most importantly feelings of helplessness or hopefulness. Those that have difficulty with positive coping strategies may draw a person without defenses like a broken umbrella or standing in a puddle.

Academic stress

Correlation results suggest that there was a small psychometric overlap between the DHS and the D-A-P-R hope score. This provides concurrent validity for both objective and projective measures of hope in identifying student coping abilities and stressful contexts. The D-A-P-R hope-based scores significantly correlated with DHS characteristics of goal pursuit and preparedness for the future. Being prepared and engaged in goal pursuit are necessary actions for any student to be successful. These two areas may have been the most present in the drawings made by the medical students and indicate the level of coping strategies and skills the student possess in negotiating their environment when faced with the external stressor of a medical curriculum. Like any successful student population, medical **students need to be able to identify important goals and coping strategies to use when goal attainment is difficult.** At times, a self-report measure of hope may not tap into all aspects of hopelessness an individual is experiencing. The D-A-P-R could help the student to visually depict their level of hope and help the student gain an understanding of how much they are struggling with maintaining hope. Once the low hope levels are identified, interventions could be developed to support the student in attaining their overall goal of becoming a physician.

The study also found that the D-A-P-R hope score was significantly higher for second year medical students than first year students. No significant difference was found for the DHS and student year. This finding may be due to the context specific nature of the D-A-P-R and reflect that second year students have accumulated more experiences of success and are more confident in achieving their goal of completing medical school. The DHS is a more global measure of hope and may not be as predictive of contextual experiences of hopelessness. In future research, it may benefit the hope literature to compare the D-A-P-R to a state measure of hope in order to determine which may best predict contextualized responses to academic stress.

Measures of hope

Practical uses for both projective and objective measures of hope can be beneficial for many classroom or counseling contexts. Based on the findings of the current study, it seems that the D-A-P-R is most beneficial when examining an individual's current hope within a specific timeframe. The D-A-P-R appears to be a quality measure of state hope levels while the DHS remains to be a global measure. The D-A-P-R is also useful for working at an individual level. For example, a counselor asks a client to draw himself or herself in the rain to assess their levels of hopelessness while experiencing difficulties in school or at home. The counselor would then use this drawing to determine whether a hope intervention is necessary based on key components in the drawing. Alternatively, when investigating the hope levels for a larger group or sample of participants, the Dispositional Hope Scale can efficiently and effectively measure the perceptions of hope experienced by many. A researcher may choose to use the DHS to find out the hope levels of a large sample to compare to other measures of well-being. These hope levels should also remain constant given the global nature of the instrument. Both objective and projective measures of hope serve different measurement purposes yet remain comparable in validity.

The keys

→ **Facilitating hope in students could reduce their academic exhaustion and potential burnout and support overall academic success.**

→ **Being prepared and engaged in goal pursuit are necessary actions for any student to be successful.**

→ **Practical uses for both projective and objective measures of hope can be beneficial for many classroom or counseling contexts.**

Sage Rose is an associate professor of Research at Hofstra University (USA). Coauthors of this article are her colleagues D. Elkis-Abuhoff, R. Goldblatt, and E. Miller. Within their research they have published the Math Hope Scale, a self-report measure that is highly predictive of math-based achievement. In conjunction to math hope, Dr. Rose is currently validating a Writing Hope Scale that predicts writing achievement in college students. She has presented her research at many national and international conferences and published several book chapters and peer-reviewed articles on hope and related topics. Personal hobbies include writing short stories and working with animals. At a young age, Sage lived on a farm and worked at a horse stable. According to her, the relationships we have with our pets can be a source of happiness and well-being, and the positive interactions experienced are mutually beneficial.

"To understand God's thoughts, one must study statistics."

Measuring hope

Can hope be quantified? For Florence Nightingale the answer was clear: "To understand God's thoughts, one must study statistics, for these are the measures of His purpose." **Keith Sykes** belongs to a special research team on hope. Over the past decade they have developed three questionnaires to measure hope, two for adults and one for children. Yes, we are able to measure hope.

Our starting point was a four-part model of hope that encompasses attachment (trust and openness), mastery (empowerment and higher aims), survival (self-regulation and perceived options), and spirituality. *(Read in this book: The Network of Hope)*

In adults, hope can be expressed as a trait or state. Trait hope is a deep, stable foundation akin to a form of resiliency. It is the hopefulness of the individual, formed from DNA, parenting, culture, and community. In contrast, state hope is a surface blend of thoughts, feelings, and behaviors; a bubbling ebb and flow of responses to attachment, mastery, survival, or spiritual challenges.

Questionnaire development is a blend of art and science. The essence of hope must be captured and rendered in plain language. This work of words must also be paired with statistical tests of reliability (consistent results) and validity (comparison with established tests as well as predictive power). Third, a good hope questionnaire should produce results relatively free from incursions of denial or social masking, which could produce reports of false hope.

Our measures of hope exceed the scientific standards for reliability and validity. Moreover, when we administer our hope questionnaires in conjunction with measures of repression, denial, or impression management, we find little overlap.

Adults

Our adult trait hope questionnaire has 56 questions. The domains of attachment, mastery, survival, and spirituality are divided into 14 smaller units (subscales) of four questions each.

Seven subscales are non-spiritual and tap micro-elements of hope such as trust, openness, empowerment, and capacity for managing fear. These elements were culled from writings in psychology, psychiatry, nursing, philosophy, and theology. Seven subscales are spiritual. We again address power, presence, and coping but now in terms of how much (or little) of each element is spiritually loaded.

Individuals who score higher in trait hope are higher in achievement strivings and trust as well as lower in their sense of personal vulnerability. They are also more likely to report working collaboratively with a higher power rather than eschewing spiritual input or conversely expecting the "spirit" to assume full responsibility.

In one experiment, we exposed both low and high hope individuals to film segments depicting the death of an individual from HIV/AIDS. **Those who were higher in trait hope reported significantly less death anxiety after viewing the film.**

Our measure of adult state hope consists of 40 questions. The format is similar to the trait hope questionnaire. However, there are 10 subscales (seven nonspiritual and three spiritual). Questions are framed in terms of recent experience instead of enduring attitudes.

Individuals who score higher in state hope report greater meaning in life as well as less loneliness and anxiety. We designed the state hope scale to serve as a measure of change (e.g., following psychotherapy or a significant life event). We conducted an experiment using the Martin Luther King Jr. "I have a dream" speech. Half our participants watched the film while another half completed a neutral writing assignment. We measured state

hope before and after each activity. **The Martin Luther King Jr. group reported significantly higher hope scores.**

Children

In children, psychologists measure states. Traits may not appear before late adolescence. Our measure of child hope parallels the adult instrument. There are 40 questions, ten scales, and content reflective of attachment, mastery, survival, and spirituality. However, the language and response format are simplified. For each question, the child is asked to circle one of three statements: "never," "sometimes," or "always." The reliability (score consistencies) for the child hope scale is a little lower than for the adult measures but still exceeds scientific standards.

In terms of validity, children's (self-reported) hope scores are highly correlated with lower ratings of depression provided by parents or guardians. This was true

for both anxious-depression and withdrawn-depression, the most common forms
in pre-pubescent children.

Two tracks?

The psychiatrist Jerome Frank, a keen observer of the human condition, suggested
that certain aspects of emotional and spiritual life, particularly transcendent states,
may be mediated by the silent right hemisphere. Ultimately, we may require a two-track
assessment, one for left-brain hope and another for right-brain hope; one that would have
pleased "the lady with the lamp" and a second likely favored by the poets, who, like Emily
Dickinson, have paid homage to the "tune without the words."

The keys

→　**In adults, hope can be expressed as a trait or state. Trait hope is a deep,
stable foundation akin to a form of resiliency. In contrast, state hope
is a surface blend of thoughts, feelings, and behaviors.**

→　**Individuals who score higher in trait hope are higher in achievement
strivings and trust as well as lower in their sense of personal vulnerability.
Individuals who score higher in state hope report greater meaning in life
as well as less loneliness and anxiety.**

→　**Children's (self-reported) hope scores are highly correlated with lower
ratings of depression provided by parents or guardians.**

Keith Sykes is a recovery pathways specialist at Community Health Resources in Manchester,
Connecticut (USA), where he conducts functional assessments and aids clients in goal setting
and developing a broader range of coping skills. Keith graduated Summa Cum Laude with a BA
in psychology at Keene State College. His research has focused on hope among cancer survivors
as well as the refinement and validation of self-report tools for adults and children and content analytic
methods of assessment. His hobbies include the acoustic guitar, song writing, and softball. "I am most
interested in the survival benefits of hope," he says. "I have always been fascinated by the resilience
of those who have faced prolonged periods of darkness and yet found a way to focus on the light."
Coauthors of this chapter are **Anthony Scioli**, **Michael Ricci** and **Thanh Nguyen**.

You can take the hope test yourself: www.gainhope.com

"Hope is at odds with ostrich behavior."

Hope is working on change

"What makes me hopeful is that more and more people and businesses are choosing—against all odds—to respect ecological boundaries and to show more solidarity, to go against materialism and egotism," says sociologist **Dirk Geldof**. "They are the vectors of greater socio-ecological justice, with respect for people and the environment." Although there are still a lot of dark clouds, hope is taking responsibility for change.

We live in a paradoxical age. The wealth and complexity of our society have never been greater than in the 21st century, certainly in this part of the world. Our lives are propelled by the pace of globalization, constant technological innovation, and the acceleration of our society. Never was our material affluence so great, never have we in this part of the world had so many means at our disposal for shaping our future. We live in the most privileged part of the world, at a temporary peak in the growth of material wealth and technological possibilities.

At the same time, social challenges have never been so great. In this global risk society—as described by the German sociologist Ulrich Beck—global warming may very well be the most underestimated risk for present and future generations. Will we succeed in the years to come in laying down a far-reaching climatological policy and limiting the rise in temperature to 2 to 3 degrees Celsius? Other risks—and hence challenges—are also waiting for answers: growing inequality, among our own societies and those of the southern hemisphere, the ongoing economic crisis since 2008, the transition to a super-diverse society... The list seems to go on and on. In the midst of our unprecedented wealth, many are plagued by uncertainty about our future. Families are uncertain of their jobs or the future of their children, and politicians (ought to) doubt whether short-term measures will be sufficient to meet long-term challenges.

Search process

Paradoxically enough, the breeding ground of hope lies precisely in these challenges. Hope is at odds with ostrich behavior, when people bury their heads in the sand so that they don't have to see the social risks around them. Hope is also diametrically opposed to perceived but at times cherished feelings of powerlessness as an excuse to not take on challenges.

Hope lies precisely in the willingness to see today's social challenges for what they are, and in the willingness to take them on. This is also the core message of what sociologists such as Ulrich Beck and Anthony Giddens describe as building up a *reflexive modernity*. Working on a process of reflexive modernization means more than just noncommittal reflection. It's about individuals and societies confronting themselves as a form of social self-criticism.

Reflexive modernization means trying to change the way we handle risks. That necessitates debate: in the 21st century, more than ever, we must determine communicatively and politically which risks we find acceptable and which not. The result of the reflexive modernization process is open. Reflexive modernization does not guarantee a better future, only a different future. It is not a blueprint—there is no commitment to specific results—it is simply a process the outcome of which is dependent on the interaction between actors. The solution grows in the search process, and precisely therein lies hope.

Making choices

Who then are the vectors or actors in this process of reflexive modernization? In industrial society, collective identities were decisive: employees came together in unions that stood up for their rights and fought for social progress. In our global risk society, however, increasing individualization results in an increasingly fragmented picture. There is not a single universal actor—such as the proletariat in Marx—on which the hopes of humanity can be pinned. In the 21st century, hope lies in a large measure with ourselves: we all have a role to play and a responsibility as citizens.

Never were we as citizens so well informed and so highly educated. Here lies great potential for personal reflexivity as a necessary reaction to the more complex society of risk. We can and must make choices: to take on global warming, to limit inequality and poverty, to better organize social diversity. At the same time, these choices are more than just a question of lifestyle—it is necessary to translate them into the structure of society. A social and political translation of this kind is necessary, because change is based on individual choices and possibilities while at the same time transcending them.

Utopian realism

Hope lies thus in recognizing the necessity of change in order to take on global warming and other contemporary risks. It is a hope that starts from reason and rationality, from a belief in the persuasive power of arguments: if we become aware of the pressing challenges in our society of risk, our growing reflexivity will lead to change. The British sociologist Anthony Giddens speaks of a "utopian realism": realistic because such a critical theory builds on current social processes, and utopian because we live in a social universe that has become permeated by social reflexivity, such that possible visions of the future also influence how we give shape to that future.

Taking the ecological and social challenges in our global risk society seriously is therefore also a call to engagement in our own lives and to social engagement in society. Anyone who wishes to consider today's risks realistically—and do we have any other choice?—has to be open to alternatives to our current society. **Hope is also shared responsibility for future generations.**

In *The Myth of Sisyphus*, Albert Camus described more than half a century ago how Sisyphus was condemned to push a heavy boulder up a hill using all his might, only for it to come crashing down again each time he reached the top. Nonetheless, Camus decided, "One must imagine Sisyphus happy." With the risks of the 21st-century society, we are all Sisyphus in terms of our responsibility to vanquish those risks and take responsibility. We must imagine Sisyphus hopeful.

The keys

→ **We are faced with enormous challenges (of which global warming may well be the most underestimated). Paradoxically, the breeding ground of hope lies precisely in these unprecedented challenges.**

→ **Reflexive modernization means trying to change the way we handle risks. This does not guarantee a better future, only a different future. The solution grows in the search process, and precisely therein lies hope.**

→ **Hope lies in the recognition of the necessity of change in order to take on major risks. It starts from reason and rationality, from a belief in the persuasive power of arguments.**

Dirk Geldof, PhD, is a sociologist and part-time instructor in the faculty of Design Sciences at the Universiteit Antwerpen (Belgium). He is a researcher and lecturer in Sociology & Society at the Hoger Instituut voor Gezinswetenschappen (Odisee, Brussels) and teaches Diversity, Poverty & the City in the Social Work program of the Karel de Grote-Hogeschool in Antwerp. He has published the books *Onzekerheid: Over leven in de risicomaatschappij* [Uncertainty: On Life in the Risk Society] and *Superdiversiteit: Hoe migratie onze samenleving verandert* [Super-diversity: How Migration is Changing Our Society].

"Anxiously attached people score lower in both the social and achievement hope domains."

The impact of hope across life domains

"Understanding childhood patterns that lead to depression is essential in order to foster resiliency in those at risk for losing hope and to develop interventions for those who have already lost it," says Prof. **Hal S. Shorey**. How can insights into domain-specific hope protect people from developing depression? And what are the implications for helping others develop and maintain hope?

My research in this area began with testing C. R. Snyder's proposition that hope develops in the context of secure attachments to supportive adults in childhood. The results of this research were powerful and revealed that having parents who were loving and available while also maintaining high expectations for their children led to secure patterns of attachment, which, in turn, led to higher levels of hope and lower levels of anxiety and depressive symptoms in adulthood. When delving more deeply into this area, however, it became apparent that **not everyone who was raised with supportive parents has high hope**, or that those raised with less than optimal parenting have low levels of hope. Rather, one's level of hope appears to differ as a function of (a) one's attachment style and basic personality dispositions, and (b) what life domain the person in question is thinking about when rating personal hope.

Nine life areas

The Trait Hope Scale, a gold standard in hope research, asks people to rate their confidence that they can achieve their goals and the degree to which they have strategies

to reach those goals. Researchers using this measure cannot tell, however, what life domain was being contemplated when any given person completed the scale. Person A, for example, could score high in hope because she was thinking about her academic pursuits when filling out the scale. Person B might not care at all about academics but scores high in hope because she was thinking about her romantic life. Both people (A and B) could score high in hope, but their experiences and the mental health outcomes emanating from that high hope would be qualitatively different.

The Domain-Specific Hope Scale-Revised that I developed with a group of my colleagues was designed specifically to solve this problem in measuring hope. It assesses hope in nine life areas (social life/peer relationships, romance, family, work, academics, sports, religion/ spirituality, physical health, and mental health). **Hope in each area relates differently to mental health and achievement outcomes.**

Depressive symptoms

In a study of how attachment styles relate to hope and mental health, I found that anxiously attached people score lower in both the social and achievement hope domains. People with avoidant attachment also score lower on hope in the social domains. But they scored higher in the achievement life areas! This finding is consistent with how attachment theorists think about avoidant attachment. It means that **when people have childhood experiences that lead them to avoid intimacy and close relationships in adulthood, they compensate by turning to achieving in the areas of sport, academics, and work.**

The problem is that having higher hope in these achievement areas does not appear to lead to less depression or better mental health in the absence of simultaneously having high hope in the social areas. This finding is supported by theoretical propositions that **people will develop depressive symptoms to the extent that the areas they are experiencing problems in are linked to their self-concepts.** One recent study among college students, for example, revealed that hope in the areas of peer/social relationships, family relationships, academics, and sports predicted lower levels of depression across a two- and five-week time period even after controlling for initial levels of depressive personality and depression symptoms. These areas of social life, family life, academics, and sports are highly germane in the lives of most college students. Overall, this means that hope for the future in these areas has the potential to override having a personality-based propensity to develop depression.

High-achievers

What are the implications for helping others develop and maintain hope? When attempting to foster resilience in those at risk or when helping others to recover from depression, it is vital to consider what life domains are central to the individual's self-concept and focus on raising the person's hope in those areas. A caveat is in order here, however, in that the person's self-concept must be deemed to be authentic and not a defense against feelings of inadequacy. Individuals with avoidant attachment styles, for example, become highly achievement-oriented as a means of feeling valued without having to risk the pain that can result from close intimate relationships. Increasing hope in academics or work for these individuals is likely to get them back on tracks of high performance and temporarily raise hope levels, but these outcomes may not be long lasting or result in long-term decreases in depressive symptoms in the absence of meaningful support from family and significant others. It is, therefore, very important to help high-achievers see that what they are really gaining through climbing the corporate ladder, amassing wealth, or becoming captain of the sports team (among innumerable other examples) is to be socially valued and appreciated by others. **One should never underestimate the importance of celebrating others as people and telling them what they mean to us.** In the absence of this type of personal validation, all of the achievement in the world will be for naught.

The keys

→ **One's level of hope appears to differ as a function of (a) one's attachment style and basic personality dispositions, and (b) what life domain the person in question is thinking about when rating personal hope.**

→ **People will develop depressive symptoms to the extent that the areas they are experiencing problems in are linked to their self-concepts.**

→ **It is vital to consider what life domains are central to the individual's self-concept and focus on raising the person's hope in those areas.**

Hal S. Shorey is an Associate Professor in the Institute for Graduate Clinical Psychology at Widener University in Pennsylvania, USA. He directs the PsyD/MBA program and Widener's Organizational Development Services. His research focuses on combining hope and attachment theory in fostering resilience in at-risk populations and optimizing performance among organizational leaders.

The rainbow of your Laws of Life

Improving hope in young people? One of the most powerful vehicles is having students write about their Laws of Life, the values to which they dedicate themselves in the present and future. You may be skeptical about children's capacity to do this, but Maurice J. Elias and his team prove it is a hopeful project. You can cultivate hope for the disadvantaged by telling your story to listeners who care for and believe in you.

Maya Angelou, an accomplished poet, credits hope with being responsible for her accomplishments in life—indeed, for her even being alive. She tells a story about slaves working on plantations who drove off despair by singing a song, inspired by the biblical Book of Genesis: "When it seemed like things are at their worst, God put a rainbow in the clouds." This, of course, referred to the biblical rains that came over the world for 40 days and 40 nights.

This story reminded her of her grandmother, who, while Maya was an elective mute in childhood because of trauma, told her that she was confident that Maya would be a great teacher one day. Maya refers to those who provide hope and caring to people who are hurting or doubting, as rainbows in others' clouds. **She urges others to be rainbows in others' clouds, even when you are not sure they can hear you, or are listening.**

Emotional skills

And so, my colleagues and I are discovering old wisdom and appreciating the central role of hope in human life and accomplishment. My work is primarily with urban and disadvantaged schools, where many children live in poverty, where they may only have one parent and even when there are two, they are beset by financial, health, and mental health difficulties. Sometimes, they are new to America and don't speak English or know the ways of schools. Hence, these children are disadvantaged.

With disadvantage comes discouragement. So our work has been dedicated to providing possibility. How? We work with schools to provide a positive, caring, supportive culture and climate; we help ensure that the

school systematically teaches all students the social and emotional skills they need to master the tasks of school and life, and we provide opportunities for students to tell their stories. One of our most powerful vehicles for doing the latter is by having students write about their Laws of Life, the values to which they dedicate themselves in the present and future. You may be skeptical about children's capacities to do this, but we have found that beginning in Grade 5, students are ready to identify their Laws of Life in meaningful ways. Most often, they tell about rainbows in their clouds—grandparents who believed in them, a parent who worked tirelessly so they could succeed, a neighbor who took them in when child protective services was about to split up abandoned siblings. We collected these stories, from 5th, 8th, and 11th graders, in the book *Urban dreams: Stories of hope, resilience, and character* (2008).

Powerful hope

It may hardly seem necessary to state that the work that brought the Laws of Life into the schools of Plainfield,

New Jersey, was found by published research to bring the expected benefits to children in social-emotional skills, reduction in problem behaviors, and improved academic performance. This has not been an isolated occurrence. Hope is powerful indeed.

And perhaps that is the message. My work has focused more than anything on providing hope, support, and skills to those at greatest disadvantage. The lessons I have learned can be distilled into one set of recommendations: **provide others with a chance to tell their story, to know that others are listening and care, and to believe in the potential for great things to happen in the future, even when it may not seem obvious in the present.** That, to me, is the definition of hope. From hope, effort and possibilities emerge.

Maurice J. Elias, PhD, professor and director of the Social-Emotional Learning Lab, Department of Psychology, Rutgers University (USA)

"What makes us happy in the short run often leaves us miserable in the long run."

A Marshmallow as a sign of hope

How do you give yourself some hope to become the person you also wanted to be? "The Marshmallow Test might be the sign of hope," says Prof. **Hanno Beck**. "It's about all those things that destroy our hopes: smoking, drinking, too much unhealthy food, procrastination… Whenever there are unpleasant things we need to cope with, we tend to dodge around them. It's so funny, I'm writing about procrastination and I nearly missed the deadline for this book myself!"

Instead of living a healthy life, exercising, or learning for the exam, we stay how we are, feeling guilty about our vices, bad habits, always aware of the way things might have been if we only had the will-power to do the things we'd like to do in the long run while sacrificing them because of the pleasure we had in the short run.

"Hyperbolic Discounting" is what economists call this strange feature of human mind: We know that it is good for us to stop smoking, quit drinking, exercising, learning for the exam, and we really want to do this—but only in the long run. In the short run, we get overwhelmed by passion, desire, or weakness of will, so we continue to smoke, drink, eat unhealthy food, and procrastinate. But what makes us happy in the short run often leaves us miserable in the long run.

Temptation

But what role does a marshmallow play in that drama? Since the 1970s researchers carried out experiments with preschool children trying to find out when and how they were willing to delay a gratification or not. The basic experiment is rather simple: The children were escorted individually into an experiment room in the school and were shown reward objects, e.g. a marshmallow. The children were told that they could eat the marshmallow immediately, but if they waited for fifteen minutes until the researcher returned without eating the marshmallow, they would be rewarded with a second marshmallow. This is the classical situation as described above: "Shall I give in to temptation and eat the marshmallow immediately, or shall I delay the smaller-sooner reward for a larger-later reward?" To translate this in the problems described above: "Shall I go for the instant reward of a drink, cigarette, or donut, or shall I resist and enjoy a larger reward later on—good health, a (almost) perfect body, or a good grade in the exam?"

What was baffling about those experiments was that researchers found out in follow-up-studies that children who were able to wait longer for the larger-later reward tended to have better life outcomes—as they grew older, they had better SAT scores (standardized tests for most college admissions in the United States), better educational attainment, a healthier body mass index, and performed better on other life measures. It seems that the children's ability to wait for a second marshmallow determined their later life and overall satisfaction with life. Are you able to wait for the second marshmallow?

Tie your hands

Is there hope in this experiment? Yes, there is, if you look at the strategies how children try to cope with temptation. They close their eyes, turn their back on the marshmallow, sniff at it, lick it, pretend only to eat it, start to dither around, put the plate with the marshmallow aside, out of their reach—and some try to cheat. Can we use such strategies for coping with our individual Marshmallows? Here are three ideas:

1. **Close your eyes and put away the plate.** Put away anything that reminds you of the temptation. Get rid of all alcohol and cigarettes at home, put away anything that reminds you of smoking, drinking, or eating. If you have to learn for an exam, put away anything that might distract you from learning.

2. **Tie your hands yourself.** A perfect strategy for losing weight is to lock the refrigerator and throw away the key. OK, this does not always work that smoothly, but the idea is perfect: Make sure that you are not able to do things you don't want to do in the long run. So what

about a bet? A bet—that you quit smoking or drinking—makes it very expensive to violate your resolutions and thereby decreases the chances that you will give in to temptation. A good means to do this are Internet-resources like www.stickk.com: You post your goal on the homepage, and you may as well choose your stakes, i.e. how much money you're willing to risk, and where you want it to go, should you fail. If you fail, Stickk.com charges your credit card with the amount you put at stake and transfers the money to your designated recipient. Moreover, you designate someone you know and trust to act as an independent third party, monitoring your progress and verifying the accuracy of the reports you submit to stick.com.

3. **Think of the reward.** OK, it's not only about austerity, but about rewards as well. Promise yourself a reward if you reach your goals—everybody needs a positive incentive.

OK, nobody said that it would be easy, but these ideas might help you reach your goals— they might give you some hope to become the person you always wanted to be. Go on, don't waste any time. There's no time like the present.

The keys

→ **Whenever there are unpleasant things we need to cope with, we tend to dodge around them.**

→ **When you are able to wait longer for the larger-later reward, you tend to have better life outcomes.**

→ **We can learn strategies to cope with short-term temptations: close your eyes, tie your hands, think of the reward.**

Hanno Beck is Professor of Economics at Pforzheim University (Germany). He has been working as an economics editor for one of the largest German newspapers. He loves sport, strolling through the woods with his little brown-furred Angel, and playing the guitar—and this is exactly what gives him hope every day.

"We are a burning candle.
But we can refuel ourselves."

In search of
inner resources

"While I was taking part in workshops for people suffering from various types of cancer I came to the realization that we all have a particular amount of energy (called vital energy) which should last us for around 120 years," says Prof. **Adriana Zagórska**. "We can compare this energy to a large candle that keeps burning out while our days are passing by." Are there any resources to refuel ourselves?

There is no chance of stopping the burning candle and there is no chance of topping it up. This candle keeps burning and one day it will completely burn out. For each day there is a part of the candle (daily amount of energy) that needs to be burned away to sustain our living and if we tend to disperse our energy then we may find that at the age of 40 there is not much left at all to keep us going.

Life energy

Nowadays people like to live on credit, forgetting that the loan once taken must be still repaid at some point in their life. **While we are spending our daily energy our immune system gets to be weakened.** If we are not careful this may lead to a critical drop in energy.

The energy that we may need for major daily problems, not even mentioning any life tragedies. And with the declining resistance a person becomes more susceptible to various diseases. The health of those with weakened immune systems can then be threatened by many types of illnesses. What struck me while listening to the stories of participants was that most of them were active people living like they can run a tab forever (live "on credit"), to some extent taking life for granted. They want to develop themselves, stay enthusiastic about their jobs and their professions; frivolously dispersing their own precious life energy like there will be a constant abundance of it, forgetting that this may need to be paid off… and then illness comes into the scenario—is this a repay day? Or maybe it is a flashing light warning and to prevent the drastic drop in energy level?

Self-efficacy

As the same time I have been conducting research on our self-efficacy consciousness level. This particularly relies on inner resources. *Albert Bandura*, the founder of the social learning theory and self-efficacy, described self-efficacy as "beliefs in one's capabilities to organize and execute the courses of action required to produce given attainments." **Self-efficacy predicts effort expenditure, persistence, and performance.** It is impossible to explain phenomena such as human motivation, self-regulation, and accomplishment without discussing the role of self-efficacious beliefs.

Self-efficacy beliefs are constructed from four major sources of information which briefly can be described as: (a) past mastery experiences—knowing one's own past makes it easier to create one's own future, (b) vicarious experiences—thanks to other people one can avoid making many mistakes as he or she can learn by other's mistakes, (c) verbal persuasion—one is open to what others are saying, one is aware of one's own fallibility, (d) physiological and affective states—one is listening to one's body and supplies it with what it needs (energy, allows the body to rest) equalizing the requirements of daily duties. Past experiences are the most influential sources of self-efficacy.

Being inspired by Bandura's theory, I decided to develop a support program for athletes within the self-efficacy area. The end effect of this work is an original program that allows us to teach and encourage athletes to reach for their inner resources and this gives them higher self-efficacy levels. The study results indicate that the program was effective. **Participants demonstrated a substantial increase in self-efficacy.** There is a need to create programs of psychological intervention focused on shaping these mental traits in athletes to optimize sport outcomes in an effective way.

New fuel

Sport is not the only arena where so-called inner resources are the key players. So, what are these "resources"? These are most of all behavioral, material, physical, social, and psychological resources, which are at hand for individuals to cope with daily challenges. These are often described as "fuel" and it could be an activity as simple as free time recreation, time spent with family, fulfilling dreams or life goals, sustaining a healthy diet, general physical activity, a hobby, spirituality, and even keeping a pet. We use resources to refuel ourselves and to compensate for the levels of energy we consume dealing with daily challenges. It is worth it then to create a list of inner resources to keep at hand—not only when our vitality is threatened and when our energy is on the edge of exhaustion, but **mainly to prevent from these drastic energy drops from occuring at all.** I think the time has come for people to realize this so they can start acting preventatively. The development of civilization accustomed people to the fact that we operate after action. The above theory and the experiences of cancer patients give us something to think about. What's more interesting, Bandura was always highlighting the importance of learning from someone else's mistakes. So what is the point of waiting until there is someone trying to learn from our mistakes? Let's prevent this by using the resources that we have been given for that.

The keys

→ **Nowadays people like to live on credit, forgetting that the loan once taken must be still repaid at some point in their life.**

→ **It is impossible to explain human motivation, self-regulation, and accomplishment without discussing the role of self-efficacious beliefs. Past experiences are the most influential sources of self-efficacy.**

→ **Behavioral, material, physical, social, and psychological resources are at hand to cope with daily challenges. Using these resources we refuel ourselves, compensating for the levels of energy we spend dealing with daily challenges.**

Adriana Zagórska-Pachucka, PhD, is currently working at the Academy of Physical Education in Warsaw (Poland). She is also a sports psychologist recommended by the Polish Olympic Committee and cooperates with soccer club Legia Warszawa, Polish champion. She is the author of many significant articles about self-efficacy among athletes. For her, "hope is something that I always have in my pocket, always to remember, never to lose."

"If you work hard enough,
you can turn an iron rod into a needle."

Ren ding sheng tian

"There are different Chinese beliefs about hope and different themes can be derived, especially in the context of adversity," says Professor **Daniel T. L. Shek**. "Primarily, there is the belief of 'ren ding sheng tian' (man is the master of his own fate), which suggests a hopeful mentality that human beings can overcome life's adversities." But there is more.

Diligence and endurance are regarded as keys to hope in adversity, as exemplified in the cultural beliefs of "chi de ku zhong ku, fang wei ren shange ren" (hardship increases stature) and "zhi yao you heng xin, tie zhu mo cheng zhen" (if you work hard enough, you can turn an iron rod into a needle). Besides, having a strong will is also the key to success, as shown in the cultural belief of "you zhi zhe shi jing cheng" (when there is a will, there is a way). In particular, seeing suffering as meaningful training in life provides motivation for one to endure and to remain hopeful. This can be seen in the thoughts of Mencius that "**Heaven gives training to a person who will be given great responsibilities.** Heaven creates suffering in his heart and spirit, makes his muscles and bones exhausted, lets him experience extreme starvation and poverty, and makes him frustrated by troubles and setbacks. Through such experiences, patience and endurance of the person will be enhanced and his weaknesses will be transcended."

Belief in the future

We have done quite a lot of research on hope and hopelessness in Chinese people. Five observations can be highlighted.

1. **Compared with people with hope, those without hope show more negative psychological symptoms** (e.g. anxiety and depression) and risk behavior (e.g. substance abuse). In addition, hopeless people have a lower level of positive mental health, such as having low self-esteem and existential well-being.

2. **Belief in the future is positively related to different positive youth developmental assets,** such as bonding, resilience, psychosocial competencies (including cognitive, social, emotional, behavioral, and moral competencies), self-determination, self-efficacy, clear and positive identity, spirituality, prosocial norms, and prosocial involvement.

3. **Several socio-demographic factors are related to belief in the future.** Compared with males, females generally have a higher level of optimism. Besides, compared with adolescents experiencing economic disadvantage, non-poor adolescents have stronger positive beliefs in the future. Furthermore, relative to adolescents growing up in intact families, adolescents in non-intact families are less hopeful.

4. **Spirituality is causally linked to belief in the future.** In particular, those with a higher purpose in life have higher optimism. On the other hand, people without life meaning tend to be more pessimistic.

5. **Different family processes also contribute to belief in the future.** Systemic family functioning attributes such as mutuality, communication, harmony, and emotional expressiveness are positively related to belief in the future; parenting attributes such as responsiveness and concern are positively related to belief in the future. Regarding parental control, while parental behavioral control is positively related to belief in the future, psychological control is negatively related to optimism. Parent-child relational qualities such as mutual trust, parent-child communication, and parent-child relationship are also positively related to belief in the future in adolescents.

Promoting hope

Unfortunately, there are very few validated programs focusing on personal, family, and cultural resources in promoting hope in Chinese people, particularly Chinese adolescents. Which practical implications can be highlighted from the Chinese literature on hope?

→   Finding a **meaningful purpose** in life and cultivation of developmental assets (i.e. personal resources) can help to promote hope in adolescents.

→ Promoting positive parenting, family functioning, and parent-child relational qualities can help to nurture hope in adolescents. Promoting the quality of family life (i.e. family resources) is also important to nurture hope.

→ Utilization of our cultural beliefs about adversity (i.e. cultural resources) can help to promote hope in people.

The keys

→ **Seeing suffering as meaningful training in life provides motivation for one to endure and to remain hopeful.**

→ **Harmonious family processes, spirituality, and a positive youth contribute to belief in the future and better mental health.**

→ **Utilizing cultural beliefs, positive parenting, and finding a meaningful purpose in life are means of promoting hope, especially in adolescents.**

Daniel T. L. Shek is Associate Vice President (Undergraduate Programme) and Chair Professor at The Hong Kong Polytechnic University in China. He is director of the Centre for Innovative Programmes for Adolescents and Families. Prof. Shek has published more than 500 articles in international journals on adolescents, health, welfare, and quality of life research in Chinese, Western, and global contexts. He is editor of the *Journal of Youth Studies* and member of the editorial board of several international journals, including *Social Indicators Research* and *International Journal of Adolescent Medicine and Health*. Daniel is interested in singing, hiking, cycling, and writing. He finds some kind of hope in human love, genuine human encounters, and serving others.

"Hope is not a fleeting emotion that escapes control."

Hope and character

Hope and optimism influence motivation and resilience.
This is shown by the research of **Charles Martin-Krumm**.
As a sports instructor and former member of the French national
rowing team, he wants to know whether hope is a personality trait
and how we can influence it.

If we investigate the historical and theological foundations of hope, we see that hope is usually conceived as a passive phenomenon, dependent on external or even divine intervention. In the 1950s, the concept of "hope" entered into clinical psychology in the treatment of the symptoms of depression, because psychologists thought that hope could have a positive effect on the patient's sense of well-being, resilience and the like. It was only at the beginning of the nineties, with the rise of positive psychology, that science no longer viewed hope as a passive phenomenon, but as a virtue, a personality trait whose foundation is largely the individual him or herself. **Today we can define hope as an active, psychological process** in which it is necessary to define the goals an individual considers important, what means and resources are needed to reach those goals, and how sufficient motivation can be developed and maintained in order to succeed. In this sense, hope is no longer a fleeting emotion that escapes control, but a cognitive process that the individual can influence by focusing on choices and motives.

Sports

Hope is a fairly general personality trait, but it is nevertheless possible to develop different levels of hope in various areas of life (for example, in sports, work, relationships and social situations) and even in specific situations. In such cases we may speak of "situational hope" in the "here and now." But as mentioned earlier, we can also posit a more general level of hope that resembles an aspect of one's character. Then it is possible to speak of "hope as a personality trait." Many studies have shown that hope in a positive sense is associated with variables such as well-being, performance and resilience.

In light of these findings, our investigation is focused primarily on two things. The first concerns the question of the extent to which hope as a personality trait plays a role in performance. In other words, does having a high general level of hope ensure that a person performs better in different kinds of activities? Or is it more important to develop a high level of hope in a particular domain (such as sports) or in a particular situation in order to perform better? In the case of sports performance in a physical education course, our results show that hope as a personality trait has no direct effect on performance. Its effect is indirect, occurring at the level of "situational hope." In other words, the general level of hope characteristic for a particular individual influences the level of hope that that individual develops in connection with physical activities, which in turn influences his or her performance.

Interventions

Our second area of investigation concerns the "mediating" variables that play a role in the relationship between hope and performance. It is clear that other psychological variables come into play in the relationship between hope and performance. We call these "mediating" entities; they function in the "interface" between hope and performance. Hope can have an effect on these mediating factors, which could have an effect on performance. Today we know that hope in general has a predictive value in various areas, but we still do not quite understand what these mediating factors are and how they interact with one another. Our goal is thus to understand which variables come into play, how they function, and whether it is possible through intervention to change the level of an individual's hope with the goal of improving his or her performance. Our investigation in practical matters of physical and athletic activities show, for example, that the individual's perception of his or her own capacity in a particular activity has a considerable influence on performance. The perception of competence influences the level of hope in practical activity, which ultimately influences performance.

Resilience

At the moment we are trying to understand how hope influences physical performance and the ability of individuals to bounce back after failure. In short, we are trying to identify the processes in which hope seems to be involved. The hypothesis is that individuals with a higher level of hope **are better able to cope with failure**, that they can find other solutions and sources of motivation in order to bounce back after a performance which they consider poor.

From a broader perspective and in cooperation with other European researchers, we are now trying to understand how different variables can influence each other, and whether there are specific characteristics or differences among the populations of diverse countries. This study was started in 2011 and is still in progress. Do people everywhere have the same sources of hope? How does an individual's level of hope develop with age? Is this development the same in all countries? Can passion influence hope, or does it have the opposite effect? There are still many questions to which we have to find answers.

Keys

→ **Hope is not a passive phenomenon but an active psychological process, which the individual can influence by focusing on his or her choices and motives.**

→ **Hope influences well-being, performance and resilience. It is also important to distinguish between "situational hope" and "hope as a personality trait."**

→ **In the interface between hope and performance, we can influence "mediating factors" (such as the individual's perception of his or her specific capacity).**

Charles Martin-Krumm is a lecturer at the Université Européenne de Bretagne (France), where he trains physical education instructors. His research has shown that hope and optimism influence motivation and resilience. The results are published in the *Traité de psychologie positive* (Martin-Krumm & Tarquino, 2011).
The co-authors of this contribution are **Yann Delas** and **Fabien Fenouillet**. Yann Delas (Université de Rennes 2) studies the relationship between hope and performance in various sports-related contexts. Fabien Fenouillet (Université Paris Ouest Nanterre La Défense) is a professor of cognitive psychology and researches the influence of motivation and well-being on cognitive mechanisms in order to understand how people can be encouraged to learn through technological means.

"Hope is the fuel that keeps the desired action going."

Hoping for hope

"Recently, my colleague suffered the tragedy of her 21-year-old daughter's sudden and unexpected death. Burying a child of one's own is undoubtedly a parent's greatest fear and deepest pain," says Prof. **Lotta Uusitalo-Malmivaara**. "How can you deal with such a loss, strive toward the hope that disappeared in the seconds policemen stood at your door?"

I knew it was early to ask my colleague to write something about hope only a few months after her child passed away. However, she promised to share something of what it is to hope for hope. No doubt she had been a high-hope, optimistic person before but all her strength had been ripped away. As a scholar working in the field she was pretty much aware of the toughness of the process that was only about to begin. "I have always been a person who doesn't give up," she said, "but the unfairness of life is crippling."

Repair

Of all the character strengths studied, hope seems to be the one that most clearly predicts well-being and happiness. Individuals having hope as their prominent strength set goals and find meaning in striving toward them. High-hope persons pursue accomplishment and seem to exceed expectations. Hope is the fuel that keeps the desired action going. Hope is associated with success and achievements in multiple areas spanning from academic achievements to social competence. Feelings and emotions are ingredients of hope, yet cognitive components drive the motivational goal-oriented process. People suffering from severe depression describe their condition as one with no hope at all. Hopelessness is best described as endless dead ends and empty goalless scenarios. Even those who have recovered from depression describe that hope needs to be refound every day, the sources of hope that worked yesterday don't seem important today.

According to scientific definitions of hope, *repair* is one of its most salient functions. We need hope to be our driving force when facing unsatisfactory, damaging, and threatening conditions. Hope is said to be at its best under probabilities of intermediate goal attainment. Hope is of no use in cases where chances of winning are 100% or non-existent. In devastating situations, the odds of winning are very low. My colleague wrote of the comfort she could find in music, of endlessly watching pictures and videos of her beloved daughter, of rereading her funny SMS and Facebook messages, and of being together with family and friends. **We learn and exercise hopeful, future-oriented thinking in the context of other people.** When we lose someone closest to our heart this endeavor is broken. Coming totally unexpectedly, the breakage is brutal and leaves one with weak odds of even surviving. So, what are the chances of hope and what can be hoped for? From an evolutionary point of view, parents' primary task is to take care of their offspring and pave the way for them to bring up the next generations. Hope and goal orientation go hand-in-hand. How can hope be kept alive if the most important goal of one's existence has disappeared? Can there ever be any comparable meaning of life?

Precious

Being grateful and savoring good memories are among the most effective happiness-increasing activities. My colleague told me about the preciousness of small acts of love and important words that were said during the time her daughter lived. These memories had proved to be indispensable in making the first steps on a path to finding hope again. Being grateful for having had a beautiful daughter for 21 years was a great source of strength. Having been given the chance to learn her personality, to love this particular girl, had given beams of light. The metaphor of hope as a rainbow of the mind was evident in the mother's voice. One day the colors would show up again when light would permeate darkness.

Traumatic and violating events can rob people of their hope permanently. Being badly mistreated and having experienced dreadful misfortune may cause people to give up the grand goal in the game of life. This may lead to extinction of interests and ambitions. "What does it matter anymore?" However, research shows that high hopers appear to find a sense of benefit and meaning even in life-threatening occasions. After a heartbreaking loss, devastating grief, guilt, and anger, hope may emerge in the form of thankfulness, kindness, and compassion that didn't exist before. Learning to live without a family member, though never totally accepting, may evolve into a deeper understanding of humanity, appreciation of beauty, bravery, and forgiveness. This journey that encompasses the very core of human strengths affects not just those closest to the family but the whole community sharing it. Having been given a chance to offer vicarious hope is a gift for those around the grieving. For the grieving, the hope of others may serve as buoyant force keeping them on the surface until they can summon up hope of their own.

The keys

→ **High-hope persons pursue accomplishment and seem to exceed expectations. Feelings and emotions are ingredients of hope, yet cognitive components drive the motivational goal-oriented process.**

→ **Hope is said to be at its best under probabilities of intermediate goal attainment. *Repair* is one of its most salient functions.**

→ **After a heartbreaking loss, devastating grief, guilt, and anger, hope may emerge in the form of thankfulness, kindness, and compassion that didn't exist before. Being grateful and savoring good memories are among the most effective activities.**

Lotta Uusitalo-Malmivaara is an adjunct professor in the Department of Special Education, University of Helsinki (Finland). Her research interests include learning difficulties, well-being in children and adolescents, especially school-related happiness. Character strengths, mindfulness, compassion, and optimal learning conditions for children with special needs also lie close to her heart. She feels deeply grateful to Terhi Ojala for sharing her story.

"Forgiveness is a generous gift."

Mandela's hope

Nelson Mandela had served 27 years in prison before he became
the first elected black president of South Africa in 1994.
He didn't choose revenge but hope, based on facing the truth
and being able to forgive. Twenty years later Prof. **Marie Wissing**
and **Tharina Guse** analyze and reflect on the processes involved
and measure hope as expressed by young South Africans.
An inspiring lesson for the world.

In South Africa our research explored psychosocial well-being, hope, and hope-enhancing
processes in many places, contexts, and forms, such as the processes of the South African's
Truth and Reconciliation Commission (TRC) as well as among individuals and groups
residing in deep rural and high-tech urban areas. We noted that higher levels
of hopefulness are byproducts of transformative experiences and processes to enhance
psychosocial well-being, and that it is associated with spirituality, future-mindedness,
meaning in life, and peace.

Twenty years have passed since the dawn of the "New South Africa." Has the hope ignited
then filtered down to the youth of the country? To a large extent this seems to be the case.
We have found South African adolescents' levels of hope to be relatively high, and similar
to those reported by American adolescents. There were also no differences in hope among
adolescents from various population groups. A similar pattern emerged when we
investigated hope among university students at a large urban institution. Further, higher
levels of hope were consistently related to psychological well-being. South African youth
seem positioned to approach the future in a hopeful and psychologically healthy

manner. Looking forward, we discover a large amount of hope among the rainbow nation's youth. Looking back, we see how hope had been seeded through South Africa's reconciliation process. An inspiring lesson for the world.

Voice to victims

A crucial role has been played by the Truth and Reconciliation Commission. How did it work? South Africa's Truth and Reconciliation Commission (TRC) was established as part of the transition to a democratic government and recognition of human rights in the aftermath of the abolishment of the apartheid regime. Looking through the lens of positive psychology, an analysis of processes and outcomes of the TRC revealed many psychosocial strengths and hope for the development of a healthier nation.

Great *leadership* was shown by Nobel Peace Prize winners Nelson Mandela and Willem de Klerk who led the negotiation process. **The strength of Mandela's leadership reverberated in his wisdom and perspective**, the integrity and social intelligence with which the choice was made of how to handle what happened under apartheid. The establishment of the TRC under his leadership was a choice of balance, fairness, justice, kindness, and hope for a better future. The victims of apartheid were put at center stage of the processes—firstly their stories of suffering and human rights violations would be heard. This process recognized the dignity of victims and communicated respect to them.

The processes of the TRC built hope by facilitating *social awareness and recovery of a lost history*. It paved the way for a future with hope for reconciliation between previous divides. By filling in gaps in knowledge of what happened to loved ones, by realizing the consequences of people's own actions for others, and by guidance towards a reconciled future, *new meanings were constructed* at individual and social levels, providing the opportunity of becoming a more positive and hopeful nation.

The TRC created the space for further *peace-making* and fueled *peace-building*. *Harmony* on both intra-personal and inter-personal levels was facilitated which also enhanced balance, acceptance, reconciliation, and the integration of opposites into a whole. *Compassion* was shown by both audience and officials in listening to the stories of victims. *Spirituality* played an (unexpected) major role in the TRC processes. Former Archbishop Tutu, as chairperson of the TRC, said at the beginning of the hearings that we need to reach deep into the spiritual wells of our different religious traditions in order to draw strength and grace with which to address the challenges of healing and becoming a more morally responsible nation. This strong spiritual theme in the work of the TRC was criticized by some, but it was seemingly accepted by victims, commission members, and perpetrators alike. By fulfilling its mandate to promote reconciliation and reconstruction, the TRC was strongly *future-minded* in its processes and the creator of *hope* for a better future.

Open windows

Individual, social, and spiritual processes were integrated in weaving the path toward the future by *telling the truth*. We listened to forensic, spiritual, and personal truths—the latter is a search for understanding, self-insight, acceptance of responsibility, healing, justice, and reconciliation. The narrative reconstruction of experiences in the socially supportive context of the TRC helped in the processing of past traumas and facilitated *posttraumatic growth* shown in remarks reflecting fuller humanness via forgiveness and repentance as part of inter-connectedness. **By telling the full truth transgressors** *accepted responsibility* and thereby the possibility to grow in integrity.

Forgiveness played a crucial positive role in the TRC's processes toward building a more positive nation. Tutu pointed out that the act of forgiveness opens a window on the future for both the forgiver and the wrongdoer. From an African perspective on forgiving, victims became the gate-keepers for reintegration of transgressors into the human community. Forgiveness is a generous gift to transgressors who are in no position to demand or deserve it. What transpired at the TRC with regard to forgiveness and growth can enrich the understanding of the concept of forgiveness in the science of positive psychology from a cultural perspective. Through the work of the TRC we noticed that, from an African collectivist perspective, *forgiveness* **is not only an individual process, but also a social process that includes reconciliation**—which is a prerequisite for growth toward fuller humanness of victim, transgressor, and society as a whole. This process was named *"interconnectedness-towards-wholeness"* by Antjie Krog, a South African poet and member of the TRC. In the words of a mother: *"This thing called reconciliation… if I am understanding it correctly… if it means this perpetrator, this man who has killed Christopher Piet, if it means he becomes human again, this man, so that I, so that all of us, get our humanity back… then I agree, then I support it all."* In this way *hope* for a better future had been built.

In the African TRC context, *gratitude* was also linked with social processes, and especially with forgiveness on an interpersonal level and the need to make restitution. There was a general thankfulness by many South Africans, black and white, that we managed to steer toward greater peace and reconciliation. **This general gratefulness and wonder united us** and inspired more efforts toward reconciliation and gave hope for a better future. *Future dreams* were made possible by the TRC processes.

The keys

→ **The transition in South Africa is an inspiring example for the development of healthy nations: showing leadership, meaning, compassion, responsibility, forgiveness, gratitude, etc.**

→ **Hope can help us to transform the negatives from the past and has a huge impact on the youth.**

→ **Building hope may be beneficial to individuals and society at large.**

Coauthor of this text is Prof. Michael Temane, deputy registrar at the University of South Africa (Unisa). **Marie Wissing** is professor at North-West University Potchefstroom and **Tharina Guse** is Head of the Department of Psychology at the University of Johannesburg, both in South Africa. They both hold doctoral degrees in psychology and are involved in teaching, research, and management. For both of them, families are important. Marie is a grandmother and Tharina a mother. They appreciate the richness of life as expressed in the beauty of nature, people, and art. Their hope for the future is not only a peaceful life for their children and grandchildren, but for greater world peace and globally more harmonious relationships among humans, between humans and their environments, and within human souls.

The Truth

The Truth and Reconciliation Commission was a court-like restorative justice body assembled in South Africa after the abolition of apartheid. Victims were invited to bear witness of their experiences in public hearings. Perpetrators of violence could also give testimony and request amnesty. The hearings started in 1996 and had an enormous impact on how the country dealt with the past and how it was looking forward to the future.

"Hope provides a platform upon which you can climb to peer farther beyond the horizon."

Gimme Hope Jo'anna

"Gimme Hope Jo'anna" is a well-known reggae anthem from the 1980s, written during the apartheid era in South Africa. The song was banned by the South African government when it was released but was widely played all over the world: "Gimme hope, Jo'anna, hope before the morning come." What about hope these days for young South Africans? Dr. **Gerard Boyce** investigates.

Few would dispute that South Africa is a tough neck of the woods in which to reside. With its high poverty and unemployment levels, one of the world's highest rates of economic inequality and prevalence of HIV and AIDS, not to mention its status as one of the most violent peacetime societies on the globe, it is relatively easy to presume that most South Africans would have fallen into despair. Presumably, young people would be most susceptible to falling into despair given the scant prospects for realizing their hopes or achieving their dreams which these indicators portend.

To explore this hypothesis further, we investigated "hope" amongst members of a multi-racial sample of young people from several schools in the port city of Durban in the province of Kwazulu-Natal, a region widely believed to be the epicenter of the global AIDS epidemic. Specifically, we investigated the relationship between respondents' hope levels and a series of attitudes which have been found to affect economic decision-making by framing the payoffs and losses which economic actors perceive to be associated with the various alternatives available to them in any given situation. The attitudes investigated corresponded to the economic concepts of discounting, subjective life expectancy, attitudes to risk under uncertainty, and career expectations.

Accepting risk

Results revealed that more hopeful respondents harbored higher career expectations than less hopeful respondents did and were more optimistic about their prospects of pursuing their chosen careers in the future. They were also more entrepreneurial. This can be gathered from the greater willingness to accept some risk in pursuit of reward under uncertain conditions that they expressed. In addition, they were more positive about their survival prospects and reported higher subjective survival probabilities than less hopeful respondents did. Notably, all these results were statistically significant at traditional testing levels and these relationships held even after controlling for a range of demographic (e.g. race, sex) and socioeconomic variables.

Taken together, these results imply that not only do more hopeful respondents expect more out of the future than less hopeful respondents do but that they are more prepared to do what it takes to ensure that these expectations are met, and they believe that they will enjoy the rewards associated therewith for a longer period than less hopeful respondents do. Seen from this perspective, hope can be said to provide a platform upon which young people can climb to peer farther beyond the horizon that is bounded by their bleak immediate circumstances, thereby enabling them to envision a brighter future.

Harnessed

Speculatively, one way in which hope might do so in South Africa is by inuring young people to the potential negative effects of psychosocial perceptions of relative inequality. By way of support for this assertion, reported hope levels were found to be related to self-assessed socioeconomic status and perceptions of relative socioeconomic status rather than objective measures of socioeconomic status.

To put these results into perspective, results drawn from an earlier study of hope levels among a national sample of roughly 3,500 respondents of all ages (Boyce and Harris, 2012) suggest that, on average, young people are neither more nor less hopeful than their older compatriots. It might thus be unfair to portray young people as wallowing in despair or to continue to peddle images of the "hopeless youth" which only serve to heighten societal fears of members of this demographic group.

Based on these findings, it is contended that a far more rewarding exercise than lamenting why young people are supposedly so hopeless would be to investigate what sustains their hope levels in the face of extreme adversity and explore how the promise they hold onto can be harnessed for the betterment of all members of society. Hopefully, the lessons that could be drawn from this could be used to strengthen our collective resolve to respond to the many daunting global challenges that, by definition, threaten all of humanity and that are capable of plunging even the most stout-hearted among us into the depths of despair.

The keys

→ **High hope levels affect better economic decision-making. Hopeful people are more prepared to do what it takes to ensure that their expectations are met.**

→ **Reported hope levels are more related to perceptions of relative socioeconomic status than to objective measures of socioeconomic status.**

→ **It is rewarding to investigate what sustains the hope levels of young people and explore how the promise they hold can be harnessed for the betterment of all members of society.**

Gerard Boyce holds a PhD in Economics and is currently employed as a Postdoctoral Fellow at the School of Accounting, Economics and Finance at the University of KwaZulu-Natal (UKZN) in Durban, South Africa. His PhD thesis investigates the relationship between perceptions of racial identity, hope, and educational aspirations among young people in South Africa. He is particularly interested in the effects which psychosocial variables, such as perceptions of hierarchy and identity commitment, have on younger persons' decision-making and how this may affect this group's potential to drive societal transformation in the future. He is also a committed environmentalist and is hopeful that young people will be brave enough to make the decisions that older generations have been too afraid to make when it comes to protecting our natural environment.

"Hope may not be something we rely on
but something that cheerfully decorates our life."

We don't talk about hope

"In Japan, hope is a very rare topic. My hope, your hope, our hope, the hope of society… these are very rarely heard in conversations," say Drs. **Naoko Kaida** and **Kosuke Kaida**. Yet the Japanese do have hope, or think about hope at least, but maybe in unique ways.

The origin of the Japanese word for hope can be traced back to Chinese literature written in the 5th century, and by the 12th century the exact word for hope, *kibo*, appears in the first Japanese dictionary. The current definition of the Japanese word for hope does not seem to be critically different from what hope means in other languages: 1) a wish for something to be realized and 2) a desirable prospect for a brighter future. How the Japanese perceive hope, however, may be pretty different from other cultures—and within the Japanese society—at different times.

Pessimistic

Hope is closely associated with optimistic/pessimistic views as it is defined with positive prospects about the future. Psychology research shows that Asian people tend to appear

more pessimistic compared to people with Western cultural backgrounds. However, these findings need to be interpreted with care.

First, people in Asian cultures may not be accustomed to expressing their optimistic or pessimistic states. For example, in general, the Japanese are hindered in expressing a positive evaluation about their performance, life, and happiness, so they tend to give more reserved self-expressions about their positive thoughts than they actually think. This may explain why the Japanese do not often talk about hope. Second, the balance of the paired psychological states is diverse between different cultures and therefore may have different implications. Optimism and pessimism have negative associations, but according to cross-cultural psychology studies, the negative association observed in Asian cultures is much weaker than that in Western cultures. This implies that, in Asian cultures, optimism and pessimism are not necessarily a conflicting bipolar pair but a complementary one. Third, in the scientific arena, we may not perfectly reflect how individuals develop and feel hope in different cultures since many psychological scales are developed based on Western values. The science of hope needs to further explore and bridge the cultural diversity of hope and its real pictures in societies.

Material affluence

Quite a number of studies, novels, and media coverage show evidence that Japanese society during the 1960s and 1980s was actually filled with a common hope from a majority of the people—that is, economic and material affluence. This strong notion of positive future expectancy was shared (though it may not have been verbally shared as often) among the post-war baby-boomer generation who were in the prime of their lives during this period. The income level had quadrupled, and the quality of life had drastically risen: their hope was achieved. After then, particularly after the collapse of the bubble economy in the early 1990s, Japanese people were no longer hopeful for economic growth. **People started searching for their *own* hope.**

Yet Japanese people in the 21st century are not hopeless. According to a nationwide survey conducted in 2006, about 80% of people have hope, and the majority of them believe their hope can be achieved. They hope for their job and career, family, health, leisure, learning, social commitments, friendship, and marriage. Other data of the same survey shows that quite a ratio of the people (60%) believe that they can live better by having hope while very few people think they cannot live without hope (7%). This finding implies an interesting guess: for Japanese people, hope may not be something they rely on so they can survive but something additional that cheerfully decorates their life and gives them a good reason to commit themselves to things that they are concerned with.

Tsunami

On the 11th of March, 2011, Japan had the devastating events of a great earthquake, a tsunami, and a nuclear accident. These events inevitably made people rethink about life and death, nature and human systems both as gifts and threats, happiness, and hope for the future. **Deep desperation overwhelmed the country immediately after the events, but soon can-do spirits grew** and spread in the affected areas and other parts of the country. People believed in hope and chose to promptly commit themselves to revitalizing their communities again rather than letting themselves soak in hopeless situations. This suggests that hope does not totally disappear even in very difficult times, and hope can be boosted even by pessimistic conditions. The year 2011 was probably the highest time during the last five decades that people in Japan seriously discussed hope.

Now in 2015, **people are back in silence again.** Our recent survey data in 2013 indicate that the Japanese people foresee that their happiness in the future will almost remain at the present level. The data also tell that the working generations are not so hopeful for their future happiness while the elderly expect a better future for their life. This contrast by generation might be a reflection of uncertainties and anxieties for the future that underlie the society's mood. It may thus not be too far until the Japanese return to talking seriously about the future, regardless of expecting hopeful or hopeless ones, but it is not certain whether they will refer to hope or any other concepts then.

The keys

→ **Asian people tend to appear more pessimistic compared to people with Western cultural backgrounds. However, these findings need to be interpreted with care.**

→ **For the Japanese, hope may not be something they rely in order to survive but something additional that cheerfully decorates their life and gives them a good reason to commit themselves to things that they are concerned with.**

→ **The public reaction after the tsunami suggests that hope does not totally disappear, even in very difficult times, and hope can be boosted even by pessimistic conditions.**

Naoko Kaida is an assistant professor in environmental economics and pro-environmental behavior at the Department of Policy and Planning Sciences, University of Tsukuba (Japan). **Kosuke Kaida** is a senior researcher in cognitive neuroscience and sleep at Life Human Technology Research Institute, National Institute of Advanced Industrial Science and Technology (AIST) in Japan. They have coauthored several papers on positive feelings, subjective well-being, and pro-environmental behavior. As life and research partners, they are hopeful and excited about integrating their research orientations further to contribute to enhancing physical and psychological well-being with quality sleep, cheerful life, and pro-social and pro-environmental engagement in societies.

"Hope is not a luxury of the privileged few."

The big five of hope

Yes, most of us want to be hopeful. But sometimes it seems we are the only ones in a desert of despair. What exactly does research know about hope? Prof. **Matthew W. Gallagher** is one of the leading researchers on hope. His research focuses on how hope and other forms of positive thinking promote mental health and recovery from post-traumatic stress disorder and other anxiety disorders. Here is the big five of what we know about hope.

1. Hope is universal. One of the most remarkable things that I have found in studying hope is the extent to which hopeful expectations for the future are universal. Skeptics of hope research sometimes argue that hope is a luxury of those who are already flourishing, but research has now demonstrated that high levels of hope are, in fact, universal. In a recently published study that I conducted with my colleagues Shane Lopez and Sarah Pressman, we examined worldwide variations in positive expectations for the future using data from the Gallup World Poll. This study included representative samples of more than 1,000 individuals from 142 countries that together represented 95% of the world's population. What we found was striking: **84% of the worldwide sample had a hopeful orientation toward the future** and 89% of the worldwide sample expected their life in five years to be as good as or better than their current life. When examining country level variations, we found that the populations of 141 of the 142 countries we examined had a hopeful orientation toward the future. Furthermore, we found that the effects of demographic variables such as age, gender, and income were quite modest. What these findings indicate is that hope is not a luxury of the privileged few, but rather represents a universal psychological resource that can be found in all corners of the world.

2. Hope is helpful. Another question that is commonly raised about hope is whether hope is a good thing or whether so-called false hope is actually a harmful delusion. What is now clear from the research that I and many others have conducted is that hope is generally a positive psychological resource that promotes healthy psychological and physical functioning. **Hope has been shown to promote a wide variety of indicators of positive mental health** such as positive emotions, life satisfaction, meaning in life, and positive relations, and to do so above and beyond other psychological constructs that are known to be helpful.

3. Hope is active. What research has consistently demonstrated is that individuals high in hope do not passively wait for good outcomes, but take an active role in pursuing their goals and engaging in activities that promote positive outcomes. They are more likely to engage in more adaptive forms of emotion regulation, **are more likely to pursue challenging tasks**, and are more likely to persevere in pursuing goals when they encounter obstacles. There is even evidence that hope provides resilience to pain, which Rick Snyder once demonstrated during a live experiment conducted with the correspondents on the television show *Good Morning America*.

4. Hope influences mental health. Hope is a robust predictor of a variety of forms of mental illness as well as an important resource in promoting recovery from mental illness. In my own research, I have focused on how hope plays an important role in promoting resilience to and recovery from post-traumatic stress disorder and anxiety disorders. It is an unfortunate reality that most individuals will experience one or more traumatic events during their life. It would be unreasonable to argue that hope could somehow prevent traumatic events from occurring, but research suggests that hope does play a powerful role in promoting recovery and a return to baseline functioning following trauma. The reason for this is that hope promotes active styles of coping and emotion regulation that are most effective at managing anxiety. These effective coping styles promote resilience to anxiety when confronted by challenging or uncertain situations.

5. Hope encourages change. There is increasing evidence that hope is a mechanism of change of cognitive behavioral therapies for Post-Traumatic Stress Disorder and anxiety disorders. Multiple randomized, controlled trials have now demonstrated that changes in hope during treatment predict changes in PTSD symptoms. It therefore appears that hope not only functions as a powerful psychological resource that can promote positive aspects of mental health, but hope also functions as an important source of resilience that makes individuals less likely to develop anxiety disorders and helps individuals to recover from adversity.

The keys

→ **Most of us have a hopeful orientation toward the future and know that hope is generally a positive psychological resource.**

→ **Individuals high in hope do not passively wait for good outcomes but take an active role in pursuing their goals.**

→ **Hope is a robust predictor of a variety of forms of mental illness as well as an important resource in promoting recovery from mental illness.**

Matthew W. Gallagher, PhD, is currently a Research Psychologist at the Behavioral Science Division of the National Center for Post-traumatic Stress Disorder at the VA Boston Healthcare System and an Assistant Professor of Psychiatry at Boston University School of Medicine (USA). His research has been awarded by the Association for Psychological Science. When not studying hope, he enjoys playing and watching soccer and is hopeful that FC Barcelona will return to winning championships in the coming years.

*"The right kind of music will help us
to build positive expectations and hope."*

Music and hope

Have you ever felt really down, and then heard a song that
all of a sudden made you feel that things aren't really so bad?
Dr. Naomi Ziv investigates this mechanism. Music psychology
attempts to empirically study the ways in which music influences
our thoughts, emotions, and behavior. Including hope.

We all know the feeling of being profoundly moved by music. We know which music
has the strongest influence on us. But what is this emotion we feel when we are moved
by the music we love? Why does music sometimes have the power to change our mood
and even our way of looking at life?

Musical structure

When we listen to a piece of music, the sounds we hear unfolding in time are integrated
into a representation of a coherent whole. The notes are not a random series of unconnected
pitches, but an organized harmonious structure. In order to perceive this structure, we use
bottom-up processes—the perception of sounds, pitches, and timbres. These are features
our brain perceives from the musical stimulus. In parallel, top-down processes are
involved. These include a set of more or less specific expectations that lead us to anticipate
the successive notes. These expectations are based on previous knowledge and familiarity
with the musical norms of our culture.

Even without ever studying music formally or learning to play an instrument, **people acquire an implicit knowledge of the structural norms of their culture's music.** This knowledge is learned through exposure to music from early childhood. A large number of studies in music cognition have shown that by the age of ten, children possess a relatively stable mental representation of the musical "grammar" of their culture. The implicit knowledge of musical structure leads us to form expectations, as we listen to music, about the direction and development of the tune. It helps us "make sense" of the piece of music we're listening to, as the music progresses in time.

Mood and emotion

Perceiving music is of course not only a cognitive process. One of the main reasons people give for listening to music is the emotion it expresses and how it makes them feel. The span and strength of music's effect on mood is extremely wide, ranging from music that just helps us pass the time more pleasantly, to being moved to tears or changing our whole perception of life.

We all learn to use music in various ways in different circumstances. We know which music will help us relax after a hard day's work, or which songs can lift us and energize us when we need to concentrate. We choose the music that will motivate us to work out, the music that will put us in the right mood before going out, or the music that will help us regulate our emotions.

Think of the times when you were sad. Sometimes in these situations we select music that we know will lift our spirits. Other times we prefer to listen to something that will help us cry and let out our emotions.

When you think about it, **this finely-tuned skill we all develop is quite amazing.** After all, nobody teaches us to do these things, yet we all develop a fine sensitivity and wisdom regarding our own reactions to music and learn to use music for our emotional needs.

Personal differences

But, of course, not all music affects everybody in the same way. We each have our own personal preferences, and our subjective ways of using music and reacting to it. **Our taste in music develops through life and is influenced by our experiences, by social factors,** and by our unique personality. A certain song may evoke a strong emotion through its association with a specific person, it may remind us of a particular event or period in life, or inspire us.

In one of the studies we conducted, we found that listening to uplifting music increased hope levels in participants who experienced failure in an experimental task. Participants who did not listen to music after experiencing failure did not feel very optimistic regarding their chances of succeeding on a consecutive task. However, a closer look revealed that the effect of music on hope was only significant for individuals who were high on trait hope. That is, the music we used helped the building of positive expectations only in people who had a stable disposition toward hope. But since there are individual differences in musical preferences, this may mean that for others a different, personal choice of music might have helped build hope.

So, think about the music you love and the emotion it evokes. Learn how to use music to inspire you, to build positive expectations and hope.

The keys

→ **The implicit knowledge of musical structure leads us to form expectations, as we listen to music, about the direction and development of the tune.**

→ **We all develop a fine sensitivity and wisdom regarding our own reactions to music and learn to use music for our emotional needs.**

→ **Our musical preferences differ. Listening to the right kind of music may build positive expectations and hope in people.**

Naomi Ziv received her B.A. in psychology from Tel-Aviv University (Israël) and her master's and PhD from Paris-X Nanterre (France). She teaches and does research in Israël. Her main field of interest is music psychology. She publishes research on the effects of music on various emotional, cognitive, and behavioral aspects. Music has always played an important role in her life. "When I was a teenager," she says, "going through the typical difficulties of this age, listening to music and playing the guitar always had a very strong positive effect on me. I always wondered how particular combinations of sounds can have such an impact. Eventually, this led me to choose music psychology as my field of research."

Positive interventions: hope in action

How do you turn dreams into goals? By adding a verb and an action to your dreams. Hope is not about wishing but about doing. Inspiring examples are the positive interventions created by Helena Águeda Marujo and Luis Miguel Neto in Portugal: the power of transformative-appreciative research.

In a pool of studies devoted to "leading by positive questions"— ranging from one involving 1,200 families living on welfare (a representative sample of the families below the poverty threshold in the Portuguese Azores Islands), to others including e.g. juvenile delinquents, institutionalized children, marginalized Gypsy communities—we created and implemented a transformative-appreciative research model. Entire families, organizations, and communities—always including several social, economic, educational, and professional layers, and intergenerational, reciprocal, and Rhizomatic configurations—are involved as research stakeholders. The aim is a dynamic and prospective-oriented awareness of their individual and collective strengths, toward enhancing relational goods, trust, and affirmation in self and others, resulting in more confidence in future life and social justice.

Positive questions

Usually, community development projects aimed at confronting real social problems of real people who live in harsh circumstances are planned using participatory approaches, to expose local tribulations, resource limitations, and unmet crucial needs and human rights. These methodologies are extremely valuable, since they boost participation, convey power, and potentiate change, while addressing the importance of local knowledge and promoting unique and crafted solutions. Nevertheless, they tend to have involuntary consequences, namely failing to sustain community participation after the implementing organization withdraws. One of the possible reasons is that when those projects end, local people often confirm the perception of their community as a needy place, filled with deficiencies and problems.

The transformative-appreciative approach **focuses on a community's achievements rather than its problems.** When the most diverse group from a community (in terms of social class, gender, age, life experience, level of education…) engage around positive questions that really matter for them, in a dialogic, appreciative way, sustainable collective meaning, action, and wisdom materialize. Qualitative and narrative action-research processes are intertwined, to promote change and research in unison.

World Café

One of the methods we use is that of the World Café (a structured conversational process for groups). This method, in connection with the Appreciative Inquiry model and the Positive Psychology/strengths-based approach, all show the capacity to bring people together in this way. As **user-friendly methods, focused on the best of people and of people at their best**, and supported in a lively network of conversations among persons that usually do not relate, the approach brings vigor to individual and shared hope. It translates into hope-in-action.

The method—which always includes communion of food, appreciative conversation among the diverse, and comic/positive emotions— invites participants to learn with each other, co-generate applicable knowledge, reciprocate in genuine ways, and profile unique paths for being a factual community. Injustice becomes palpable and conscious through people's individual and communal stories.

Co-constructed hope

The creative, sustainable projects that have been emerging from these processes are amazing— from groups of women organizing activities to enhance their commu-

nity's health in face of high levels of obesity, to building communi-tarian ovens, to creating techno-logical-based projects to promote engagement with school and meaning in life in teens.

They show a vigor of solutions, warm and respectful collaborative relationships, and benevolent visions of the future, that compel for the triumph of an invincible co-constructed hope.

Helena Águeda Marujo and **Luis Miguel Neto** coordinate the Executive Master in Applied Positive Psychology at the University of Lisbon (Portugal).

"Inconsistent or controlling parents
have kids with lower resilience when they are adults."

Resilience, hope, and growth

Watch children and their parents in the playground. Bring people in for 520 days of isolation for a mock-flight to Mars. Put crew-members and tourists together in a long and extreme transoceanic cruise on a sail-powered freighter. What happens to their emotional state? Scientists **Iva Šolcová** and **Vladimir Kebza** draw their conclusions regarding resilience, growth, hope, and education.

Through our research, we learned several important things about resilience. The first three come from scientific writings and concern resilience in general:

1. The most important thing is that **resilience is nothing exceptional.** In the words of Ann Masten, it is an "ordinary magic" that does not require anything rare or extraordinary. It is common and it arises from ordinary human capabilities, relationships, and resources.

2. The second important finding is that **resilience is not a definite, universal, limited human capability and/or trait.** It is rather a process in the course of which you can fail in one situation, and carry over in another. After feeling unresourceful in one situation, you can feel resourceful in another.

3. The third important piece of knowledge is that **you can learn to use your strengths and virtues to battle with adversity.** As Nelson Mandela put it: "The greatest glory in living lies not in never falling, but in rising every time we fall."

Parenting styles

In our studies, we were striving to contribute to a list of factors associated with resilience with interesting results. When you look at children playing in the playground and at their parents you are in fact observing two potent factors determining adult resilience: *child behavior and parenting style*. Our longitudinal study (which started in the fifties of the last century in Prague and in the sixties in Brno) showed the relation between *active behavior in early childhood* as measured by observation and *resilience in adulthood* (as measured by questionnaires). Active behavior was represented by general activity, nonconformity/disobedience, general reactivity, and violent behavior against things at 12, 18, 24, and 30 months of age.

The question of how parents impact child development has been investigated for a long time by developmental psychologists. Our findings suggest the **positive relations of perceived warmth in parenting and involvement in parenting to resilience in adulthood** (and a negative link of inconsistent parenting style and controlling parenting style to resilience in adulthood).

On the base of our data on resilience in adulthood, we concluded that personality resilience might comprise two factors. The first factor is represented by control over one's individual life, personal and professional efficacy, and competency (this factor was labeled *Competence-Control*). The second factor that was labeled *Vitality/Well-being* appears to be represented by energy, involvement, dedication, and commitment. We did not study hope in this research, but it can be hypothesized that hope could indeed be a part of the Vitality/Well-being factor. **The Vitality/well-being factor seems to us essential in the promotion of resilience**; that is, it is important to seek the ways by which the Vitality/Well-being part can facilitate resilience when included in strategic interventions.

Mars and cruise

There are promising results in our study addressing the question of possible positive changes in the condition of the MARS 500 experiment, which is the longest hi-fidelity spaceflight simulation to date (520 days of group isolation). Our results show that **the majority of crewmembers were capable of personal growth** in the conditions of demanding and stressful simulation of extended space flight. Even though the experience of a simulated spaceflight cannot be as rewarding and powerful as an actual spaceflight, it had a positive impact on crewmember personality. Most marked was *social* growth.

Another highly demanding situation in which we detected positive growth was a transoceanic cruise on a sail-powered freighter. The crew of 16 people (8 professional crewmembers and 8 tourists; 9 males and 7 females; representing 9 different countries) participated in the cruise. The transoceanic voyage meant for the crew to handle 4,732 nautical miles from Mauritius Island to port Fremantle in Australia, as well as five weeks of isolation and confinement in extreme conditions. All the tourists were administered a questionnaire on stress-related growth after the trip. All respondents displayed positive growth after the cruise experience. **Most marked was cognitive and social growth.** The most frequent responses indicating social growth in both groups were represented in these answers: "I developed new relationships with helpful others," "I realized I have a lot to offer other people," "I learned to appreciate the strength of others who have had a difficult life." The most frequent responses indicating cognitive growth were "I gained new knowledge about the world" and "I learned to look at things in a more positive way."

Common goal

In our two studies, we observed the phenomenon of personal growth and improved psychological functioning after a shared experience of a challenging situation. We can try to trace why it happened. One important thing is that they were the "right staff"—well selected people for the purpose given. The feeling of being a part of a well-functioning team probably played an important role.

The participants worked together as a group, originally drawn together as outsiders, within a shared place and they shared a common goal. Thanks to solidarity experiences based on face-to-face interaction, shared emotions, and a shared common goal, the participants were capable of emotionally investing in relationships with others. This has probably been the engine of marked social growth in both groups, as L. Vygotsky phrased it: "Through others we become ourselves." And as G. Vaillant summarized his seventy-year-old findings: "The only thing that really matters in life are your relationships to other people."

Our advice for improving resilience, hope, and growth? Support your children in active and exploring behavior. Be warm, understanding, and responsive parents. Be attentive to your relations with other people; they are the most important in life.

The keys

→ **Resilience is nothing exceptional and not definite. You can learn to use your strengths and virtues to battle with adversity.**

→ **A warm parenting style results in more resilient children than a controlling or inconsistent style. Resilient adults need to feel vital well-being and control over their personal life.**

→ **We are all capable of cognitive and social growth, especially through interaction with others, shared emotions, and a common goal.**

Iva Šolcová is a senior scientist at the Institute of Psychology of the Academy of Sciences in Charles University of Prague (Czech Republic). She deals with stress resistance and resilience in different contexts and has published more than 90 studies in highly appreciated peer-reviewed scientific journals. In 2004 she received the National Psychiatric Award for the best theoretical and research work on the theme of psychological stress. With her husband Miloslav, who is also a psychologist, she has three adult children and she is the proud owner of two Irish Wolfhounds. Her motto? "With all the evil in the world I do believe in the good in man."

Vladimir Kebza is Professor of Clinical Psychology at the Faculty of Economics and Management, Czech University of Life Sciences and Faculty of Philosophy and Arts, Charles University in Prague (Czech Republic). He is the principal investigator and coordinator of several national and international grant projects, including "Psychosocial Determinants of Health." His main research interests and results include mental health and psychological aspects of health-related behavior.

"For Nietzsche, hope is the worst thing on earth."

Time perspectives

Besides philosophy and psychology, hope is treated in sociology, especially in Quality of Life research. What's the attitude toward hope in this field of science? Sociologist **Jennifer Gulyas** explains how hopes and fears are part of the time perspectives of subjective well-being. They influence our lives in different dimensions.

The German philosopher Nietzsche (1844–1900) wrote about hope and referred to the Greek myth of Pandora's Box. The box was a present from Zeus to Pandora, the first woman on earth. She was warned not to open the box, but she did, and all the evils of mankind poured out of the box. Before she had opened the box, mankind had not known any evil or bad things. However, there was something left in the box, and that was hope. Pandora opened the box again and hope came on earth, like Zeus had intended. He wanted people to continue desiring life even though they might be tortured by bad and evil things. He wanted mankind not to throw their lives away. Nietzsche's point of view is that hope is the worst thing on earth because it prolongs the torment of man.

Another German philosopher, Bloch (1885–1977), wrote in his "Principle of Hope" that hope has to be differentiated from dreams. Hope is connected with rational plans to fulfill the contents and make them real, whereas dreams are irrational.

Future expectations

Besides philosophy and psychology, hope is treated in sociology, especially in Quality of Life research. What's the attitude toward hope in this field of science? One approach is that hopes and fears are part of subjective wellbeing, and subjective wellbeing is threefold: it has three time perspectives, namely past, present, and future; and three components, namely positive well-being (happiness and satisfaction), negative well-being (worries), and future expectations. The future expectations may be hopes, or fears, or they might be neutral, which means that the expectations remain unchanged. And we have different dimensions. On the one hand, we refer to private dimensions (like health, work, income, leisure, family, and so on) and on the other hand, to public dimensions (like the health of the nation, the economic situation, poverty, and so on) and the general dimension, which is a combination of the two dimensions named above. **The three components and within the dimensions vary independently of each other.** How does this concept refer to the reality of life? I would like to give an example. Somebody may be satisfied with his family life, but he has worries about his working life; his future expectation for each domain is hopeful. Another person might also be satisfied with his family life and have worries regarding his working life, but he is fearful for the future regarding both dimensions.

Self-fulfilling prophecy

How does this influence life? The attitudes of these two people might influence their future, because of the phenomenon of self-fulfilling prophecy. The self-fulfilling prophecy implies that I behave in a way that encourages the prophecy to become real. Hope sets personal, social, and economic resources free, whereas fears block these resources, which is why **future expectations can produce a self-fulfilling prophecy.** But having hope where there is no hope would be false as well. Fears regarding the future can also function as warning signals and can lead to a change in behavior so the fears will not come true. We can transfer this thought also to a society as a whole. A hopeful society is good for each individual living in this society because it supports positive and constructive behavior of all.

In our lives there will be situations where you need to have hope so you can continue. These situations may be sickness (your own, a family member, or a friend), the possibility of losing a job, a bad accident, and so on. Whether you have hope or not influences your behavior. Hope is not something bad, as Nietzsche suggested. Hope is necessary for life and a chance that what you hope for will come true.

The keys

→ **Hopes and fears are part of subjective well-being. This has three time perspectives (past, present, and future) and three components (positive and negative well-being and future expectations).**

→ **The future expectations may be hopes, fears, or neutral. The three components and within the dimensions (private, public, or general) vary independently of each other.**

→ **Through self-fulfilling prophecy hope sets personal, social, and economic resources free, whereas fears block these resources.**

Jennifer Gulyas graduated in 2011 in sociology and worked since then at the Goethe-University Frankfurt am Main (Germany) for Wolfgang Glatzer's *Global Handbook of Quality of Life* (2015), where she wrote articles about hope. She has been speaking on hope at different Quality of Life conferences. Now she is working in the private sector. Hope is her companion in life.

"Radiant assurance is beyond hope, which implies a degree of uncertainty."

Hope: between despair and radiant assurance

"Hope occupies a place on the spectrum of confidence ranging from despair to radiant assurance. Despair implies that hope has vanished. Radiant assurance is beyond hope, which implies a degree of uncertainty," says Prof. **Jeffrey Wattles**. His publications on courageous willing, teleology, philosophies of history, and peace contribute to the worldwide mosaic of reflections on hope.

This reflection on our attitudes toward the future begins with a look at our consciousness of the past. Edmund Husserl distinguished (1) explicit *remembering* from (2) *retaining* the past as a receding dimension of the present. Reading or hearing a sentence, we retain but do not consciously recall earlier words as we perceive later words. Thus explicit, active memory is distinguished from *retention*.

Husserl described a parallel distinction about our consciousness of the future: there is (1) a definite, conscious act of expecting or predicting a future event and (2) a tacit *"protention,"* a dimension of the present that does not explicitly predict or hope for anything. **Reading or hearing the beginning of a sentence, we protend the completion of the sentence** with a vague sense of its grammar and content. Or imagine a boy who goes out one day and meets an older boy, and they get along wonderfully well. Because of the protentions and hope launched by their day of friendship, when evening comes and the younger one must return home, it would be a shock if the older boy said, "Good-bye. I won't be seeing you anymore."

Protention

Radiant assurance is a *present* experience: "Taste and see that the Lord is good." The taste of divinely good Presence also includes protentions without any future boundary, since the experience of radiant assurance does not phenomenologically involve this body of flesh. It is conceivable that death could end a wonderful relationship with the spiritual Friend, but such an end would violate the momentum of friendship already begun. There are no quantitative limits on the dimensions of the present "moment," the now.

Radiant experience can significantly modify our sense of past and future. A radiant experience of forgiveness refreshes the sense of self and modifies memories associated with shame and guilt. Remembering the radiant experience reawakens the retention, as though the retention persists as an underground river, ready to surface at any time. The sense of self as restored nourishes faith and hope for our future.

Assurance

Radiant assurance can encompass the future. People report near-death experiences and visions of the heavenly life to come. Experiences of radiant assurance regarding life after death or our planetary future erase all doubt about destiny. But most of us live with a measure of uncertainty and rely on hope to bolster courage.

On the spectrum of certainty, hope can lean either way. When hope is weak, fear and discouragement hamper constructive responses to uncertainty. When hope is nourished by radiant assurance, then the experience of uncertainty gets transformed. One way is to contemplate possible outcomes, prepare vigorously for each of them, and heartily embrace the uncertainty. Another way is to channel the energy of radiant assurance into efforts to bring about the desired outcome.

Flow

Effort at the level of optimal performance has been described by Mihaly Csikszentmihalyi as "flow." In the paradigm case, an athlete of high skill faces a high challenge, at the level that calls forth his best. "The main dimensions of flow—intense involvement, deep concentration, clarity of goals and feedback, loss of a sense of time, lack of self-consciousness, and transcendence of a sense of self, leading to an autotelic, that is, intrinsically rewarding experience—are recognized in more or less the same form by people the world over." A figure skater does not know whether some competitor will score higher, but her experience of flow brings its own radiant assurance along with it. **Flow is neither an assurance of victory nor a guarantee against a fall.** But optimal performance does not get distracted by worries about competitors, but enters into the flow of excellence cultivated by thousands of hours of training. Confident of something good in our future, we can savor it in advance. In savoring, the uncertainty that calls for hope is increasingly supplemented by assurance.

The keys

→ **In our consciousness of the future there is a tacit "*protention*," a dimension of the present that does not explicitly predict or hope for anything.**

→ **When hope is weak, fear and discouragement hamper constructive responses to uncertainty. When hope is nourished by radiant assurance, then the experience of uncertainty gets transformed.**

→ **Confident of something good in our future, we can savor it in advance. In savoring, the uncertainty that calls for hope is increasingly supplemented by assurance.**

Jeffrey Wattles is a (mostly) retired professor of philosophy and religion at Kent State University (USA). He studied at Stanford, in Louvain and Toronto. His academic life project is to help construct a philosophy of living in truth, beauty, and goodness. His main publication is *The Golden Rule* (Oxford University Press). He finds hope in his students' transformative experiences with the experiential approach to teaching he developed and in a complement to his approach at an inner-city middle school in Cleveland, Ohio.

"Sometimes we have to give up to move forward."

The dark sister of hope

Don't we all dream of making the world a better place? So does **Ella Saltmarshe**. She has spent over a decade working in international development and public policy. Increasingly she is focused on maximizing the impact of interventions to build a better world. She has discovered that to do this work, hope alone isn't enough; she also needs its dark sister, doubt.

Hope. It's part of my operating system. I'd never start those crazy, overambitious projects without a heady dose of hope. I'd never try and intervene to make the world better, if I wasn't feeding myself hope. I'd never persevere through the tough, icky work, if it weren't for hope. I read books that help me hope more. I watch films that help me hope richer. I listen to music that helps me hope deeper.

Dangerous opiate

But for hope to function as a force for good, it needs its dark sister: doubt. When used well, doubt helps us act intelligently; when used badly, it stops us from acting at all. But without doubt, hope becomes a dangerous opiate. Years ago, I was attending a noisy panel discussion when an Afghan woman criticizing US intervention in her country shouted out, "Hope is not a policy." She stated that all too often American foreign policy had prized hope over doubt, optimism over intelligence. Over the years her words have kept resonating in my ears. They have led me to dissect hope, to understand where it can help and where it can hurt. Because make no mistake, misplaced hope can be as damaging as a lack of hope.

For most of us, the battle between hope and doubt doesn't play out on the landscape of global geo-politics, but in the minutiae of our daily lives. Not every project we do, or every relationship we have, will work. Sometimes we have to give up to move forward.

Over-hope

Those of us who want to make the world better are often prone to over-hoping. We see challenges as opportunities to overcome. We see relentless difficulty as a chance to dig deep, to use our tenacity and grit. When the going gets tough, we definitely don't get going. These character traits that lend themselves so well to positive change can also trap us in projects and relationships that are going nowhere. Knowing when to let doubt trump hope is a vitally important skill. Do it too early and you'll never succeed at anything, do it too late and you might waste years on something that will never work.

These are such easy words to write and such difficult words to live. Making these ideas real requires the inner-awareness to recognize your own predilection to over-hope or over-doubt, and then the outer-awareness to truly recognize the situation you're in, without filters (either of the rose-tinted or darkened variety). It requires us to have F. Scott Fitzgerald's "ability to hold two opposed ideas at the same time, and still retain the ability to function." We need to be able to hope both wildly and rigorously.

The keys

→ **For hope to function as a force for good, it needs its dark sister: doubt. Without doubt, hope becomes a dangerous opiate.**

→ **Misplaced hope can be as damaging as a lack of hope. Those of us who want to make the world better are often prone to over-hoping.**

→ **Knowing when to let doubt trump hope is a vitally important skill. We need to be able to hope both wildly and rigorously.**

Ella Saltmarshe is trained as an anthropologist. She is a writer and strategist. Her journalism can be found in *The Financial Times, Wired, Monocle,* and *Creative Review.* As a strategist she advises NGOs, donors, and governments on public policy and social change. For Ella, this means taking a systems approach, whether that's through co-founding the Systems Changers initiative, working on strategic philanthropy with organizations like the ClimateWorks Foundation, incubating innovation labs, or co-founding The Point People to build and connect networks.

"We rarely manage to lift ourselves out of the swamp of hopelessness that bogs us down."

The relational nature of hope

"Hope is fundamentally relational," says Prof. **Patrick Luyten**. "The development of the capacity for hope is embedded within early attachment relationships and remains intimately tied to relationships with others." He studies the relational nature of hope in relation to the placebo effect. Where psychology and biology meet.

Despite its centrality in human existence, hope remains a somewhat elusive concept. As this volume attests, hope is central in many areas of life. In their personal lives, people hope that their relationships will work out, that their job will be exciting and will bring personal fulfillment, that their children will be healthy and happy, and that they will live a long and prosperous life. Those confronted with illness or disease hope that they or their loved ones will become better. In business and sports, people hope that they will be successful. Religious people hope that there will be an afterlife. Politicians hope that they will be elected and in turn often proclaim that their political program offers hope for a better life for their voters.

Two brain circuits

Psychology has provided important insights in what hope is. Yet, without reference to the biological underpinnings of hope, our understanding of this complex emotional state is likely to be incomplete. Like any complex human emotion, hope involves the brain, and complex brain processes for that matter. Indeed, while research on animals suggests that non-human primates and some other animals may experience a state of hopelessness, it is highly unlikely that they know the experience of hope.

This may be explained by the fact that in humans, **hope is associated with the activation of two closely related brain circuits: the so-called reward system on the one hand and the mentalizing system on the other.** The former system is also present in many animal species besides humans and is activated whenever we experience something that is pleasurable. Chronic frustration of this system leads to feelings of hopelessness and depression. The latter system is present only in rudimentary form in most animals with the exception of humans. This system underpins our capacity to reflect on ourselves and others. Both systems point toward the key role of relationships in explaining the feeling of hope in humans. Or better: our fundamental dependence on others and their *minds* to help us understand ourselves, navigate our complex social world, and project ourselves into a hopeful future.

Hopeless swamp

For those who have grown up in a warm and supportive climate, the feeling of being related to others is one of the most rewarding experiences in life. For these individuals, relationships are rewarding; they really like other people, as is evidenced by the activation of the brain reward system when they interact with others. These individuals, who are often described as securely attached, typically also have solid reflective capacities, precisely because they are open toward others, their opinions, and their understanding of the world. They are eager to learn from the minds of others. **For individuals who have lacked positive attachment experiences, relationships are not rewarding.** By contrast, relationships are either a source of anxiety (e.g. fears of being abandoned or rejected) or are associated with considerable discomfort.

With secure attachment and reflective capacities comes the capacity for realistic hope rooted in rewarding experiences with others and a capacity to reflect on oneself and one's own life. Those with insecure attachment often lack the capacity to develop realistic hope, particularly when their capacity for reflection is impaired. Feelings of meaninglessness, helplessness, and hopelessness, key features of depression, may ensue or be constantly looming in the background. Once depressed, they feel stuck in a gloomy scene without any future, let alone a hopeful future.

Hope is therefore fundamentally relational. The development of the capacity for hope is embedded within early attachment relationships and remains intimately tied to relationships with others. Indeed, we need others to open up our mind and free us of the gloomy hopeless scenery in which we may find ourselves when our hopes and dreams have been thwarted. We rarely manage to lift ourselves out of the swamp of hopelessness that bogs us down. We typically turn to others and their minds when we feel down and without hope. As we have seen, this, however, presumes that **we must have the belief and the capacity to turn to others when we lose hope.** Unfortunately, feelings of hopelessness cloud our thinking. We may feel completely stuck in painful feelings and we have the feeling or often, rather, the *conviction* that there is no hope and that others can do little or nothing to help us. This is the drama of depression and hopelessness: those who may benefit most from relationships in restoring hope often have the fundamental belief that others cannot help them.

Placebo

This is not mere speculation. In the medical sciences it is well known that hope alone may be associated with a positive response to treatment. This is the essence of the so-called *placebo effect*. Studies have shown that the placebo effect is associated with the activation of the brain reward circuit and the mentalizing circuit. It is typically only observed when the placebo is embedded within a relationship with a trusted other (e.g. a doctor or shaman). Hence, in humans, hope entails a relationship with a trusted other and the capacity to reflect on oneself and others. This is also the basis for psychotherapy. While hope therefore comes with many advantages as it allows us to project ourselves into the future, even and perhaps particularly when we are in dire straits, there is also a downside to hope. When our hopes are shattered or when there is no more hope, a sense of hopelessness may ensue. Further, poor judgment may also lead us to naively believe in our dreams or those of others. Like a placebo, we may later find that we have been deceived. Again, this shows that we may therefore do well to turn to others to evaluate our beliefs and hopes in the pursuit of happiness and well-being.

The keys

→ **With secure attachment and reflective capacities comes the capacity for realistic hope rooted in rewarding experiences with others and a capacity to reflect on oneself and one's own life.**

→ **The drama of depression and hopelessness is that those who may benefit most from relationships in restoring hope often have the fundamental belief that others cannot help them.**

→ **We may do well to turn to others to evaluate our beliefs and hopes in the pursuit of happiness and well-being.**

Patrick Luyten is Associate Professor at the Faculty of Psychology and Educational Sciences, University of Leuven (Belgium) and Reader at the Research Department of Clinical, Educational, and Health Psychology, University College London (UK). He serves on the editorial board of several scientific journals and heads a treatment service for patients with depression and functional somatic disorders. He finds hope in his profound admiration of those who have succeeded against all odds and those who continue to hope, even when life has dealt them major blows. These individuals continue to remind us that hope ranks among the most powerful emotions and motivations of human beings. They remind us that positivity, benevolence, and generativity are also part of human nature.

"Hope helps us to help ourselves."

Fortune of hope

"All else being equal, we would all like to be hopeful, in the sense that hopelessness or resignation does not sound attractive," say Prof. **Andrew Clark** and Prof. **Conchita D'Ambrosio**. They both study hope from an economic point of view.

Having hope is good for our well-being, in the same way that job insecurity or economic insecurity in general are bad for it. Hope underlines the key role played by our perception of what will happen to us in the future in determining how well we live our current lives. But where does hope come from? Very likely in part from within yourself, but from others as well. We would like to briefly think about the latter here.

Tunnel effect

In the first instance, the observation of others' good fortune may lead you to be more hopeful about your own future. This is sometimes referred to in the context of Albert Hirschman's "tunnel effect." Imagine that you are stuck in two lines of traffic inside a tunnel. After a while, the lane next to you starts to move. Whereas it might be thought that this would lead you to curse your misfortune, Hirschman suggests that you will instead see this as good news: if their lane is moving now, then my lane will start to move soon as well.

As such, seeing that others are doing better may well lead you to feel more hopeful about your own future prospects. This phenomenon is probably all the more likely as the others are more similar to you (in terms of where they live, or some individual characteristics).

This hope that comes from others is the opposite of the envy that social scientists imagine that we may experience when we observe others' good fortune. **This "fortune of hope" is then something of a more pleasant way of thinking about how we interact with others in society than one in which we are constantly jealous of each other.** Even so, it is worth underlining that we don't want others to do well here because we have altruistic feelings about them, but rather because their good fortune makes us feel better about our own future.

Our parents

A second likely source of hope is more individual: our parents. In British data (from the British Household Panel Surveys), respondents whose parents were higher-class, rather than lower-class, report being more hopeful. Overall, only just over one third of respondents whose parents were in the lowest quarter of the social-class distribution said that they often thought that the future looked good today. For respondents whose parents were in the top quarter of the social-class distribution, this figure was close to 50%.

This might be thought to be unsurprising. We know that there is intergenerational transmission of income and education, among other things. So those whose parents were better-off are undoubtedly better-off themselves. This is indeed the case. But **with respect to hope, the effect of having better-off parents persists even when we factor out how well-off the respondents are today.** In other words, respondents with higher-class parents have on average better outcomes today and, independent of today's outcomes, more hope for the future.

The poor

A last point is that if we receive hope from others around us, then inequalities might be exacerbated. My good fortune will lift me up, and my neighbor's as well. But those who live in poorer areas will not benefit from any such positive neighbor effect and will suffer a double whammy: they are poor, and so are their neighbors. **The positive effect of others' good fortune cuts both ways.** The same unpleasant arithmetic applies to intergenerational transmission: respondents with better-off parents both have better current outcomes and greater hope for the future.

The societies in which we live are redistributive: we take from the richer to give to the poorer. The analysis of hope reveals that the poor are deprived in more than just the income dimension: this accumulation of low income and low hope arguably makes the poorer even more deserving of our hope. But even beyond that, there are good reasons to believe that the poor need help. Esther Duflo, in her 2012 Tanner Lectures, argues that **the lack of hope is crippling for the poor**, in that it actively prevents them from being able to carry out actions that would help them exit poverty. Policies which are targeted at helping the poor can then have spectacular returns, partly because they directly increase their income, but also because they bring hope back to the poor: hope helps us to help ourselves.

The keys

→ **Seeing that others (especially when they are similar to us) are doing better may well lead us to feel more hopeful about our own future prospects.**

→ **People with higher-class parents have on average better outcomes today and, independent of today's outcomes, more hope for the future.**

→ **Policies which are targeted at helping the poor can have spectacular returns because they bring hope back to the poor: hope helps us to help ourselves.**

Andrew E. Clark holds a PhD from the London School of Economics. He is currently a CNRS Research Professor at the Paris School of Economics (France). His broad area of study is social interactions and social learning. He has published across a variety of journals in economics and psychology and refereed for 160 different journals. Outside of work, he enjoys reading, trying to memorize all music released prior to 1990, and playing the guitar.

Conchita D'Ambrosio is Professor of Economics at Université du Luxembourg (Luxembourg). She is an economist with a PhD from New York University. Her research interests revolve around the analysis and measurement of individual and social well-being. She has been a member of the editorial board of the *Review of Income and Wealth* since 2001 and managing editor of the same journal since 2007. Outside of work, she enjoys swimming and pottery.

"The beauty of a good fantasy is hidden in its capacity to bridge a dream world with a real world."

The benefits of daydreaming

You have probably often been told to stop daydreaming:
"It is fun but it is useless." Prof. **Joar Vittersø** doesn't agree.
Daydreaming is not only pleasant. The mental theatre produced
by a daydream can be very functional and useful as well.
But not any fantasy will do the trick.

To daydream means to play with plans and hopes for the future. And a good daydream
is able to create mental models of possible activities and identities for the person whose
dream it is. Although hedonistic in the sense of being pleasant in the here and now,
fantasizing about the future is more than amusing drifts of thoughts. Rather the contrary,
daydreams are essential for reaching goals that are important but hard to get—they are
simply a clever trick evolution invented to make it more likely for our hopes to come true.

This may sound strange, particularly to goal-oriented and time-urgent individuals.
True enough, **on the surface, fantasizing about possible futures may look like
a massive waste of time.** And people who give themselves up to their emotions have
never been regarded highly in the history of western thinking. Plato, for instance,
considered emotions and feelings as impediments to rational behavior. Similar
perspectives have dominated theories in medicine, social sciences, behaviorism,
and the humanities ever since.

Simulation

But today we know better. Science has taught us that emotions are part and parcel of the machinery that guides us through the labyrinths of life. Emotions are simply very useful, and both positive and negative feelings have important roles to play in our lives. The delightful experience that sometimes arises when thoughts are drifting from idea to idea is one such example. The pleasantness of a lovely fantasy motivates us to keep on fantasizing. There is, of course, nothing controversial in the idea that pleasure attracts us to hang on to whatever it is we are doing. It is far more provocative to say that daydreaming itself is functional. But that is the argument put forward in this chapter and here is why.

Think of a daydream as an opportunity to make possible futures real in your own mind. By simulating different options and ideas you have about the future, the details of their quality and possible effects in your life become more real and concrete. And in the process of making the future more tangible, the different steps needed to actually get there become clearer. The thinking through of these steps creates plans that can be tried out as doable ways to act. Possible errors and flaws may be detected before they are carried out in real life, thus preventing small or big adversities. And it all takes place as a kind of play—a mental theater produced by a daydream. In this imagined drama your mind is simulating how the plans should be executed and what their consequences might be. Just like athletes or musicians or chess masters who, in their minds, go over the phases of an upcoming competition or contest over and over again. The simulation in your mind of what you have to do in real life means, at least partly, to exercise what you need to do in particular situations in order to succeed with your plans and achieve your goals. The beauty of a good fantasy is hidden in its capacity to bridge a dream world with a real world.

Emotions

But not any fantasy will do the trick. To be helpful, the daydream must deal with the steps that lead toward achievement, not only with the rewarding outcomes of it. Randomized control group experiments have demonstrated that those who are instructed to only imagine the pleasant consequences of a much hoped for future get no better at reaching their goals than those asked not to daydream at all. Only individuals who are instructed to include planning details in their fantasies seem to benefit from the daydream. One way researchers make sure that the process toward goal achievement becomes part of the imagination, and not only the sweet end state, is to ask participants explicitly to focus

their attention on the difficulties and obstacles they expect to meet when executing the plans needed to reach their goals.

Doing things that bring pleasure comes natural to humans, and it is good that we are like that. It would have been dangerous indeed if our forefathers were attracted to food that was poisonous and ran away from food that was nutrious. Today we can learn about healthy meals in more sophisticated ways, and the role played by pleasures in regulating food intake has in many respects become dysfunctional. But **increased knowledge does not imply that we no longer depend on our emotions.** In many respects the world is still too complicated to be fully grasped, and we need assistance in order to realize what is important in our lives and what is not. The emotions help point out these directions.

Hope is one such direction, and daydreaming can assist in reaching it. But fantasies are not very helpful if they only include the pleasure of reaching the goals we wish for. Daydreams are useful when they deal with the plans that describe how to reach our goals. Fantasizing about possible futures are only functional if the images we create in our minds include the operations needed to overcome the challenges that stand between where we currently are and where we hope to be.

The keys

→ **Daydreams are essential for reaching goals that are important but hard to get. They are simply a clever trick evolution invented to make it more likely for our hopes to come true.**

→ **To be helpful, the daydream must deal with the steps that lead toward achievement, not only with the rewarding outcomes of it.**

→ **Fantasies are not very helpful if they only include the pleasure of reaching the goals we wish for.**

Joar Vittersø is a professor of social psychology at the University of Tromsø (Norway) and has been a well-being researcher for more than 25 years. His work deals basically with conceptual and measurement problems in the study of happiness. Joar is Research Advisor on well-being issues to the Gallup Institute in Washington, DC, a Scientific Advisor to EU's framework program on mental health research in Europe (ROAMER), a board member for the International Positive Psychology Association, and he has published more than 100 articles, book chapters, and scientific reports. As a researcher, his biggest hope is that scientific knowledge will inform politicians and decision makers to make better and wiser choices in the future than they have taken until now.

"Hope requires first of all the recognition and intrinsic valuation of the human person in their present situation."

Hope and expectation

What about hope in contexts in which people cannot get what they need to live with dignity? **María José Rodríguez Araneda** sees the poor conditions in lots of regions in Latin America. Hope plays a vital part over there in its different expressions: resilience, faith, dreams, perspectives… "But is it such a good idea to *prescribe* hope as a virtue in a context in which frustration is due to injustice and the beneficial interest of others?"

Talking about hope inevitably implies recognizing the implacable nature of the experiences of despair and hopelessness for the psyche. The attack of both is closely related to frustration. In this scenario, hope offers a way out. The feeling of hope provides a positive outlook, serenity, and the strength to carry on with life.

In this respect, I think it is very meaningful to differentiate between *hope* and *expectation of success*. In other words, *optimistic hope of satisfaction* or *expectation of seeing one's desire fulfilled*. This *hope-expectation* will precede a new satisfaction or frustration in a circle that is sometimes agreeable, and other times disagreeable. By hope I mean trust in a future that has something good in store.

Vanity

When we look at places where social conditions are more frustrating, we begin to see that people are prouder of their faith and inner strength than of their expectations, to which they accord less importance. Let us review some data from a comparative study we have undertaken with Chilean and Italian samples (2013), which showed that for Chilean men and women, hope turned out to be an aspect of greater importance in life than it was for the Italians, for whom expectation was more important. The discourses suggested hope was based on faith and belief in God, which allows confidence in a future that will, one way or another, be for the good, giving people the strength to overcome adversity. Accordingly, this notion of hope is more related to the theological virtues of Catholicism, in other words trust in the omnipotent help of God. "A virtue that prepares one to have confidence and the certainty of achieving eternal life and the necessary means, both supernatural and natural, to achieve it, based on the omnipotent help of God. The very reason for hope is God, inspired by God. Too little hope is despair and too much is vanity" (Martí Ballester, 2014).

Let us distinguish the above notion from that of *persevering towards the fulfillment of goals in order to achieve success*, a notion offered us by authors who work from a utilitarian viewpoint (like Fred Luthans, 2008). This latest equivalence of hope with the *satisfaction of expectations* fits in with the parameters of late modern capitalism. From there, satisfaction has become the new paradigm of what is valuable, in terms of experience, life, and person, the achievement of which is seen moreover to depend on the individual and on his personal capacity. But this is not a true meaning of hope, but rather of optimism in the achievement of expectations according to the efforts and values of each person.

Adversity

Having made this distinction, I would like to reflect on *hope* in contexts in which people cannot get what they need to live with dignity. This is often connected with injustice, ill-treatment, and the casualties of the happiness of others. (An allegory based on the song *Pequeña Serenata Diurna* by Silvio Rodríguez, which goes: "I am happy, I am a happy man, and I want to be forgiven this day for the casualties of my happiness").

The data from the study shows that in the face of insecurity, hope becomes more important. For this reason it is of key importance to question the ethical dimension of hope. From the point of view of the social sciences, especially psychology, is it such a good idea to *prescribe* hope as a virtue in a context in which frustration is due to injustice and the beneficial interest of others? **Can it be right to *announce* the benefits of hope— on a psychological level—if social life is regulated and controlled from abuses of power, inequality, and exclusion?**

To take this discussion further, let us remember the poverty and exclusion in Latin America. What is healthy at an individual level is not necessarily appropriate to be prescribed in an expert discourse, in rights (associated with duties), or in public policies. The fact that hope is beneficial in facing up to the adversity of life does not mean that it is advisable to prescribe it if it tempers awareness of injustice or reduces social action. This is particularly significant, since it is the normalizing institutions of everyday life themselves that legitimize and perpetuate conditions of injustice.

Given all of the above, hope requires first of all the recognition and intrinsic valuation of the human person in their present situation. To promote it from the social sciences without considering this ethical minimum, without questioning the implications or considering contexts, or worse still, identifying it with expectations of success, seems to me detrimental to society and to individuals.

The keys

→ **We need to differentiate between "hope" and "expectation of success." At places where social conditions are more frustrating, we see that people are prouder of their faith and inner strength than of their expectations, to which they accord less importance.**

→ **Achievement of expectations is not the true meaning of hope. There are contexts in which people cannot get what they need to live with dignity.**

→ **The fact that hope is beneficial in facing up to the adversity of life does not mean that it is advisable to prescribe it if it tempers awareness of injustice or reduces social action.**

María José Rodríguez Araneda is Associate Professor, School of Psychology, University of Santiago de Chile (Chile). Her research focuses on meanings of happiness, ethics, quality of life, and social and organizational psychology. Her recent study is titled "Social representation of conditions for happiness and living experiences source of happiness in Chile and Italy."

"Close relationships play a vital role in shaping people's self-concept."

The magic mirror

"Magic mirror in my hand, who is the fairest in the land?" Setting vanity aside, many people might dream of owning a magic mirror which reflects an ideal version of themselves and provides a regular affirmation that their most cherished hopes and dreams will come true. Dr. Madoka Kumashiro explains where to find that mirror.

In fact, many people already have access to such mirrors: their close relationships. Over the years, my collaborators and I found that close relationships play a vital role in shaping people's self-concept, by helping them move closer to the kind of person they ideally hope to become.

Michelangelo

Based on the "looking glass self" theory, which suggests that people come to see themselves as reflected in their interaction partner's eyes, the Michelangelo phenomenon uses an analogy to propose that such interactions result in positive outcomes when others' reflections match the individual's own hopes and wishes for themselves. Michelangelo allegedly remarked that as a sculptor, he chipped away the outer layers of stone to unearth the ideal form lying within. Analogously, the Michelangelo phenomenon theory suggests that people often need such a skilled sculptor to help reveal the "ideal self," or the kind of person they most aspire to become.

The "looking glass" does not always reflect the ideal self: close relationships can bring out the best or worst in us. For example, Mary might initiate steps to realize her dream of opening her business if her friends believe she has entrepreneurial qualities, but she might choose to stick with her unhappy job if her friends believe that is all she is capable of achieving. When close relationships elicit their desired characteristics and behaviors, individuals not only feel closer to their ideal self, but they also feel better about their lives and their relationships that brought about such transformation. Thus, close relationship partner's expectations and beliefs about the self can become a self-fulfilling reality, influence the kind of qualities people display or the kind of goals they choose to pursue, and affect both personal and relational well-being.

Locomotors

Of course, the Michelangelo metaphor is not meant to be taken literally. Unlike passive blocks of stone, people are dynamic beings who may also keep adopting different sets of values and goals as they accomplish or abandon some goals and experience developmental changes across their lifespan. In particular, personality appears to play a large role in the sculpting process. We have shown that individuals can contribute to their own sculpting process by creating an optimal or suboptimal social environment in which to experience personal growth. Continuing with the metaphor, some stones may make it easy for any amateur sculptors to work on, whereas some stones may be so brittle or too hard that it would take an extremely skilled, dedicated sculptor like Michelangelo to elicit its ideal form. Similarly, people can make it easier or harder for others to help bring out the ideal self and support their desired goals.

One such personality process involves individual differences in how people generally approach their goals. High "locomotors," or individuals who are quick to take action on their own goals, tend to make it easy for others to elicit their ideals. They pick realistic, flexible goals, take action, and seek out help in a positive manner. In contrast, high "assessors," or individuals who like to critically evaluate and analyze their goal pursuits, tend to act in ways that make it difficult for their close relationships. They tend to pick overly difficult and unrealistic goals, are passive and critical, and reject help and advice. Consequently, locomotors report feeling closer to their ideals, higher life satisfaction, and better relationships compared to assessors. Moreover, this personality trait also affects the sculptor as well: locomotors tend to be more effective than assessors in helping their partners move closer to their ideals.

Partners' eyes

The proliferation of books, magazines, websites, and apps on self-improvement reveals a vast appetite. Rather than try tackling it on their own, it may be important for people to also pay attention to their close relationships. If they like how they see themselves through their interaction partners' eyes, **with the reflection mirroring one's ideals, there is a good chance of achieving one's most hoped-for self.** If they do not like what they see, they may need to work on changing the interpersonal dynamics and the social environment. Fortunately, it may take only one special sculptor—a friend, family member, romantic partner, colleague, or mentor—who believes in their potential to set them on the path toward their desired future.

The keys

→ **Close relationship partners' expectations and beliefs about the self can become a self-fulfilling reality, influencing the kind of qualities people display or the kind of goals they choose to pursue.**

→ **People can make it easier (high locomotors) or harder (high assessors) for others to help bring out the ideal self and support their desired goals.**

→ **Fortunately, it may take only one special sculptor who believes in their potential to set them on the path toward their desired future.**

Madoka Kumashiro is an Associate Professor of Psychology at Goldsmiths, University of London (United Kingdom). While pursuing her PhD at the University of North Carolina at Chapel Hill under the direction of Professor Caryl Rusbult, who originally proposed the theory of the Michelangelo phenomenon, she became interested in integrating the previously disparate fields of self and close relationships. She has published many journal articles and book chapters. Her research examines self in interpersonal contexts—how close relationships can bring out the best or the worst in each other, how individuals struggle to achieve a work-life balance, and how personality affects one's relationships and goal pursuit behaviors.

Happy city, hopeful city

Hope is a very practical concept. It is your way to go if you have a goal you want to achieve. The Happy City Initiative, which started in Bristol (UK), does exactly that: campaigning to build the willpower for happiness to be taken seriously and delivering training, projects, and tools to reach the goal of growing happier communities.

Happy City is based on a simple idea: being happier needn't cost the earth. The world needs a new story: less "stuff for stuff's sake" and more "life for life's sake." It's about changing priorities to put people before profit, to redefine what it means to prosper. From the start, the plan has been to grow happiness by helping people to live more, share more, and enjoy life, for less. **The initiative is working at all levels from the grassroots of small community groups to the high table of government policy.** The inter-connected projects include the Happy City Index, a new tool to measure, understand, and influence the true prosperity of a city and its people. Alongside the Index, there is an interactive online Happiness Bank—signposts to what there is in the city to grow your well-being

from choirs to gardening groups and yoga to laughter. There's the annual Happy List, the antidote to the Rich List, which celebrates the people who make a difference to the well-being of their city. Upbeat Streets is a social media project that invites people to share pictures of the places in their neighborhood that makes them happy, creating a digital gallery of happiness.

Contagious

Since the goal is to grow a sustainable happiness, training is an important part of what the Happy City Initiative does. As an applied positive psychologist specializing in the practice of positive psychology, I feel strongly that the knowledge needs to go beyond the university campus to serve communities in very practical ways.

Positive psychology has shown us that it is possible to learn to be happier, and the science has given us evidence-based tools to train our minds and emotions.

I have collaborated with the Happy City Initiative to create the Happiness Habits, a program that puts the science into action with simple actions that anyone can do to

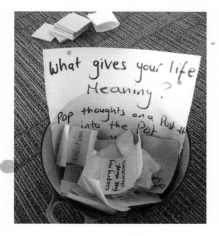

The 8 Happiness Habits

Here are the 8 Happiness Habits – try them for yourself and encourage others to do so as well.

1. **Savor positive experiences** to maximize the enjoyment from life's good times.

2. **Practice gratitude** to notice and appreciate the things that are good in life.

3. **Use your strengths.** Your strengths are the positive self. Use them to reach goals and resolve issues.

4. **Live life with purpose** and find the meaning in the everyday.

5. **Nurture your relationships.** Good relationships are what characterize the happiest people on the planet.

6. **Learn optimism** – the thinking tools that protect you from depression.

7. **Build your resilience** by doing all of the above!

8. **Set positive goals** so that you move forward and gain a sense of progress and achievement.

grow their well-being. It has been delivered to communities, schools, and organizations to support workplace well-being. The evidence shows that the Happiness Habits are beneficial for the broad range of people who've completed the program, which includes professionals, refugee parents, and pensioners. **The benefits go beyond the individual to spread well-being across the community.** It's a fact: happiness is contagious. It spreads from person to person to up to three degrees of separation. And what I do on a one-to-one basis, the Happy City Initiative is doing on a city-wide basis. This gives me hope for the future.

Miriam Akhtar, positive psychologist specialized in practical interventions
More information: **www.happycity.org.uk**

"Hope is the better side of happiness."

Two sides of the same coin?

"When I started my work in primary care I soon realized that people also want to see a doctor for problems to which there are no immediate, strictly medical solutions," says medical doctor **Sakari Suominen**. He sees his patients struggling with hope and happiness. Are they two sides of the same coin?

Such problems could, for instance, be exhaustion due to strain from working or their private life. First, that observation led me to the work of Professor Aaron Antonovsky on Salutogenesis, and that gradually led to the initiation of my own research in the field. Professor Antonovsky published his book *Health, Stress and Coping* in 1979 where he introduced his theory of Sense of Coherence. It is still inspiring me.

According to his ideas, all individuals continuously use resources in the theory called "Generalized Resistance Resources" in order to solve problems of everyday life. The resources can be bound to one individual—as, for instance, acquired occupational training or social skills—or they can be provided by the environment—as, for instance, opportunities to attain occupational training or social support provided by other people as friends, relatives, or colleagues. **Sense of Coherence (SOC) could be characterized as representing an individual's readiness to administrate these resources in order to make them function in a coordinated manner to solve a particular problem.**

Adverse life events

So the central issue is not how much of various resources we have at our disposal at a precise point of time, although this aspect also plays a role. The essential issue is more about whether an individual manages to coordinate his or her resources for a common goal or aim, even when they are relatively scarce. SOC is further categorized to three sub-components called comprehensibility, manageability, and meaningfulness. More generally, one could say that these components stand for three universal qualities of human beings: the thinking, acting, and feeling woman or man. Of these three, Antonovsky considers **meaningfulness the most central one as it has a motivational function.** In other words, a perception of one's life having a deeper meaning extending beyond the ordinary routines of everyday life helps us to keep up the two other ones, i. e. comprehensibility and manageability, should, for instance, adverse life events occur. Thus, meaningfulness comes conceptually close to what we can mean by hope.

Antonovsky makes the assumption that strong SOC can protect health and, indeed, numerous studies in which SOC has been measured by a set of closed questions, have provided support to this. Moreover, Antonovsky gives health a broad content and thus the conclusions can be considered being as applicable to well-being as well.

Fighting spirit

Based on what has been said, could strong SOC then be considered as standing for or even as identical to what we generally call happiness? Not necessarily. Happiness is an emotional state of mind. The stronger the emotion the more we tend to call it happiness; the more this state comprises intellectual appraisal the more we tend to call it life satisfaction. On the other hand, SOC again could be characterized as readiness to handle problems of everyday life, which does not necessarily imply happiness or even feeling satisfied. Examples to illustrate this are not hard to find. If a person due to break-up of an intimate partnership or unexpected unemployment is in crisis, he or she does not perceive the situation as happy or satisfying but can, in spite of this, if soc is at a strong enough level, keep up a fighting spirit and be convinced that she or he will be able to find some kind of solution, even if problems seem huge. So in real life most people with strong soc tend to be happy but, in a theoretical sense, these two dimensions do not necessarily coincide.

Then again, does this theoretical distinction have any practical relevance? I would say yes, it matters, and even add that hope is the better side of happiness. Why so? Because **happiness can be considered a double-edged sword and then again hope not.** Naturally, it is acceptable to thrive against happiness but while doing so it is possible to forget about the happiness of others or at least about the happiness of those who do not belong to one's own close circle. So thriving ruthlessly toward one's own happiness can jeopardize the conditions for happiness of unknown others.

Support

On the other hand, life is full of unexpected events, some of which can be arduous and hard to deal with. Here again, examples are not hard to find. Anyone can, all of a sudden, be traumatized in a traffic accident or be fired. These are no easy situations to handle and are far from happy, but keeping up hope is essential when dealing with them. If hope can be maintained in these situations there is a greater probability it can lead to successful coping and, because of that, offer better chances of development and recovery for the individual. **Losing one's hope, or the hope of ever being able to regain hope, hides solutions from us, even if they were available.**

Finally, I would like to add that becoming a happy and balanced person is an individual challenge for everybody. Happiness cannot be given to one person by others in a permanent way, although sometimes situations can be perceived so. However, anyone can support another person, even an unknown one, to maintain her or his hope and by that again support that person's individual development to gradually gain personal and genuine happiness.

The keys

→ **Sense of Coherence (SOC) has three sub-components: comprehensibility, manageability, and meaningfulness. The last one comes close to what we can mean by hope, as it has a motivational function.**

→ **Most people with strong Sense of Coherence tend to be happy, but these two dimensions do not necessarily coincide.**

→ **Anyone can support another person, even an unknown one, to maintain her or his hope and by that again support that person's individual development to gradually gain personal and genuine happiness.**

Sakari Suominen lives in Turku (Finland). He is a medical doctor and a public health scientist. Concurrently he is part-time Professor of Public Health at the Nordic School of Public Health in Gothenburg (Sweden). He has published over 100 scientific referee-approved papers of which most are international in the field of epidemiology, public health management, and health of children and adolescents. In 2009 he was awarded the Adolph G. Kammer Merit in Authorship Award by the American College of Occupational and Environmental Medicine. He has a passion for wooden boats and enjoys sailing in the summer time. When he gets overwhelmed by negative thoughts ("as everybody can sometimes lose hope") he searches for comfort in playing singer-song-writer music on his acoustic guitar.

"More optimism is not always better."

Hope and happiness

"Hope and happiness are obviously related. Hope will typically add to happiness and happiness will feed hope. Yet empirical research does not always find strong positive correlations and sometimes even negative links. To understand these differences we must first define the concepts and consider the measurement of these," says Prof. **Ruut Veenhoven**, one of the world's leading experts in happiness research. Hope is the expectation that things will turn out well in the future.

The higher the perceived probability of a good outcome, the more hope. Expected "things" can be trivial, such as a sunny day tomorrow, or of major importance, such as surviving an illness. In the context of this analysis of the relation of hope with happiness, I will deal with the expectation that major things will turn out well. Such "major things" can be a specific part of life, such as one's career, or life as a whole. In this paper, I focus on hope in the sense of expectation that life as a whole will turn out well.

This kind of hope has been measured in several ways. In one approach, hope is seen as a personality trait and measured with questionnaires that tap a general tendency to be optimistic about the future. A related approach is to think of hope as an attitude to the future, which is often measured using single questions. A variant of this approach is asking people how happy they think they will be in the future, typically in the next 5 years. In that context, people are typically also asked to rate their happiness in the past 5 years and in the present, so that hope for a better life appears in the difference.

Happiness is the subjective enjoyment of one's life-as-a-whole as experienced in the present. A synonym is "life satisfaction." Like hope, happiness is a subjective phenomenon that is measured using questioning. A common question reads: "Taken all together, how satisfied or dissatisfied are you with your life as a whole these days? Please express in a number between 0 and 10, where 0 stands for 'totally dissatisfied' and 10 for 'totally satisfied.'" Such questions are often used in survey studies, and the research findings obtained with them are stored in the World Database of Happiness. This "findings archive" developed during the past decade now contains some 13,000 research results.

Moderate optimism

One of the categories in the World Database of Happiness is "Hope." To date, this category counts 84 research findings. Each finding is described on a finding page using a standard format and terminology. Going through the finding pages, the following patterns catch the eye.

Hope and happiness tend to go hand in hand, but not always. Studies all over the world found positive correlations, especially when hope was measured as an optimistic stance or as a positive attitude to the future. A recent study in Germany found that optimistic people score about one point higher on the 0–10 happiness scale than pessimists and that this difference exceeds the effects of unemployment or divorce (Piper, 2014). The difference was greatest for moderate optimists, which suggests that more optimism is not always better. Yet correlations are much smaller and sometimes even negative when hope is measured by the expectation to get happier than one is now.

More resources

Hope can affect happiness in several ways. One reason for the positive correlations is obviously that hope is rewarding in itself, a bleak outlook on the future generating stress. Next to that, hope will mostly encourage behavior that feeds happiness in the long run, if you do not hope for success in love you will never try to succeed. Trait-hopeful people will thus have built more resources in the past. Yet unrealistic hope can also reduce happiness, for instance, if it holds you captive in an irreparable marriage.

Likewise, happiness will affect hope. Positive experience of the present will affect perception of the future. Happiness also has beneficial consequences, such as better health, which in turn feeds hope. Yet happiness can also work out negatively on hope. If you are happy already, you can hardly get happier in the future and are even at risk of getting a bit less happy. When it comes to getting happier than one is at present, the unhappy have a better chance.

The keys

→ **Hope is the expectation that things will turn out well in the future. Happiness is the subjective enjoyment of one's life-as-a-whole as experienced in the present.**

→ **Hope and happiness tend to go hand in hand, especially when hope is measured as an optimistic stance or as a positive attitude to the future. Correlations are much smaller when hope is measured by the expectation to get happier than one is now.**

→ **Hope can affect happiness in several ways. Likewise, happiness will affect hope. But when it comes to getting happier than one is at present, the unhappy have a better chance.**

Ruut Veenhoven is emeritus-professor of social conditions for human happiness at the Erasmus University in Rotterdam (The Netherlands). His current affiliations are Erasmus Happiness Economics Research Organization (EHERO) and Opentia Research Group of North-West University, South-Africa. He is often called the "Happiness Professor" and is respected worldwide for his lifelong research on the subjective quality of life. His major publications are *Conditions of Happiness* and "Informed pursuit of happiness." Ruut Veenhoven is a founding editor of the *Journal of Happiness Studies* and founder and director of the World Database of Happiness. More at www.worlddatabaseofhappiness.eur.nl.

> *"Some attempts to cope with anxiety*
> *can be seen as a fight against its hope component."*

Fear and anxiety

It is often said that fear and anxiety are the opposites of hope.
Prof. Maria Miceli offers a more nuanced approach.
Anxiety seems to be a combination of hope and fear.

An anxious state of mind actually implies the belief that the outcome might be negative,
but also the opposing (though often more feeble) belief that the outcome might be positive.
This mixture of, and conflict between, hope and fear can be considered as typical of anxiety.

The difference between fear and anxiety lies in their different objects. Whereas the object of fear is a possible (or probable or certain) danger, the object of anxiety is an event that implies a possible and uncertain danger. The trepidation and restless wait typical of anxiety depend on this alternation between fear and hope. Actually, a basis component of anxiety is the epistemic goal to "know whether the danger will come true" so as to put an end to the uncertainty. If this goal is satisfied, even in favor of a negative certainty, anxiety should be reduced accordingly.

Fight or flight

No doubt, uncertainty might be present also in fear. However, it does not seem to be its object and focus. Everyday language offers some hint in this regard. For instance, whereas "I am afraid of…" does not communicate any alternation between hope and fear, "I am anxious about…" conveys precisely this alternation. The typical mind-set of a state of anxiety is likely to elicit such statements as "I don't know what to think or expect, I don't know if I can hope for the better or I must despair." In the clinical domain, some evidence indirectly supports this mixture of fear and hope as typical of anxiety. For instance, whereas negative affect is shared by both depression and generalized anxiety disorder, low levels of positive affect appear as specific only to depression. The behavioral inhibition system, which is supposed to be the neuropsychological basis of anxiety, is activated by sources of conflict between aversive and appetitive stimuli, and is characterized by risk assessment and caution. In contrast, the neuropsychological basis of fear is provided by the fight-or-flight system, which is activated by threats that don't imply any approach orientation, and just produce escape or defense reactions.

Avoiding hope

When anxiety and depression appear strictly related, it might be supposed that one moves from an anxious to a depressed state whenever uncertainty becomes (subjectively) unbearable. At this point, some individuals "prefer" to give up any positive prospect and associated hope, and deal with negative certainty. In such cases, anxiety may vanish and be replaced by hopelessness and depression.

Worry is a crucial component of anxiety. As far as the cognitive anticipatory activity is concerned, anxiety and worry coincide, whereas anxiety typically includes other components, such as autonomic overactivity, restlessness, and irritability. Dwelling on negative hypotheses and scenarios helps the worrier to divert from positive hypotheses, thus defending from a disturbing alternation of positive and negative emotions. Though here negative certainty is not necessarily achieved, **the worrier tries to enter an "as-if" state of mind where the negative possibility is temporarily taken as a negative certainty.** This stimulation is meant to be a sort of rehearsal of what would happen if the worst comes to the worst, in order to get used to such negative possibilities, be able to better endure them, and reduce suffering if the blow does fall. In other words, some attempts to cope with anxiety can be seen as a "fight against its hope component." Either by actually promoting despair or by trying to simulate what would happen if the threat comes true, one is trying to avoid hope, because of the pain implied by its alternation with fear.

Conversely, other coping attempts imply a fight in favor of hope and against fear. An optimistic and self-reassuring "nothing bad will happen" promotes hope by minimizing the likelihood of the negative outcome. More precisely, it is an endeavor to turn mere hope into a more solid positive expectation, which cannot coexist with a negative one about the same fact.

The keys

→ **The difference between fear and anxiety lies in their different objects. A mixture of fear and hope is typical for anxiety.**

→ **In terms of their cognitive components, anxiety and worry coincide, whereas anxiety typically includes other components, such as autonomic overactivity, restlessness, and irritability.**

→ **An optimistic and self-reassuring "nothing bad will happen" promotes hope by minimizing the likelihood of the negative outcome.**

Maria Miceli is a senior researcher at the Institute of Cognitive Sciences and Technologies of the Italian National Research Council (ISTC-CNR) in Rome (Italy). Her research focuses on the cognitive aspects of social mechanisms and processes and their interplay with motivational and emotional components. Coauthor of this text is Cristiano Castelfranchi. Maria's most recent book, also coauthored with Cristiano Castelfranchi, is *Expectancy and Emotion* (Oxford University Press). Fond of music, she sings in two choruses. "It gives me hope," she says "when I see that people (myself included) sometimes learn something from experience, and don't keep making the same mistakes; that is, when, at least, their (and my) current mistakes look different from the usual ones."

> *"Loss and powerlessness are close cousins to hopelessness and hope."*

Maintaining hope in the face of an incurable disease

Carol J. Farran has been a professor for over thirty years, dealing with the aging process. She felt she was fortunate to be at the right place at the right time when the Rush Alzheimer's Disease Center was funded by the National Institute on Aging (USA). Here, she built on what she had learned from older adults who were depressed, with family caregivers of persons with Alzheimer's disease and related dementias. And she once again found that family caregivers and their family members with dementia poignantly expressed feelings of hope and finding meaning.

Alzheimer's disease and related dementias have existed for many years but oftentimes were called by different names or were thought to result from "just growing old." Despite the recent advances made by modern medicine, there are still no cures for these diseases and most often, it is up to the family—spouses, adult children, grandchildren, or others, to assume responsibilities of caring for their family member with this disease. Much of the research done with family caregivers in the United States has focused on the stress and ill-health related to providing this care. At the same time, how is it that family caregivers frequently give voice to hope and making sense out of this process of caring for their relative?

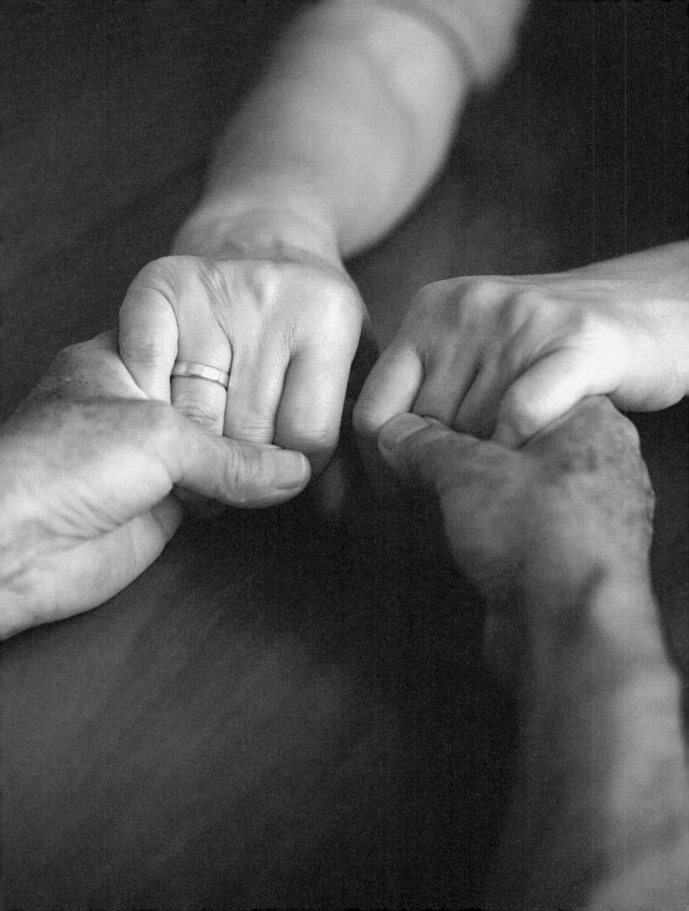

Lost and powerless

Loss and powerlessness are close cousins to hopelessness and hope. It has sometimes been said that one cannot fully experience hope without also having experienced hopelessness. The realities of *loss* for family caregivers of persons with dementia are always present— they have lost their relationship with the person whom they love, they can no longer communicate with this person in the way they did in the past, and they observe their family member gradually losing their mental and physical capabilities. They deal with their own and other's responses to these losses and have said, **"we lost our future plans."**

At the same time, they may experience a sense of powerlessness over their situation—they may describe themselves as fulfilling a sense of duty, responsibility and obligation. They may also experience a loss of freedom in doing what they would have done in the past. Their world is more constricted—environmentally, physically and mentally. They describe a loss of freedom, and their life is described as "boring and living in a limbo." They "hope" for a cure through research, "wish" things were different, and experience a seemingly endless situation.

The option to choose

At the same time, caregivers learn that they have *the option* to consciously choose their attitude toward family caregiving. They may experience the paradox in their situation— how is it that their mother, who was a kindergarten teacher and taught many children over the years, now needs help with her daily personal needs, does not recognize her own husband and children, and cannot complete the simplest of tasks related to her care? Who is she then, and how do they relate to her? They find that in order to develop hope, they must draw upon their own personal skills and fortitude, learn to appreciate the small positive things in their lives, take one day at a time, and generously use their sense of humor.

Even in the small daily experiences, family caregivers have the potential to experience hope as they relate to their family member with dementia and others who support them. **Caregivers have the option to cherish each moment of what they still have.** A husband caregiver described his experience of trimming the Christmas tree with his wife. He said, "We communicate all the time, even though I do all of the talking." With each Christmas ornament they added to the tree, he would tell his wife when they received it, and who gave it to them. He experienced her love when she told him "thank you" after doing something for her. Other caregivers have expressed hope when they are confident they are providing *the best care* for their relative, even though it was not perfect, and when they see how well their family member responds to this care.

Inner strength

Hope is a feeling, a way of thinking or behaving, and a way of relating to ourselves and our world. It enables us to deal with escapable situations where our needs or goals, or our desired outcomes, are not met. **It is a process of accepting a potentially "hopeless" situation and allowing a creative and imaginative process** to occur where boundaries are wider than they initially seem. It involves a sense of inner strength in someone or something, which helps us to move through, and even grow, despite this difficult situation.

What persons with dementia most need are sensitive and caring persons who are willing to enter into interpersonal relationships that foster hope. There are no pills to enhance or sustain hope. It is the daily work of persons who care for those who have dementia to observe, direct, and comfort persons who suffer from the effects of misfortunes such as dementia, and invest their time, effort, energy, and love into being hopeful and making every moment the best it can be each day.

The keys

→ **Family caregivers of persons with dementia often feel loss (of persons, freedom, and future) and powerlessness (fulfilling a sense of duty).**

→ **They learn that they have the option to consciously choose their attitude toward family caregiving. In order to develop hope, they must draw upon their own skills, cherishing each moment.**

→ **Hope involves a sense of inner strength in someone or something, which helps us to move through, and even grow, despite this difficult situation.**

Carol J. Farran, has been a Professor in the Rush College of Nursing and The Nurses Alumni Association Endowed Research Chair in Health and the Aging Process at Rush University Medical Center, Chicago (USA) for over 30 years. While her initial clinical work focused on older adults with depression in hospital and community settings, she was moved by the moments of hope expressed by these individuals, even when they were very depressed. She built on that experience in the Rush Alzheimer's Disease Center. She enjoys opportunities to interact with persons of many cultures, participate in musical and cultural activities, as well as playing and making memories with her three grandchildren.

Stories of hope

"An Information Technology Company in Japan was facing
a serious problem. It had been praised as a place where women
especially made remarkable achievements. But in reality,
the company held a very strong sense of crisis, as many of
its significant female employees were leaving suddenly," tells
Prof. **Yuji Genda**. He discovers two different stories of hope.

To cope with the situation, the company decided to ask former employees to speak frankly about the considerations that had led them to leave. There were various reasons behind their resignations, but the person in charge of the survey finally concluded that the reasons could be classified into two main categories.

The first was, **"I left because I could not foresee what would happen in the future if I continued working there."** The IT industry was undergoing drastic changes, and the tough work environment required workers to quickly respond to rapidly changing circumstances on a worldwide level. The female employees were making their utmost efforts to keep up with this situation, but they could see no stable future no matter how hard they worked. As a result, they became exhausted and decided to leave.

What was the other category? It was **"I left the company because I could see what would happen in the future."** These female employees had various experiences and acquired knowledge and skills. They could foresee the future and do their work strategically. They were satisfied and fulfilled by their situation initially, but quite a few gradually lost interest in their work and finally left the company as they could see what would happen in the future.

These two reasons stand in stark contrast. However, the common issue is that the fundamental cause of the departure of female employees from a clearly prestigious company was not discontent with incomes or personal relations but rather a loss of hope in working itself.

Visible

People may decide to change their jobs in search of better working conditions such as higher wages, or to escape from difficult personal relations in the workplaces. However, the reasons mentioned here involve neither low salaries nor troubles in human relations. The women felt that they "could not see" the future or "saw the future." They left the company because their imagination could not be stimulated there.

Even when people face an uncertain future, they can feel hope toward a future challenge if they can see something bright ahead. On the other hand, even when they can forecast the future to a certain extent, they can still find hope if they have expectations toward something they have not yet seen. People may feel a story such as "It hardly seems visible but something can be in sight" or "It seems like I'm seeing it, but I don't quite see it." Such ambivalent situations, which can stimulate the imagination, can be a force for hope that is different from affluence or human relations.

Like many classics, stories that have been handed down contain contradictory and ambivalent elements and leave room for multiple interpretations. All classical stories, including works of literature, music, and performing art, continue to be shared through the ages as they continue to have the power to be interpreted in a variety of ways. The story of hope is ambivalent in many cases, and its contents contain diversity, which may be interpreted as contradiction.

Imagination

Returning to the example of the workplace referred to at the beginning, what was lacking was a shared fiction or story of a desirable direction, which was neither false nor true. A workplace filled with bumps and detours, setbacks and redundancies, is by its very nature a good mine for stories. Some members of the workplace overcome setbacks thanks to their friends and colleagues. Even if it is a slow process, these people become more confident in their work. At the same time, they become interested in work in a true sense after finding "something invisible." If they encounter such a story that gives them the will to face the looming future beyond their own interest, they will maintain their hope for work.

As it is impossible for a company to prevent excellent individuals from leaving through human strategies alone, only a human story nurtured in the entire workplace can improve the atmosphere, leading to hopes regarding work. Individuals and groups living in society need not only strategies but also such a story of hope.

Hope is a story that is needed when confronting an uncertain future. A certain story exists wherever there is hope. Hope is also like a story in that its ending does not always bring happiness in the future. Just like tragic-ending stories, attaining hope is not necessarily equal to future happiness. But a story can stimulate the imagination at the same time, so that it can be a force for hope

The keys

→ **People can feel hope toward a future challenge if they can see something bright ahead or if they have expectations toward something they have not yet seen.**

→ **The story of hope is ambivalent in many cases, and its contents contain diversity, which may be interpreted as contradiction.**

→ **What is mostly lacking is a shared fiction or story of a desirable direction. And that is exactly what we need to encourage hope.**

Yuji Genda is a Labor Economist and Professor in the Institute of Social Science at The University of Tokyo (Japan). He is a Japanese leader for the Social Sciences of Hope Project. Recent publications include: *Hope and society in Japan*, *Have jobs and hope gone forever in Japan?*, and *Japan in decline: fact or fiction?* What is according to him the most important advice for hope? "Play!"

Hope in Japan

Hope is a subjective representation that is wanted as something desirable in the future. It can be categorized according to factors such as achievability and sociality. How about hope in Japan?

In a Japanese nationwide questionnaire of approximately 2,000 people in their 20s to 50s, conducted in 2006, about 80% of respondents said they had some type of hope and 60% said that they believed their hope was attainable. The largest number of respondents described hopes regarding work, far outnumbering those who suggested hopes regarding family, health, or leisure.

Hope that is considered attainable is strongly defined by three social factors. This makes it possible to explain why a loss of hope spread between the 1990s and the beginning of the 2000s. First, **hope is influenced by the degree of choices available**, which depends on affluence. Analyses have shown that people who are elderly and perceive their remaining time as limited, and those who have been marginalized in education and/or employment and/or who have low income and/or poor health, are more likely to report an absence of hope. Social changes, such as the falling birthrate, increase in low income population or unemployment, worsening health conditions, and stagnating school advancement rates, have led to a rise in the percentage of people who lack hope.

Secondly, **hope is influenced by interpersonal relations** based on exchanges with others, such as family members and friends. Individuals who grew up in an environment where they experienced expectations and confidence from their family are more likely to report having hope. Individuals with an awareness of having many friends are more likely to have hope. Further, those who interact with friends outside of work colleagues and family members are more likely to have hope regarding their work. Thus, friends have a great deal to do with the generation of hope not only quantitatively but qualitatively as well. The spread of loneliness among the Japanese population as a whole, symbolized by unstable family relations, bullying, social reclusiveness, and the solitary death of senior citizens, has accelerated the spread of a loss of hope.

In addition to economic and sociological factors, we must focus on **the narrative structure of society**, which is believed to be necessary for facing an uncertain future, as a social facet of hope. Statistical analyses show that individuals who have experienced setbacks that forced them to modify their hopes, and who, with the background of having overcome such obstacles, do not hesitate to make apparently vain efforts, are more likely to have attainable hopes. If the society in the story consists mainly of people who have had such experiences and or who have such characteristics, people are more likely to have hope. We also need to have foresight about the direction of society beyond simply acceleration and efficiency, while being expected to make strategic judgments to avoid failures and to use non-wasteful problem-solving thought. Social circumstances in which there is no shared new value in the story to provide such foresight can also contribute to an expansion of the loss of hope.

Professor Yuji Genda,
The University of Tokyo

> *"High hope managers, employees, and organizations lead to better attitudes, behaviors, and performance."*

Hope in effective workplaces

Despite the acceptance that having hope is good, up until recent years it has been a very vague and fuzzy concept. It has lacked theoretical understanding, operational definition, valid measurement, and empirical research of its impact. This all changed with the arrival of positive psychology at the end of the previous century and then its introduction into the workplace as a vital part of well-known management professor **Fred Luthans's** concept of psychological capital.

In 1999, as a management professor at the University of Nebraska and Gallup senior scientist, I was lucky to attend the first Positive Psychology Summit in my hometown of Lincoln, Nebraska. This summit was sponsored and held at the Gallup Organization the year after Martin Seligman's famous presidential address at the American Psychological Association where he charged the field of psychology **to give more balanced attention to the positive and what was right with people,** instead of the field's almost sole focus on the negative and what was wrong with people. Seligman organized the Summit and had contributions from other founders such as Ed Diener and Barbara Fredrickson. Their presentations and insights served as a trigger moment for me to bring positive psychology to the workplace.

The following fall the second Summit was held at Gallup Headquarters in Washington D.C. and this time I was especially stimulated by academic presentations on the concept of hope by University of Kansas professors C. Rick Snyder and his close colleague Shane Lopez. They carefully laid out the rich theoretical grounding of hope, the operational definition of hope, including both the goal-oriented, agency-based "will-power" and the proactively determined pathways to goal attainment or "way-power." They also indicated there were valid measures of hope and research showing the positive impact of hope in a variety of human endeavors. These two Positive Psychology Summits and follow-up relevant reading served to launch my presentation at the third Summit in 2001 and publication of my seminal articles on positive organizational behavior (POB) and positive psychological capital (PsyCap).

The hero within

In order to make a distinction from the non-research based, feel-good positive approaches found in the popular business literature, in formulating POB and PsyCap I set up the following inclusion criteria: (1) grounded in theory and research; (2) valid measurement; (3) open to development and thus "state-like" as opposed to fixed and "trait-like"; and (4) desirable impact on employee attitudes, behaviors, and especially performance in the workplace. After carefully analyzing the large number of potential positive constructs for inclusion in PsyCap, four clearly emerged as best meeting the criteria: **Hope, Efficacy, Resilience, and Optimism**, or the "HERO within."

Although in positive psychology there is considerable research that has established the positive relationship between hope and various life domains, only a few workplace studies have been conducted to date. For example, we have found **a significant positive relationship between the level of hope of employees in all types and levels of organizations and their attitudes** such as job satisfaction, work happiness, commitment and engagement, desired behaviors such as retention, and individual and organizational performance. I have found the profile of high-hope managers is not only that they are good at the classic functions such as planning, organizing, and controlling, but they are also very goal oriented and have the motivation (i.e. the will-power) and proactive pathways determined (i.e. the way-power) to attain these goals. I commonly encounter managers and employees who tell me they "hope" to do better, improve their performance. My quick response is to ask them if they have set stretch goals, established the pathways to these goals, identified real and potential obstacles, and have proactively determined alternative pathways around these barriers. If they answer no, or "not really," as they commonly do, then I say, you don't really have hope. Importantly, the goals, and communicated paths to them, excite and motivate not only the high-hope managers, but also their followers. In other words, hope has a contagion effect that creates a climate of openness, trust, and motivated performance that also characterizes hopeful employees and hopeful organizations.

Wise investment

Besides this beginning empirical evidence of the positive impact of hope per se on workplace outcomes, in conjunction with the other three components of PsyCap, there is now overwhelming evidence of at least the supporting role hope can play in effective workplaces. Our research clearly shows that PsyCap as a core, higher-order construct has tremendous impact on desired outcomes. For example, a few years ago we conducted a meta-analysis of 51 PsyCap studies and found a strong average relationship between PsyCap (that includes hope) and desired employee attitudes, behaviors, and performance. In addition, these findings have been verified in a recently published review of 66 PsyCap articles. In other words, employee hope, by itself, has a significantly positive impact in the workplace, but especially when it is combined and is in synergistic interaction with the other PsyCap HERO psychological resources of efficacy, resilience, and optimism.

Since hope as a PsyCap resource is state-like and thus is open to development (unlike trait-like personality or more "hard-wired" talents and intelligence), **it can be managed and increased by short human resource development programs.** We have found through experimental, control group research designs that these programs lead to an increase in employee participants' PsyCap (including their hope) and cause their performance to improve. Using utility analysis in one such study, we found over a 200 percent return on development. In other words, developing one's PsyCap (and hope) is a very wise investment.

High hope

In closing, the intent of this chapter was to take a more "hard-headed" pragmatic approach to hope. Just like Lopez and Snyder's *Handbook of Positive Psychology* has only my and Carolyn Youssef's chapter on the workplace, the same is largely true of this *World Book of Hope*. Unlike most of the other entries in this book which have wonderful, inspiring perspectives and stories of hope, I have tried to give an evidence-based portrayal of hope as a valuable positive resource for psychological capital in today's workplace. High-hope managers, employees, and organizations lead to better attitudes, behaviors, performance, and competitive advantage that are needed in order to thrive or even survive in today's dynamic, global economy.

The keys

→ **Hope is more than a feel-good, fuzzy concept. It is grounded in rich theory and research, has valid measures, is open to development, and has been demonstrated to have positive impact in various life domains.**

→ **For employees and managers, high hope in combination with efficacy, resilience, and optimism (HERO) has a significantly positive impact in the workplace.**

→ **Psychological Capital (which includes hope) can be developed and has causal impact on performance with very high return of development.**

Fred Luthans is University and Distinguished Professor of Management at the University of Nebraska (USA). A former President of the Academy of Management, he has written the generally recognized first texts in the field of *Organizational Behavior* (now in its 12th edition) and *International Management* (now in its 9th edition). A prolific researcher, he founded the field of Positive Organizational Behavior (POB) and originated the concept and research foundation of Psychological Capital (PsyCap). He is an avid recreational golfer and huge fan of his university's football and basketball (men's and women's) teams. He feels his biggest accomplishment is being part of a large, loving family.

"The most extraordinary characteristic among top workers is the hope they express in their work."

Hope at work

"Success at work is not a synonym of cold-heartedness and opportunism," says Dr. **Satu Uusiautti**. "We can also see it as a manifestation of well-being. And hope is one of the important elements in boosting success at work. Search for meaning and you will be finding hope."

What is success? Whose definition of success counts? Nicki Baum has defined that "success is as ice cold and lonely as the North Pole." But instead of seeing success as an outcome of self-centered behavior, a state in life filled with envy, cold-heartedness, and opportunism, could success be a manifestation of positive development, happiness, and well-being? With these questions in my mind, I started studying the phenomenon of success over ten years ago through awarded top workers from various professions all the way from cleaners to doctors, from farmers and artists to police officers and priests.

Every human being's life abounds with promises and opportunities. **Strengths and positive resources are not attributable only to certain people.** The discovery of human strengths, a balanced life, satisfaction, and support can lead a person to a path that is not only filled with feelings of happiness and a meaningful life but also shows the way to success.

Positive strategies

When considered from this perspective, success at work (1) is dependent on certain factors, (2) necessitates action, and (3) is manifested through certain outcomes. The first means that success at work can consist of various elements that can be roughly divided into individual-bound factors (such as motivation and competence) and context-bound factors (such as opportunities or limitations, and demands or obligations) that form the preconditions of success.

However, **success is not a state that will miraculously materialize if the conditions are good; it requires action.** A push toward success can be a sum of many factors engendering a sense of purposeful doing and, consequently, a sense of finding the right path. It means that when the individual-bound and context-bound features are synchronized, the individual can seize the opportunities, use his or her strengths, and actively pursue personal development.

Success at work in this perspective is manifested as positive emotions and attitudes, which means a good feeling about oneself, one's capability, and one's place in the world. Therefore, success is not defined as the achievement of a certain goal or position (e.g. becoming a CEO) but considered a combination of feelings of expertise, accomplishments, and top performances, and the use of positive strategies within a particular context leading to a sense of purpose and meaning.

223

Top workers' advice

Wondering how to deal with hope at work and how to be more successful? Here are four key points adopted from top workers:

1. Seize challenges and dare to indulge in your work
Everyone's work includes challenges of some sort. Consider them as opportunities to develop yourself and your work, and you start to see the potential in you. Eventually, you will start hoping for such opportunities.

2. Be prepared to work—there is no free ride for anyone
Top workers cannot avoid mistakes, difficulties, or boring and routine-like tasks at work. No one is infallible and, with an optimistic attitude, you can find pleasure from accomplishing the most tedious parts of your work.

3. Believe in yourself
Whatever happens at work, trust in your expertise and your ability to cope with it. James E. Maddux has wisely said: "Believing you can accomplish what you want to accomplish is one of the most important ingredients—perhaps the most important gradient—in the recipe for success."

4. Search for meaning and you will be finding hope
Finally, the attitude that is taken in work life makes daily work meaningful. Having realized the importance of your work and your ability to do it well, you have found the right track. That's the real success, and something worth hoping for.

Positive expectations

It is worth noticing that realistic, positive expectations closely relate to an expectation that one's behavior will be effective. When considering the phenomenon of success at work, hope is particularly important, especially in the light of achieving future goals and plans and how certain life events—especially the negative ones—are experienced. Positive expectations can partly result from a hopeful attitude. My studies have shown that the most extraordinary characteristic among top workers is their positive attitude, the hope they expressed in their work. **Successful workers do not give up in the face of conflicts.**

Instead, they see such situations as opportunities to reassess their occupational skills and, if necessary, to study and develop. They are persistent, which means they have *willpower*.

Furthermore, top workers see conflict situations as challenges that they expect they can solve, instead of hopeless dead ends. An awarded Finnish Police Officer of the Year told me: "So, first you try again, if it's worth it. But sometimes you have to look in the mirror, admit that this won't lead anywhere, and find another route. I have done it many times during my career." This kind of proactive attitude, willingness to strive for success, is at the very core of top workers' characteristics and means that they have *waypower*, the other important element of hope in addition to willpower. If one expects the best (has the will), and is ready to work for it (has the way), success at work can be, thus, achieved by anyone and in any profession—whether it was the widening expertise in a cleaner's profession or climbing up the career ladders from a rank-and-file police officer into a chief of police.

The keys

→ **Success at work (1) is dependent on certain factors, (2) necessitates action, and (3) is manifested through certain outcomes.**

→ **Success at work is manifested as positive emotions and attitudes, which means a good feeling about oneself, one's capability, and one's place in the world.**

→ **Successful workers do not give up in the face of conflicts. They see them as challenges.**

Satu Uusiautti, PhD, is Researcher at the University of Lapland (Finland) and Adjunct Professor of Educational Psychology at the University of Helsinki (Finland). She has written dozens of articles about success at work and in life in general, positive development, human strengths, and flourishing at work. She is the author of *The Psychology of Becoming a Successful Worker*. What shows hope at its best in her own work? "The collaboration with my closest colleagues and my students. They are so filled with enthusiasm with their research topics. That provides me joy and a sense of meaning, especially when I see the long-term perspective and the positive influence of my work."

*"We need not limit ourselves to changes
to things happening outside of us."*

Can leopards hope to change their spots?

Can we hope to lastingly change who we are and how we relate to the world around us? In the film *As Good As It Gets* Jack Nicholson portrays a man experiencing severe difficulties in his relationship to the world around him, and his character poses the rhetorical question, "what if this is as good as it gets?" But is this depiction of the human condition fair? Can we change? Is there any cause for hope? **Christopher Boyce** has been trying to understand these questions.

An area of research I have been developing in recent years concerns an individual's personality—the psychological component of ourselves that remains from one situation to another, tending to direct how we might generally behave or react in our day-to-day lives. I've been interested in whether personality changes and how understanding personality might provide us with hope in regards to how we deal with difficulties in life.

The Big Five

Psychologists have spent decades understanding the core aspects of individual personality. A particularly influential model, known as the Big Five model of personality, suggests there are five main components of an individual's personality—agreeableness (e.g. our tendency to be cooperative and considerate of others), conscientiousness (e.g. our tendency to be orderly, methodical, and dutiful), extraversion (e.g. our tendency to seek stimulation and experience positive emotions), neuroticism (e.g. our tendency to experience negative emotions), and openness (e.g. our tendency to be intellectually curious and creative)—with each of us having a score on each of these dimensions. But is there any hope for our personalities to develop?

A popular belief in personality psychology has been that personality is more or less fixed over the life-course. It was thought that people change due to more or less biological factors up until about the age of 30, at which point personality is "set like plaster." This is a belief that has permeated throughout society and many people might therefore believe that it is impossible to change—a belief that may itself inhibit change.

Personality change

However, while personality is, on the whole, stable from one situation to the next this does not mean it cannot and does not change over time. Traditionally, personality researchers have paid little attention to aspects of change, but now substantial evidence exists to show that personality does change and that this happens in part in response to our environments. **Personality development is beginning to be viewed as a fluid process of individuals engaging dynamically with their environments.** This provides us with a more hopeful attitude toward personality as we may be able to change aspects of ourselves simply by cultivating the environments that support such change.

An understanding of personality change is important since our personality is one of the strongest and most consistent predictors of higher well-being. If people believe incorrectly that personality does not and cannot change, then it may result in an over-focus on external factors that perhaps they feel they have a better chance of changing (a promotion at work, more money, or a new relationship). However, our work shows that our personalities are just as likely to change as these factors yet contribute substantially more to changes in many indictors of well-being. Thus we need not limit ourselves to changes to things happening outside of us—there is, therefore, hope!

Internal resources

Another reason for hope when it comes to personality is that our personality helps us deal with difficult life circumstances. While good things do happen, almost everybody will have to deal with difficult and traumatic situations at some point in their life. How will we deal with them when they do happen? In fact, **how we deal with difficult events such as becoming disabled, unemployed, or experiencing a loss of income depends on our personality.** For example, being agreeable, perhaps due to better quality relationships, seems to help individuals when they become disabled, and being open to experiences mitigates the negative effect of an income loss on well-being. While life may at times be difficult, if we have cultivated helpful internal resources we can hope to cope much better than we think.

So, is this as good as it gets? Can we hope to change? It seems that we can change, and by understanding and considering our personality there may be direct and indirect benefits to the quality of our lives. Modern societies often give us expectations about how our external circumstances should or could be. However, these expectations are rarely met and focusing more on how we relate to the world around us is more likely to bring profound benefits to our lives.

The keys

→ **Many people believe that it is impossible to change—a belief that may itself inhibit change.**

→ **We may be able to change aspects of ourselves simply by cultivating the environments that support such change.**

→ **It seems that we can change, and by understanding and considering our personality there may be direct and indirect benefits to the quality of our lives.**

Christopher Boyce is a Research Fellow with the Behavioural Science Centre at Stirling Management School. He also holds an honorary position as a Research Associate in the School of Psychological Sciences at the University of Manchester (United Kingdom). His research attempts to understand how an individual's health and happiness is influenced by the world around them. When does he feel hopeful himself? "When I look around and see people taking small simple steps that help to make the lives of themselves and others better, it inspires me to make small simple steps in my own life."

Out of poverty: Project Hope in Boston

Thousands of volunteers all over the world are involved in local and global projects offering hope to the most vulnerable. Worldwide, the most popular words in the name of these organizations are not "help" or "aid" but "hope" and "future." Let's have a look at Project Hope in Boston, where families move up and out of poverty.

"Hope is like a road in the country; there never was a road, but when many people walk on it, the road comes into existence," says the author Lin Yutang. Every day, countless women and children come through the doors of Project Hope, each at a different point on the road of their journey, each

facing their own challenges. Every day, these families walk the road laid down by so many before them. In each step, there is hope in the knowledge that others have traveled the same road, and have transformed their lives. Our job at Project Hope is to help the road remain clear.

Transformation

Project Hope was founded in 1981 when the Little Sisters of the Assumption opened the doors of their Magnolia Street convent so homeless women and children could live with them. Over the years, the mission expanded beyond sheltering families and providing childcare to a multi-service agency at the forefront of efforts in Boston to move families up and out of poverty. We do this by providing low-income women with children access to education, jobs, housing, and emergency services and fostering personal transformation and work with the community and state for broader systems change.

When you work with the poor, they're your family. You don't do it for them; you do it with them. This concept of mutuality is a core value

at Project Hope and drives all the work we do empowering families.

Ambassadors

We recently asked the women in our program, our Ambassadors, to tell us how they define hope. Their determination and successes are what fuels our hope.

When **Denisha** was 23, she became homeless after leaving an abusive boyfriend. Determined to change her life, she enrolled in Project Hope's Workforce Development & Employer Partnerships (WDEP) program and found a job that helped her afford an apartment in a safe neighborhood for herself and her daughter. Today, she is enrolled in college. She says: "Hope is when all the roads have led to dead ends and you finally are led to a new path. Hope is believing after all the dark days that your better tomorrow is on its way."

When **Rhonda** was 32, she was laid off and realized she did not have the skills she needed to find a job to support her three children. After graduating from WDEP, she landed her dream job at a local hospital. Six years later, her career path will allow her to own a home. To Rhonda, hope is "the inspiration of know-

ing one's self worth and the impact you make on the lives of many."

Being laid off at 34 was an opportunity for **Claudette** to take a leap of faith and begin a new career as a child care provider. She enrolled in Project Hope's Family Child Care Business Enterprise program and opened her own daycare. Today, she owns her own home, her successful daycare is always full to capacity, and she is working toward a bachelor's degree. For Claudette, "Hope is a better tomorrow. Hope is waking up each morning."

What does hope mean to me? I see hope every day in our project. I see it in the faces of the children learning to read, the tears of a mother getting her apartment keys, a student understanding English for the first time, and a job training participant hearing the words "you're hired."

Sister **Margaret A. Leonard**, executive director of Project Hope in Boston, Massachusetts (USA) More information: **www.prohope.org**

"Parents' ability to focus on the bright side shapes children's early learning."

Young children's hope

How about young children's beliefs about optimism and hope?
Are they naïve? And what is the influence of their parents' attitudes?
That is the research field of Prof. Kristin Hansen Lagatutta.
It seems that we can all benefit from learning to perceive the world
from the vantage of a young child.

In the well-known children's classic *The Little Engine that Could* by Watty Piper, the little
blue train is faced with a daunting challenge: she needs to traverse a steep mountain
to deliver toys and food to children on the other side. Although the objective situation
is bleak—she has never done such a feat before—she decides to think optimistically,
repeating the mantra, "I think I can, I think I can," over and over until she achieves her goal.

These messages of the power of optimism and hope are pervasive across many cultures,
and we, as adults, know that thinking positively can improve emotional well-being (indeed,
hundreds of scientific studies have documented significant relations among optimism,
mental health, and physical health). The question that has intrigued me is what do young
children know about the influence of the mind on emotions, including the benefits
of positive thinking?

How you look at it

My research investigates young children's understanding of mind-emotion relations; particularly, their growing knowledge that people's emotions and decisions are powerfully shaped by how they interpret situations, reflect on the past, and think about the future. Consider this scenario: two children are riding a bicycle, hit a bump in the road, fall off and break their arms. Clearly, this is a negative event. One girl thinks about how fun it will be for friends to draw on her cast, whereas the other girl thinks about how itchy the cast will be and how she won't be able to play with friends. Five- to 10-year-olds predicted and explained each girl's emotions using a 7-point picture scale ranging from "very bad" to "very good." Children further responded to additional trials featuring characters with optimistic versus pessimistic thoughts in negative, positive, and ambiguous situations. Parents and children also completed surveys measuring their individual levels of optimism and hope.

Results showed that as children grow older they better understand the impact of optimistic versus pessimistic thinking: they more often explain emotions in relation to characters' thoughts, and they predict greater differences between the emotions of positive and negative thinkers. Notably, the strongest predictor of children's knowledge about the benefits of positive thinking (besides age) was parental optimism and hope. **Children with more optimistic and hopeful parents predicted greater improvement in emotions following positive thinking in negative situations,** judged a larger difference between the emotions of the optimists versus pessimists, and more often explained emotion differences as caused by thought focus compared to children whose parents were lower in optimism and hope. Thus, parents' style of coping with setbacks—their ability or willingness to focus on the "bright side" of negative events—shapes children's early learning about the power of thinking on emotional well-being.

Letting go of the past

In other studies, we have investigated developmental changes in how 4- to 10-year-olds reason about people's future-oriented thoughts, emotions, and decisions in situations where they re-encounter someone who previously harmed them, helped them, or both harmed and helped. Of interest is how children connect people's mental states and experiences over time, using their knowledge that people's past events shape how they react to current situations as well as anticipate what the future will bring. Although even 4-year-olds forecast differently given different past events (for example, they anticipate a more positive future in the consistent-help versus consistent-harm situations), they show a greater positivity bias compared to older children and adults. That is, in situations involving negative past experiences, 4- to 5-year-olds still often anticipate positive outcomes.

For example, a person can feel happy seeing someone who destroyed his picture and locked him in a closet, because now he thinks, "that boy is really ready to say sorry for those bad things!" These data correspond with related studies showing that children younger than age 7 have a more positive outlook than older children and adults, especially in adverse situations. Although risky, this willingness to anticipate the good has clear benefits: young children are in a point in their life where they greatly depend upon others and need to build their social networks. Being more trusting, forgiving, and hopeful can aid in forging these relationships.

When to expect the best

This is not to say that young children are naïve optimists who always expect positive futures. We are finding, for example, that even 4- to 5-year-olds recognize that desired outcomes are more likely in high (for example, picking a winning coin with 75% chance) versus low probability situations (for example, rolling the winning number on a 6-sided die). Thus, they modify optimistic expectations depending upon the situation. Despite this ability, 4- to 7-year-olds greatly overestimate the chances that desirable, yet unlikely, outcomes will occur—often more than doubling the objective probability. This seeming "error" may actually serve an adaptive purpose: it may make young children more willing to try new things without fear of failure or negative outcomes.

As a final note, I do not want to leave the reader with the false impression that all is positive in the life of a young child. Many children around the globe face atrocious injustices, trauma, and neglect. Even in low-risk, highly educated American samples we find that parents view their 4- to 10-year-old children as much more optimistic and less worried than children self- report about their own thoughts and emotions. Thus, although young children do interpret situations more positively and think more optimistically about the future than older children and adults, they can experience troubling emotional lows, negative emotions frequently undetected by caregivers.

In closing, from the research evidence it appears that we do not need to inspire optimism and hope in young children as much as *preserve* it as they grow older. We, as adults, can also benefit from learning to perceive the world from the vantage of a young child—even when faced with negative circumstances, we should always look for and anticipate the good… and, perhaps, even try something new.

The keys

→ **As children grow older they better understand the impact of optimistic versus pessimistic thinking. The strongest predictor of their knowledge about the benefits of positive thinking (besides age) is parental optimism and hope.**

→ **The willingness of young children to anticipate the good is risky but has clear benefits. Being more trusting, forgiving, and hopeful can aid in forging their basic relationships.**

→ **Children modify optimistic expectations depending upon the situation. They overestimate desirable outcomes, but that makes them more willing to try new things. Adults can benefit from this way of perceiving the world.**

Kristin Hansen Lagattuta is a Professor of Psychology in the Department of Psychology and the Center for Mind and Brain at the University of California, Davis (United States). Her research has been funded by the National Science Foundation and focuses on age-related changes and individual differences in emotion understanding. She has published empirical articles in top-tiered journals such as Child Development and Developmental Psychology. She is the editor of the book *Children and Emotion: New Insights from Developmental Affective Science* (2014). Outside of work, Dr. Lagattuta enjoys photography and has fun spending time with her husband, three children, and menagerie of pets. What inspires her and gives her hope? "Watching my children and students become passionate about what they are learning—their enthusiasm and drive to explore, take risks, question, invent, and work hard."

"The new perspective can sometimes have more value than the old one."

Hope during illness

Suddenly the verdict falls: you're seriously ill. Or it happens to your child or your partner. No one saw it coming. From one day to the next you have to rethink all your expectations for the future. Prof. Jan Walburg investigates people's reactions in such situations. They vary greatly, but hope and perspective always play a crucial role.

In the course of our lives we build up expectations for the future. And everyone has a few inner representations of that future. Sometimes these representations are very specific (a house, a family, a profession) and sometimes they are vague ideas of what our future will look like. They could also be several ideas or representations. We can see ourselves in several roles—for example, in a profession, and in several situations, such as living in the city or maybe in the country, in a family or alone.

Gradually we prepare to realize those expectations, armed with better information, motivated by the hope that we can bring them within our reach. And slowly but surely we know whether those expectations are real. We evolve in the direction of our goal: our training goes well, or a relationship stabilizes. This can reinforce our goal-oriented behavior. Or it can be disappointing. Perhaps we cannot marshal sufficient willpower, or we are not intelligent enough. Or we don't succeed in finding a partner who makes us feel good. This can also lead to adjustments in our expectations. This is usually a gradual process, with all the space and time needed for adaptation, reflection, and reorientation.

Unprepared

But what if circumstances are suddenly very different? This is the case with a chronic illness, for example. Suddenly we have to adjust our perspective. First there is the process of taking in the knowledge that the illness will influence our life. But then comes the realization that the future scenarios we have formed, consciously or unconsciously, and been working toward for years, are no longer valid. The future is very different. Shorter. Or determined by a decreasing ability to develop ourselves, a greatly reduced mobility, or an increasing dependence on others. We are never prepared whatsoever for this new scenario. **It is likely that we will really lose our way for a while.** Suddenly we are no longer working step by step to refine and realize our anticipated future; instead, our life is determined by the path to and from health-care providers.

In such circumstances, how do we preserve our hope in a future that has a positive meaning for us?

Some people react differently than you would expect. **The illness becomes a reason for reflecting on your life,** for rethinking your current values. It gives insight into new values. Sometimes this leads to people looking right through the pain and difficulty to see new perspectives that make life worth living again. The value of friendship and love is experienced more intensely, or the hectic rush of daily working life is gladly set aside. Suddenly a new perspective arises, one that has more value than the old one. You might say that events have helped someone to find his or her destination. **And hope once again acquires the powerful role that it has for everyone:** the hope that new expectations will be realized.

New perspective

Most people need a lot more time. Sometimes, years after the sorrow, the rage, and the dejection, they still build a future that has value. Their hope recovers slowly but steadily, often aided by conversations with others who can understand how difficult it is to find something new to hold onto while still contributing.

And some people don't succeed in doing that, but bitterly latch on to the old expectations that can no longer or can only partially become a reality. **They don't succeed in making a new representation of the future that gives them hope.** Every scenario is a disappointment when compared to their original image of the future. Fear of pain and lower quality of life, resistance to a life requiring constant care, and reduced mobility hinder the formation of a new perspective. Hope is at best focused on the possibility that maybe, just maybe, everything will be all right.

Scientists have attempted to investigate the effects of the manner in which people are or are not able to build up new hope. With people whose prognosis is not too bad—and who have a reasonable outlook—and also a bit more time, the ability to develop new perspectives leads not only to an improvement in their well-being, but also to an improvement in their health. To put it in technical terms: **their morbidity and mortality are lower and their immune system functions better.**

Therefore, there are many reasons for health-care professionals to pay special attention to the resilience and perspective of people with chronic illnesses. Many people are able to adapt, but there are just as many people who could use a nudge in the right direction to experience hope again in terms of realizing their desired future.

The keys

→ **People react differently when they become seriously ill. Some look right through the pain and difficulty to see new perspectives that make life worth living again.**

→ **Most people, however, need a lot more time. Their hope recovers gradually. Others do not succeed and bitterly latch onto the old expectations.**

→ **Among people with a reasonable outlook, the ability to develop new perspectives leads to an improvement in their well-being and their health.**

Jan Auke Walburg is a professor of psychology at the Universiteit van Twente (the Netherlands). He studies the circumstances in which people flourish, in their personal lives, at work or school, in their relationships, and in their communities. Jan was previously chairman of the board of directors of the national institute for mental health and addiction, the Trimbos Institute. He has written several books, among them *Mentaal Vermogen* and *Jong van Geest*. His passion for music has found expression in a book on the emotional significance of Gustav Mahler's symphonies.

"Recognize that the thing that you do well,
YOU DO WELL! And enjoy it."

Stumbling with hope

"More than an encounter, my first experiences with hope were
a few stumbles. I found myself hitting the ground over and over
again searching for hope," says Dr. Alejandro Tapia-Vargas.
"Moreover, my mother's name is Victoria (Victory) and my aunt
is Esperanza (Hope). Why wasn't I more successful in this topic?"

The first time I fell

I used to consider myself a "realistic" person. I used to analyze situations and think about
the possibility something was about to come. Some friends used to call me "pessimistic"
and I denied it, saying, "I am basing my opinions on data. If something seems quite unlikely
to happen and there is no evidence for it, it is not going to happen." To my surprise,
a colleague gave me an instrument that measures optimism. When I saw my results,
some assumptions changed about me and my knowledge of hope.

Hope implies two mental processes: 1) it is a cognitive evaluation about future events,
and 2) people do this evaluation based on the confidence they have in themselves. **Hope is
the result of a reasoning that implies assessing a possible situation to come (point one)
and our own implications (point two).** Could it happen? What does it depend on? What
factors are related with it? Does it depend on me or on something else? These questions
are related to something that psychologists call self-efficacy, mastery, or agency. If it depends
on me, do I have the ability to deal with it? Can I start now or do I need to develop
something first? Do I have the capacity? These aspects imply what psychologist name
self-image or self-concept.

In this sense, my hope depends on two elements: the opinion that I have about me and the prediction that I have made evaluating the possibility that something might happen.

My second fall

I used to see hope as synonymous with faith. But that was my mistake; faith is a certainty. A certainty with no evidence, which implies a confidence that something will be real or is going to happen. The base of faith is believing. With hope, there is some data that allows us to predict something in the future and to make us feel confident.

Yes, hope is related to faith in religion. Both are virtues that are mostly worthy and are promoted by institutions. Actually, hope is almost a requirement for religious practice, to believe in a better life to come and a better life after death. Hope and faith usually come together; faith makes us believe, and hope makes us feel sure. But hope is not limited to religion and its practices.

That's because hope is a positive feeling oriented to the future. In order to understand feelings as a human variable, psychologists understand that **every emotion that we have (positive or negative) is time oriented.** We feel satisfaction or bitterness over something related to the past, and feel joy or anger over something that is happening right now in the present, and we feel hope or insecurity over something to come in the future.

Rising up

When I was a child and I fell down, my mother used to say to me, "Now what? Up! Come on, up." I would rise up, get a hug from her, and go on walking. So, what did I learn from my hoping falls?

1. **Center your daily activities on things that you master.** With this, you will develop more confidence in what you do and what you are.

2. **Enjoy.** Recognize that the thing that you do well, YOU DO WELL! And enjoy it. It is a pleasure or reward for you, even if someone else will receive a benefit for it (a client, a relation, or a neighbor). Many people can benefit at the same time as you. Enjoy it!

3. **Go on!** Whatever you do, keep working. The things to come are not yet here and they will be the outcome of, precisely, whatever you are doing right now.

The keys

→ **Hope depends on two elements: the opinion that I have about me and the prediction that I have made evaluating the possibility that something might happen.**

→ **Hope and faith usually come together; faith makes us believe, and hope makes us feel sure.**

→ **Some good advice? Center your daily activities on things that you master. Enjoy! Go on!**

Alejandro Tapia-Vargas, PhD, works at the Department of Psychology in the University of Monterrey (Mexico). He is a researcher and psychotherapist in the Center of Treatment and Research of Anxiety. He is editor of *Momentos de historia en la psicología* (Moments of history in psychology) and coeditor of *Psicología positiva* (Positive Psychology) in Mexico. Nowadays his main research interest relays on the relationship between scientific writing and fictional literature. He is now working on a biography and enjoys life, practicing photography, mountain biking, journaling, cooking, and spending the weekends with his children.

"Too much hope doesn't work in love."

The hope for perfect love

Elaine Hatfield, a life-long expert in studies on love, confirms that hope has lots of positive effects, but she warns us that hoping and searching for perfect love can be a mistake. In the arena of love, unrealistic self-confidence and reckless hope can create misery. Some couples hang on too long in the hope that things are bound to get better.

Passionate love is an extremely powerful emotional state that is generally defined as a state of intense longing for union with another. It is a complex emotion that is marked by its extreme highs and lows, as well as its tendency to cause the afflicted person to think obsessively about the person for whom they desire. Passionate love is a fleeting emotion. It is a high, and one cannot stay high forever. Starting shortly after marriage, passionate love has been shown to steadily decline, with long-married couples admitting that they feel only "some" passionate love for each other.

Fortunately, there may be a bright side to this seemingly grim picture. **Where passionate love once existed, companionate love is thought to take its place.** Companionate love is said to be a gentle emotion, comprising feelings of deep attachment, intimacy, and commitment. Some researchers have argued that, as passionate love decreases, companionate love actually increases. We didn't find support for this theory. Couples reported that both romantic and companionate love tended to decline (and to decline equally) over time.

Passionate love

The *APA Dictionary of Psychology* defines optimism as "the attitude that things happen for the best and that people's wishes or aims will ultimately be fulfilled." Generally, **the hopeful are blessed.** As the research of C. R. Snyder (2002) and others has demonstrated, the hopeful typically possess higher self-esteem, are more confident, more persistent, achieve more, possess sunnier dispositions, and are healthier. All to the good, **except in the arena of love.** There, unrealistic self-confidence and reckless hope can create snares and delusions.

Almost everyone in the West hopes that someday they will find love. Hope runs high that they will attract a person who is good looking, charming, witty, kind, wealthy, and sexually desirable to boot. And, typically, at first, in a romantic relationship the seekers convince themselves that they have found the man or woman of their dreams. But time takes a toll and all too often, passionate affairs don't work out. **Reality replaces fantasy and disappointment follows hope.** People sigh and grieve, but having convinced themselves that they have learned a valuable lesson, they resurrect the fantasy and move on to the next. And sometimes on and on.

Eventually, though, many come to abandon the fantasy of ever finding a fiery romance. Instead they settle: they make a commitment. After all, the folklore assures them that although passion may burn itself out, it will be replaced by a mellow, slow burning fire. Things will get better. Yet, even with these now modest expectations, many are disappointed.

Companionate love

There is considerable evidence that passionate love does, in fact, tend to erode with time. We have interviewed, for example, a random sample of nearly 1,000 dating couples, newlyweds, and older women in Madison, Wisconsin. We assumed that although passionate love would decline precipitously with time, companionate love would hold its own or even increase. We were wrong! As predicted, passionate love did plummet with time. Both steady daters and newlyweds expressed "a great deal of passionate love" for their mates. But after many years of marriage, women reported that they (and their husbands) now felt only "some" passionate love for their mates. And what of companionate love? Here, contrary to our predictions, companionate love declined at almost exactly the same rate as passionate love.

The conclusion one draws from these data depends on whether one is an optimist or a pessimist. On the positive side, contrary to some portrayals in the mass media, a few lucky older persons, married for a quarter of a century or more, still felt a great deal of love (both passionate and companionate) for their mates. (Of course, even when love has flickered out, couples may still reap the advantages of a loving family and a lifelong relationship, with someone who knows and cares for them.) On the negative side, with the passage of time, most couples felt less and less love (passionate and companionate) for their partners. Passionate and companionate love remained "coupled" together, for good and for ill, longer than was previously thought.

Marital problems

How do people respond when their deepest hopes are dashed? It is here that too much optimism might prove a disadvantage. Often times it is all to the good when people assume they can make improvements in their faltering marriages. But **some couples go too far.** Buoyed by a lifetime of hope and optimism—and with a supreme confidence in their ability to solve any problem given enough effort and time—they hang on for far too long. Romantic and marital problems are often far more challenging than solving a Megaminx.

Personalities are amazingly resistant to change. Emotional problems are almost impossible to fix. Drug addiction, alcoholism, character flaws, and abusive personalities rarely respond to loving care. Often, for the optimistic—successful in every other realm of life—it takes far too long to realize this. But if one is lucky enough to possess a relationship that does work (and some do), the joys are endless, and very much worth hoping for.

The keys

→ **Generally, the hopeful are blessed, except in the arena of love. There, unrealistic self-confidence and reckless hope can create snares and delusions.**

→ **During marriage, passionate love and companionate love mostly decline at almost the same rate.**

→ **It doesn't help waiting too long to solve marital problems. Some couples go too far in relying on mere hope for the better.**

Elaine Hatfield is a Professor of Psychology at the University of Hawaii and past-president of the Society for the Scientific Study of Sex. In 2012, the Association for Psychological Science (APS) awarded her the William James award for a Lifetime of Scientific Achievement. She has written numerous studies and a dozen novels. What she still hopes? "Fernand Braudel, an eminent French historian, once observed that his most profound hope was for a world with a bit more justice, a bit more equality, a bit more freedom, a bit less violence, and a good deal less poverty. Those modest achievements would be worthy of celebration. That is what I hope for in the world of the future too."

Richard L. Rapson is a Professor of History at the University of Hawaii. He came to Hawaii in 1966 after teaching at Amherst College and at Stanford University. He has written more than a dozen books, most of which focus on the psychological side of American life, past and present. He is working on a new book that points out the many global advances that have been made since the end of the Second World War. He hopes he's right and that the progress in democracy, women's rights, and the escape by billions from millennium-long poverty will continue.

Paul Thornton is currently a doctoral student in Social Psychology at the University of Hawaii at Manoa, where he also works as a Teaching Assistant. Paul's research interests include emotional contagion, persuasion, and cognitive dissonance. Paul finds hope and meaning in the pursuit of scientific and self-discovery and in fostering a love for learning in his daughter.

"Hope? In order to keep it you have to give it away!"

Hopeful couples

A couple faced with divorce. Another couple struggling with fears and anxiety. Dr. Charlie Azzopardi talks to them. He is a systemic practitioner with more than twenty years of experience in the field of mental health. Does he have hopeful advice?

Hope has as many meanings as there are people in the world. It often comes packed in a soothing set of feelings that may feel like the relief you experience immediately after the struggle to surface for breath when you thought you had drowned. You're not saved, you're not sure, but something inside tells you that you can make it. Hope, dreams, aspirations, ambition, anticipation, wish, and faith can all be said to have a synonymous meaning, as the color of hope is so camouflaged and so matching with practically any context.

Hope saves the lives of those who experience it. The hope that life can turn out good in the end distinguishes those who stay alive from those who commit suicide. I recently worked with a couple who consulted me because the husband had an affair. He was undecided whether to stay with his family or leave with the new woman he had come to know. His wife had given up on the idea that he loves her and attempted suicide three times. When I saw them, she was visibly angry, sad, hopeless, and resigned. She had not identified her potential to bring him back.

We talked and my work centered around tapping on her personal resources: her beauty, her love, their history together. While reconnecting with these, she increasingly realized that she is still part of the game and that **the more hopeless she feels the more she neglects herself and the more difficult she becomes for him to stay with.** So while she gradually understood, she became increasingly hopeful. She started seeing her personal resources, which helped her use them more. A few sessions later she returned more radiant, better looking, calmer, better able to connect with her man, and definitely easier to be with. He told me he had made his mind up, to stay with his wife of 15 years. The reasons: he said he loves her and that they have two children together. He also added that he's seen her changing radically and profoundly.

Sharks

Hope is what keeps people alive in tough situations. People stranded in deserts, stranded in coal mines, or fighting for their lives in any way experience great relief and change. As they hope that things will turn out well they become empowered to act. Another couple I worked with visited me because of bouts of anxiety and depression. In their attempt to circle the world with a yacht they got stranded with broken equipment in the middle of a shark-infested ocean. **Looking back at the terrifying experience, they recalled how hope empowered them to look forward to life.** Rather than let go and hopelessly wait for fate to take its course, hope energized them to do something and try to fix the equipment. They managed to safely reach the next port some 19 days later. That same hope is the same hope they now use to beat their anxiety and those debilitating moments of depression so characteristic of post-traumatic stress disorder. It is hope that gives people on the edge of cataclysms like impending death the power to move on and face their fears.

I remember reading Albert Camus's book on the plague and thinking, "How can one hope amidst all that devastation?" Yet hope's amazing chemistry does exactly that: It provides the chemicals of hope exactly when one needs them. **Hope's chemistry fosters a desire toward life.** Talk to terminal cancer patients. Many have never thought of life as they do now after the discovery of their illness. The chemistry of hope is so powerful too. In my 22-year-long career in drug addiction I encountered many clients who felt very hopeless about ever quitting drugs. They may have felt hopeless, yet the discovery of a terminal disease triggers the hope chemistry in a way that their recovery is spontaneous. They now not only want to live but also live healthily. They hope and they act on hope's behalf toward a better future. They claim strength straight from hope.

The lifeline

My assumption that hope is a physiochemical reaction of the body is based on the fact that hope is transcultural. You find it wherever you go. It must, therefore, be a very fundamental emotion. This makes hope, in my view, part of the autonomous nervous system and an automatic chemical reaction in the primitive brain triggered by some contextual event. I am sure, however, that people can work to learn to become better hopers. Cultures of hope can be created and fostered with the aim of eradicating hopelessness and the negative experiences associated with it.

In short, hope is akin to oxygen. It is the lifeline of life. Maybe these suggestions can help you:

1. **Look ahead and dream.** Teach yourself to transcend time by looking ahead and fantasizing about what you want to achieve, your aspirations, your dreams. We call it visualization. This seems to provide a greater impetus on the chemistry of hope and makes your dreams more realizable.

2. **Think positive.** Hope breeds hope and hopelessness breeds hopelessness. Thinking positive means you teach yourself to become optimistic and to see more of the bright side of experiences. This positivity definitely helps in the release of endorphins.

3. **Support hope in others.** Hope, like all of the other feelings, is contagious. The more you help others feel hopeful the more hopeful you are likely to be. Remember the saying? In order to keep it you have to give it away.

The keys

→ **Hope's amazing chemistry provides the chemicals of hope exactly when one needs them. It fosters a desire toward life.**

→ **Hope is a part of the autonomous nervous system and an automatic chemical reaction in the primitive brain triggered by some contextual event.**

→ **We can become better "hopers": look ahead and dream, think positive, and support hope in others.**

Charlie Azzopardi is a Family Therapist and Systemic Consultant at the Institute of Family Therapy in Malta. He develops new therapeutic techniques that make working with families and individuals more accessible. Charlie has published several articles and books on marital problems, addiction, marital separation, and parenting.

"Evidently, despair is not the rule in old age."

Hope in old age

"If one thinks about old age, one may question if there is room left for hope with advancing age. Lifetime is limited and the older we get the closer we get to death," says Prof. **Dieter Ferring**, an expert in autonomy of older people. "We need to differentiate between hope and our future time perspective."

The tasks associated with old age are described by different theoretical models. Very early models—such as the "disengagement" theory—underlined that withdrawal from social life and preparation for death are the specific tasks of old age. A more positive approach comes from Erikson who proposed a model of psychosocial crises underlying individual development across the life span in the 1950s. In his model, Erikson describes the tension between "ego integrity" versus "despair" as a crisis characterizing old age that covers the years from 65 to death. Integrating one's life experiences and having a sense of personal fulfilment describes the solution to this conflict; despair about one's life described by unfulfilled needs and goals characterizes the less successful result. Although not directly, this model elaborates the notion of hope in old age since despair indicates a loss of all hope and confidence.

Perspective

Evidently, despair is not the rule in old age. This is convincingly demonstrated by studies showing that older and younger generations do not differ with respect to indicators of subjective well-being. This is most intriguingly described by the term "satisfaction paradox," which depicts that older people report comparatively high satisfaction with their lives in spite of age-related losses and impairments. These findings indicate the effective use of adaptive processes that older persons use to regulate their subjective well-being. These processes also serve the construction of hope even though one's lifetime may be limited.

In order to understand this, one needs to differentiate two concepts that play a crucial role here: the term of future time perspective on the one side and the concept of hope on the other. Future time perspective stands for the temporal space that one perceives for setting individual goals. This perspective evidently differs considerably across the human life span: the young ones looking ahead over decades to live; the old ones counting the years that will be left to achieve their goals. Similarly, hope also implies important goals and needs but here the person wishes them to come true and is not sure if this will be the case. Hope is, thus, always characterized by uncertainty, whereas future time can be comparatively easily estimated. Consequently, one may have a limited time perspective but on the other hand still have hope of achieving important goals.

New goals

The second common aspect that future time and hope share is the content of the goals projected in the future. Again, there are considerable differences across the life span here. The young person hopes to find a partner; the old person hopes to live as long as possible with one's partner. Goal contents and profiles thus differ depending on the period of life and its predominant needs. It is an important adaptive capacity of the aging person to say good-bye to goals that are no longer achievable due to irreversible losses. Imagine a person who has always been proud of his or her physical fitness doing a lot of sports during the week who suffers now from degeneration of joints and arthritis. Or, more dramatically, imagine a person who has always been proud of being independent and not needing anyone's help who suffers a stroke and now has to rely completely on the help of others.

Breathe

Giving up goals and finding new ones that are attractive are therefore crucial for individual adaptation, and hope plays a major role here in many respects. First, a "hopeful" person may more easily find another goal and this may reflect different the lifetime experiences of a person who may be either optimistic or pessimistic. Finding a goal also depends on individual aspirations and ideas about the "Is" and the "Ought" of one's life.

A person can thus change the criteria for estimating their well-being by calibrating his or her goals. The person addicted to sport may find satisfaction in a reduced activity; the person with a stroke may find that the event changing his or her life was a necessary warning sign to live more healthily and change their lifestyle. Identifying new goals indicates as well that one has found or assigned meaning to the loss of a former important goal. All these processes indicate the effectiveness of hope.

Last but certainly not least, hope in old age also has a transcendent meaning for many of us. Life after life may sometimes be a consolation for those who are challenged by illness and impairment (not only in old age) in their current life and help them cope with this.

Thus, life is full of hope "even in" —or better, "just as much"—in old age. As Cicero put it, "dum spiro spero"—"as long as I breathe there is hope."

The keys

→ **Older people use effective adaptive processes to regulate their subjective well-being. These processes also serve the construction of hope even though one's lifetime may be limited.**

→ **We need to differ between hope (which is always characterized by uncertainty) and future time (which can be comparatively easily estimated). One may have a limited time perspective but still have hope of achieving important goals.**

→ **A person can change the criteria for estimating their well-being by calibrating his or her goals.**

Dieter Ferring is Professor and Head of the Integrative Research Unit on Social and Individual Development (INSIDE) at the University of Luxembourg. His main research areas lie within life span developmental psychology and geropsychology; his research and publications focus on personal and social factors contributing to autonomy and dependence in old age. His personal statement on hope? "Watching my son grow up, playing with him and his friends, gives me hope for tomorrow. In my work context, research on care giving and observing the solidarity and compassion of caregivers gives me hope for mankind."

> *"Hope is a conviction that there is meaning irrespective of how things turn out."*

The wisdom of the nurse

"I have learned that the ability to perceive hope is fundamental to the human being," says **Ania Willman**, President of the Swedish Society of Nursing. The lived experiences of hope among elderly in an acute care setting are based on envisioning possibilities, persistent expectancy, and nurturing affiliations: the wisdom of the nurse.

As a researcher I have worked with the theoretical concept of hope within nursing science from a humanistic, holistic perspective with the help of the Human Becoming theory. From the Human Becoming perspective, hope is a dimension of the paradoxical rhythm, hope-no-hope. It is a chosen way of living in the moment that is the structured meaning of a situation.

Hope is fundamental to the human being. Hope is always present but comes to the fore during difficult circumstances, such as serious disease, pain, or sorrow—moments that also contain glimpses of "non-hope." **Perceiving hope is a precondition for a person being able to experience health,** as hope is closely linked to a person's conception of a possible future, trusting that there will be a tomorrow. In difficult situations, even in the very last moments of life, hope can be a source of trust and joy for many people. Hope is an expectation and a conception of future opportunities. It is a conviction that there is meaning irrespective of how things turn out.

Lived experience

The lived experiences of hope among Swedish elderly in an acute care setting can be described as envisioning possibilities amid adversity, as persistent expectancy arises with nurturing affiliations.

1. The core concept envisioning possibilities amid adversity is an essence of the lived experience of hope. Each participant, men and women between the ages of 74 and 91, described this in a unique way. Ingrid said: "Sometimes you have hope without knowing what you are hoping for." And another woman, Elly, said: "Hope is the thing that makes you go on and look forward in difficult situations. You can push hard times away by participating in activities. Hope is something you feel within yourself."

2. The second core concept, persistent expectancy, can be described as living a particular way, while not knowing all that is yet-to-be. For example, Allan, a former sailor, said: "You have hope that the way life turns out is the best way." Lisa, an 82-year-old widow, who had lived in poverty with four children, said: "There have been some misfortunes, but it should not be too easy for you. There ought to be days with sunshine but also some dark days. Otherwise you will not find your life valuable." In the Human Becoming theory, change is a continuous, unitary human-universe process. Within this process, persons co-participate in change, choosing meaning and reaching to what is not yet.

3. The third concept, nurturing affiliations, can be viewed as propitious involvements and connecting-separating. This concept was also described in unique ways by the participants in the study. For example, Tor, an 82-year-old widower, former carpenter, and stone carver, said: "It is important to know people, hope comes from knowing people." Ruth, an 84-year-old widow, said that hope is knowing that her family can manage without her and that "it is important to have friends and fun" as well as having a person who understands and pays attention to your feelings. The participants spoke of experiences that were despairing but they added that at the same time experiences of contentment and nurturance were present. Their stories enhance our understanding of the lived experience of hope, thus of health and quality of life since hope is a lived experience of health. Hope was described as a rainbow, as an inspiration, as a feeling of loneliness, and at the same time a feeling of belonging.

Not giving up

Hope is an expectation and a conception of future opportunities and is usually described as a stance of life. Hope is not giving up, as the opposite implies not finding life worth living. Health is a subjective experience of meaning and therefore a sense of hope is vital for the patient's well-being, thus **the utmost care is necessary in order not to extinguish hope but instead to strengthen it.** Great wisdom, experience, and competence are required from nurses and others, to encounter each patient individually with the aim of nurturing his/her hope irrespective of health status or phase in life.

The keys

→ **Hope is a dimension of the paradoxical rhythm, hope-no-hope. It is a chosen way of living in the moment that is the structured meaning of a situation.**

→ **The lived experiences of hope among elderly people in an acute care setting is described as envisioning possibilities amid adversity, as persistent expectancy arises with nurturing affiliations.**

→ **Great wisdom, experience, and competence are required from nurses and others, to encounter each patient individually with the aim of nurturing his/her hope irrespective of health status or phase in life.**

Ania M. L. Willman is Professor and Head of the Department of Care Science, Faculty of Health and Society, Malmö University (Sweden) and President at the Swedish Society of Nursing. She has published professional articles on nursing in numerous publications. Dr. Willman worked as a nurse for 13 years before she became a teacher and researcher. She has worked with nursing all her life, in practice and theory. Her main interest? "My husband and my work, my two daughters and their families, including five grandchildren." She said, "If I am not reading and writing, you can find me on the sofa knitting or in the woods picking mushrooms and berries."

"Almost 20% of the adult population has some kind of chronic pain."

Chronic pain

How can we build hope, optimism, and resilience in people with chronic pain? That's what the research of Dr. **Brian McGuire** is about. He is codirector of the Centre for Pain Research at the National University of Ireland. "While no one would ever volunteer to have a life of chronic pain, for those who have this condition, there is every reason to be hopeful."

Pain is an evolutionary process designed to alert us to tissue injury so that we can take action to minimize damage, for example, by removing a hand from a hot surface or changing position in bed to avoid muscle cramping or bed sores. This protective mechanism is so intrinsic in our adaptation to the environment that we often engage in these health-preserving behaviors without even noticing. Having pain also highlights to us the need to seek help such as medical attention.

Pain is an almost universal phenomenon. I say "almost" as there are a small number of individuals who have a congenital insensitivity to pain. Not surprisingly, such individuals tend to have shortened lives that are marked by multiple injuries and illnesses, as the normal warning mechanisms are not operational. For the majority of people, however, pain is experienced quite regularly but is typically of mild intensity and a short-lasting experience.

Unfortunately, that is not the case for everyone. In fact, a sizeable minority of the population has an experience of pain whereby it is persistent for a long period of time. This form of pain is known as *chronic pain* and is generally defined as pain that lasts for three months or longer. A large European study suggested that almost 20% of the adult population across multiple countries has this form of pain. So, while it is not the norm, it is nevertheless relatively common.

Self-management

People who endure chronic pain are truly remarkable individuals who daily demonstrate the unique resilience of the human spirit. Humans are not designed to have long-term pain and, not surprisingly, the quality of life of people who have chronic pain tends to be reduced.

As you might expect, people with chronic pain have reduced capacity to partake in a range of activities in everyday life such as sport and leisure, employment, and social activities. Having chronic pain also affects the psychological well-being of people—one of our studies shows that depression is five times more common in people with chronic pain than in those without pain. As well as the human cost, chronic pain also costs a lot in terms of health service usage and reduced productivity. People with chronic pain visit the doctor more often, use more medications, are more likely to miss work, and even when they attend work are likely to be less productive.

This all appears to be quite a hopeless story so far. However, that is not the case as researchers have started to understand the nature of chronic pain and to develop more effective ways of treating it. Although most people having chronic pain for a year or longer are not likely to ever be free of some level of pain, those individuals can learn to manage and cope with the pain quite well and lead a better life than might be expected based on the description of the impact of chronic pain earlier in this paper. Because people who have chronic pain tend to have it for a very long time, there is now a focus in psychological research on helping people to develop ways of dealing with the pain. The psychological approaches generally promote a self-management approach, that is, they encourage people to become experts in monitoring their symptoms and in developing a range of techniques and coping strategies to deal with the pain. Indeed, this approach is now expressly endorsed by a number of prominent pain management organizations.

A better life

So, how does this self-management approach help people with chronic pain? A central element of the treatment is to try to help people to think about the pain in a different way. It is a natural response to be fearful of pain and to be worried that participating in activity might cause more damage to the injured part of our body. However, the risk of injury is actually very low. Most people have what is known as benign chronic pain; that is, there are no major injuries to the body and no "red flags" that would be a contraindication to increasing one's level of activity. So, these approaches teach people how to gradually increase activity while building one's confidence to do so and becoming less fearful of the pain.

What about the effectiveness of these approaches—are they worthwhile? Generally the answer to this question is a resounding "yes." These approaches have been shown to be effective in reducing the level of interference or disability arising from the pain.

They also help to improve mood and reduce fear of activity, and they help people to think in a more helpful way about the pain. Sometimes they also help to reduce the intensity of pain, but almost all pain management programs say that this is not a central goal of the program, but instead **they focus on helping people to do more activity despite the pain.** Achieving a reduction in the pain is considered a bonus—but living a better life despite the pain is the central aim.

New approaches to treatment are also targeting resilience—that inbuilt toughness and flexibility that enables us to cope with new challenges and persistent difficulties. These resilience-building programs are now being evaluated in people with chronic pain and are proving to be effective.

While no one would ever volunteer to have a life of chronic pain, for those who have this condition, there is every reason to be hopeful. New treatments are emerging all the time, and people show an amazing capacity to adjust to the most challenging experiences, including chronic pain.

The keys

→ **The self-management approach helps people with chronic pain. A central element of the treatment is to try to help people to think about the pain in a different way.**

→ **These approaches teach people how to gradually increase activity while building their confidence to do so and becoming less fearful of the pain.**

→ **Achieving a reduction in the pain is considered a bonus—but living a better life despite the pain is the central aim.**

Brian McGuire is Senior Lecturer in Clinical Psychology at the National University of Ireland, Galway (Ireland). He is director of the Doctor of Psychological Science program in Clinical Psychology and Joint Director of the Centre for Pain Research. His clinical work is primarily in behavioral medicine, such as pain management and diabetes care. His research interests are in pain management, diabetes, and adjustment to chronic physical illness. He has published numerous articles and the book *Feeling Better, a cognitive behavioural pain management programme for people with an intellectual disability*. What does hope mean for him? "Never giving up looking for a better way. What gives me hope is that each day I meet people in my professional life that have so much hardship but they keep fighting on."

The active part of hope

"Most of us are familiar with media images of refugee children from conflict and post-conflict countries. Such portrayals often imply there is little room for hope in their lives given the many losses and traumatic experiences their families have endured," says Dr. **Sophie Yohani**, born and raised in Tanzania. "But there is another, more hopeful side to these portrayals. Knowing this opens possibilities for building resilience in children who are exposed to trauma and mass violence."

I discovered the power of hope (from a professional perspective) at the age of 22 while working with street youth in Dar es Salaam, Tanzania. I worked as a teacher and counselor at a youth center, where I became intimately aware of the experiences of street-involved youth in Tanzania. The boys' resilience and sense of hope, despite a life of tremendous adversity, made a significant impression on me and went on to shape much of my professional life, which upholds a strengths-based philosophy.

Children's voices of courage and hope are often missing in children's mental health literature, which seems more often to speak of their pain and despair, and often from the perspective of adult researchers. So what happens when we invite refugee children to explore and share their experiences of hope during early years of resettlement? What happens when such an invitation is given in a setting that is safe, familiar, and space is made to explore personal experiences of hope using creative approaches such as photography, drawings, quilting, and child-centered interviews? We learn that despite the many pre- and post-migration challenges faced by refugee children, hope is not foreign but an enduring presence and that children are also able to identify sources of hope in their lives. In fact, hope appears to be crucial during post-trauma adjustment as it is associated with an increased sense of personal empowerment and security—which are critical for healing from trauma. The following understandings of hope in children emerged from one of my research studies with a group of children (ages 8 to 17) in an early intervention program designed to assist children from post-conflict environments with adjustment in Canada.

The heart of hope

Children's descriptions of hope suggest hope has two different but reciprocally related aspects. One part, the "heart of hope," seemed to be a core experience. When asked, most children described hope as being present in their hearts. Children had some difficulty articulating this aspect of hope, but they were able to relay that it was within them and had an enduring presence: "hope never goes away" or "it can get bigger and smaller" were common responses. Children admitted to difficulties and challenges that decrease hope such as missing loved ones who were deceased or left in countries of origin, learning difficulties at school, and parental unemployment—but hope was nevertheless present. **Hope did not take the struggles away, but instead gave the ability or motivation to cope.** "Hope makes me feel I can do it if I try harder," was one 10-year-old girl's comment regarding difficulties with learning at school, after three years of missed school in a refugee camp.

Hope engendering sources

Another aspect of hope emerged in the children's descriptions of themselves and others involved in personally important activities that sustain the heart of hope—essentially hope-engendering sources. **One individual hope source (engaging in self-empowering activities) and two relational hope sources (secure relationships with people and with nature/spirituality) were identified** in children's work. For example, hope was experienced by a child when a safe and caring teacher helps them to read, when they have the opportunity to care for plants or animals, and when learning to ride a bicycle or cuddling a soft toy to reduce anxiety. These sources of hope act as fuel to support an internalized sense of hope, which in turn activates the child to engage further with these sources. In other words, a sense of empowerment and security are key contexts for the development of hope for this group of children.

Basic trust

The descriptions of hope by refugee children support the famous development psychologist Erik Erikson's (*Childhood and society, 1950*) notion of the importance of basic trust in the development of hope in children. The enduring part of hope (heart) may well be closer in nature to what Erikson described as basic trust. It appears to be an intangible yet vital foundational experience that is linked to a generalized sense of safety emanating from important relationships. **Unlike basic trust that is often described as a one-dimensional enduring sense of safety, hope, as depicted by refugee children in my study, has another part that is active and dynamic.** This active part helps children to feel empowered and to engage in activities that connect them to other people and to nature as an extension of their world. This active part of hope may well be closer to Erickson's description of hope that emerges from having an established sense of trust.

Thus, we learn from refugee children that hope is crucial for adjustment after difficult life experiences because it is closely linked to basic trust that can be shaken during life-changing experiences. We also learn that hope can be engendered by identifying and then facilitating sources of hope such as nurturing secure relationships with family and community members, providing opportunities to connect with nature and/or spiritual activities, and facilitating experiences that empower children's sense of mastery.

The keys

→ **We learn from refugee children that hope is crucial for adjustment after difficult life experiences because it is closely linked to basic trust that can be shaken during life-changing experiences.**

→ **We also learn that hope can be engendered by identifying and then facilitating sources of hope such as nurturing secure relationships within families and communities, providing opportunities to engage with nature and spirituality, and facilitating experiences that empower children's sense of mastery.**

→ **Hope has a reciprocal quality and is nurtured in supportive relationships.**

Sophie Yohani, PhD, was born and raised in Tanzania and currently resides in Canada. She is Associate Professor of Counseling Psychology at the University of Alberta and the Director of the Faculty of Education's Counseling Centre, a university-based community training center for graduate students. She is a registered psychologist with expertise in counseling/community psychology, refugee mental health, and community-based research. Sophie maintains a special interest in childhood and adult trauma and the experiences of hope and resiliency in adversity. Her research focuses on the mental health of refugee and immigrants and program/policy implications in educational and community settings.

Supportive relationships

Hope appears to reside deep within us, as part of our human nature. Hope then makes herself visible through our actions and words that indicate a mental and emotional connection to others, to ourselves, and to our natural and/or spiritual environment. Through our responses, we identify what is meaningful to us.

We all have the ability to hope, it is the outside manifestation of hope or how we are able to connect, that varies depending on our circumstances. A hopeful person who finds herself in a difficult situation is able to look for alternative ways to connect to what is personally meaningful, thereby ensuring the continuation of hopefulness. Most people do this without being aware of their actions.

It is in times when our hope is significantly challenged that finding ways to connect become difficult, and so hope is not visible to us or others. These are times when we feel disconnected from ourselves, others, and nature and/or spirituality. We feel helpless, worthless, and eventually hopeless. Yet, these are also the times when we are deeply invited to receive hope from others. For **hope has a reciprocal quality and is nurtured in supportive relationships.** Both the enduring and reciprocal qualities of hope form the foundation for building hopeful communities toward a better world.

"A leader is a dealer in hope."

Political hope

Politicians love hope. Throughout the ages, in every corner of the globe, and across the political spectrum, leaders have sought to present themselves as hope providers, capable of delivering empowerment, unification, and even salvation to the masses. **Kristen Wallin** and her colleagues set out to learn whether the hopes expressed by an American president in his first inaugural address might be related to job performance, public approval ratings, or policy initiatives.

Hope has long been viewed as a form of "political capital." Napoleon realized this fact ("a leader is a dealer in hope") as did John Gardner, former US Secretary of Health, Education, and Welfare ("The first and last task of a leader is to keep hope alive"). Philosopher Loren Goldman, drawing on Kant, argued that beliefs about what is possible in the future are essential for social action and without them "politics itself cannot exist."

Promises

We grounded our research in a model of hope encompassing mastery, attachment, survival, and spirituality (*see in this book: The Network of Hope*). These are the same hopes described in classic reflections on leadership. Aristotle exalted rulers who could release the potential of a citizenry. John Quincy Adams declared, "If your actions inspire others to dream more, learn more, do more and become more, you are a leader." Emerson agreed, "Our chief want is someone who will inspire us to be what we know we could be."

Leaders cultivate trust and openness. Marcus Aurelius wrote, "Never value as profitable to thyself that which shall compel thee to break thy promise… to act the hypocrite, to desire anything that needs walls and curtains."

Leaders inspire perseverance and resilience. Publius Syrus suggested, "Anyone can hold the helm when the sea is calm." Many are familiar with Churchill's 1940 speech to parliament: "We shall fight on the beaches, we shall fight on the landing grounds, we shall fight in the fields and in the streets, we shall fight in the hills; we shall never surrender."

Leaders inspire faith in transcendent truths. Confucius exalted rulers who followed "heaven's mandate." Lincoln appealed to "the better angels of our nature." On the eve of his assassination, Martin Luther King, Jr. reflected, "I just want to do God's will… I've seen the promised land… I may not get there with you… [but] we, as a people will get to the promised land."

Hope scores

We studied the last ten elected US presidents, from Eisenhower to Obama, yielding an even number of Democrats and Republicans.

To score each inaugural address, we divided the "hope domain" into 12 scoring categories (four hope dimensions multiplied by three themes). One point was given for each recorded theme.

Hope Scoring Categories

A. Mastery References
1. Successful planning; goal setting; productivity
2. Collaborations (past, present, or future)
3. Pursuit of transcendent collective or personal goals

B. Attachment References
1. Connection; trust; unity; equality
2. Continued presence and availability (of administration)
3. Two-way openness (administration and public)

C. Survival References

1. Protection or liberation
2. [American] resilience (past, present, or future)
3. Fear reduction (reassurance; dispelling specific fears)

D. Spiritual References

1. Spiritual inspiration (justification; blessings; empowerment)
2. Spiritual presence (past, present, or future)
3. Spiritual assurance (past, present, or future)

Two raters (liberal and conservative) agreed upon (reliably scored) the hopes in each speech. We derived hope rankings and profiles. For example, Obama scored highest in total hope whereas Eisenhower ranked fifth. The highest scores in mastery, attachment, survival, and spiritual hope were recorded, respectively, for Obama, Nixon, Kennedy, and G. W. Bush. Eisenhower's profile reflected low mastery, high attachment, moderate survival, and high spiritual hope. Obama's profile consisted of high mastery, moderate attachment, high survival, and moderate spirituality.

Profiles

We relied on historian's ratings of presidential effectiveness gathered by the *London Times* and CSPAN. Public Approval Ratings were collected from the *Wall Street Journal*. We reviewed summaries of presidential initiatives written by presidential biographers. What did we find?

High survival-oriented hope (promising protection and liberation, reducing fear, and stressing American resilience) is related to estimations of greatness. As for public approval, we found that *greater* survival-oriented hope is linked with a higher nadir (low point) while *lower* mastery-oriented hope is associated with a higher zenith (ceiling). From a hope perspective, great presidents have embodied saviors more than architects.

Finally, we were able to relate hope profiles to policy initiatives. To cite one example, Kennedy, who scored highest in survival hope ("liberating hope"), vowed to "pay any price, bear any burden, meet any hardship, support any friend, oppose any foe, in order to assure the survival and success of liberty." In the Bay of Pigs, the intent was the liberation of Cuba; in Vietnam, to curtail the perceived loss of liberty from spreading Communism. Hesitant at first, he committed to the Civil Rights movement.

The keys

→ **Beliefs about what is possible in the future are essential for social action, and without them politics itself cannot exist.**

→ **High survival-oriented hope is related to estimations of greatness. As for public approval, greater survival-oriented hope is linked with a higher nadir (low point) while lower mastery-oriented hope is associated with a higher zenith (ceiling).**

→ **From a hope perspective, great presidents have embodied saviors more than architects.**

Kristen Wallin received her BA in psychology from Keene State College (USA). She found herself captivated by positive psychology and delighted in the renewed interest in character and virtues. Kristen finds great pleasure and hope in setting aside time for reading to her children in the bustle of the local library, and in the quiet privacy of the evening. For her, hope is what emboldens humanity to conquer the most seemingly impossible obstacles. It is the fire that can release our inner potential. Coauthors of this article are **Anthony Scioli, Sarah Stevenson** and **Daniel Graham**.

HOPE XXL:
the future is now

"Making the world a more decent place has long been on the list of things I want to do," says **Chris van de Ven** (the Netherlands). Together with a few young people, he pondered what we could all do to make real improvements in the world. Naïve? **"Doing nothing is much worse,"** he says. In the meantime, **HOPE XXL** has grown into an inspiring initiative that has even managed to reach the United Nations.

HOPE XXL started as a youth initiative with the goal of having everyone rate his or her life an average of eight out of ten. In the Netherlands, that average was already just under eight, but in a country like Bangladesh, the feeling of well-being hovered around five. "In order to give people around the world a better outlook on the future, we need innovative and inspiring ideas. That is why HOPE XXL is developing a new vision of the future together with young people around the world, with input from the older generation," says Chris van de Ven. The organization calls its list of focal points the Liemers List, named after the region in which HOPE XXL was started by a group of ten young people. It is a "list of things that have to happen," with articles on sustainability, human

rights, international cooperation, and much more. In 2015, after six years of work, HOPE XXL offered the worldwide Liemers List to the United Nations.

Happiness

HOPE XXL looks for things that connect people and focuses on the similarities, not the differences—because in the end everyone wants

the same thing: a happy life. Martin Luther King Jr. already pointed out in 1967 that an international perspective is necessary to achieve this goal. For this reason, HOPE XXL seeks to give insight into the universal "basic package" of necessary preconditions for a human existence. All the articles in the Liemers List serve this goal. Particularly important is that the younger generation can point to the focus on a long-term perspective. At present, a great deal of policy is oriented toward the short term, and international organizations are largely occupied with putting out fires. We all want a high quality of life, but that requires a greater engagement from everyone in order to keep the long term in view. HOPE XXL has also asked many young people what kind of world they want to

pass on to their grandchildren. The answers to this question form the basis of the Liemers List.

Youth worldwide

HOPE XXL may have its roots in the Netherlands, but the organization has in the meantime talked with people around the world. In 2012, a European conference was organized for young people from twenty-five European countries to come together. Kofi Annan, former secretary-general of the United Nations, opened the conference. He said: "Dreams are necessary for a better world. Everything begins with a dream; without ideals we'd be nowhere." Later, at the Peace Palace in The Hague and other locations, separate conferences were organized with youth from Africa, Asia, and North and South America. In addition, eighty professors in the Netherlands have endorsed at least eighty percent of the Liemers List.

In January 2015, HOPE XXL organized the conference at which the worldwide Liemers List was finalized. The conference was organized in cooperation with the UN-mandated University for Peace (UPEACE) and took place at their campus in Costa Rica. Immediately afterward the delegation traveled to New York to present HOPE XXL to the United Nations: an important milestone!

Future

Now that the Liemers List has been finalized and presented to the United Nations, it is time to make it a reality. In the coming years, HOPE XXL will be working on the implementation of the list in the Netherlands and elsewhere, beginning in Liemers, where various parties will cooperate at the regional level to increase well-being. Nationally and internationally, HOPE XXL will remain active in order to contribute to a world in which everyone gives his or her life an eight or more out of ten.

More information: **www.hope-xxl.com**

"Hope serves to motivate us,
as individuals and as a collective society."

Learning to dream

"Hope is an important aspect of our lives. It provides us
with the basis to reflect, to articulate, and to dream," says
Prof. **Huy P. Phan**. "It enables us to contemplate, persist,
and anticipate." Abilities that are worth learning, for all of us.

Hope, from my point of view, is a positive dimension of life that enables all of us to dream,
feel inspired, and project long-term goals for accomplishment. It is positive because we
envisage the possible and impossible for fulfillment and accomplishment. How often do
all of us make this general saying to someone: "I hope Dad is going to meet us there, later"?
Hope, however, is more than just a word that we use to depict a casual saying in conversations
with others; rather, hope is a dynamic motivational system that allows us to aspire
and work hard toward our goals in life.

Confidence

So, what is hope? Hope, in its simplest terms, is defined as a *sense of determination for one
to reach a particular goal in life* (i.e. the agency of hope). Goals in life, for example,
may entail a desire for you to obtain a good education or to retire comfortably. Hope also
requires that we consider and *structure plans that would enable us to reach and fulfill
our goals* (i.e. the pathway of hope). These two theoretical tenets form the premise of hope

as a psychological construct. Hope has been researched over the years by a number of scholars, and evidence as such indicates that hope associates positively with self-esteem, perceptions of control, optimism, positive affectivity, and outcome expectancies.

Previous research has shown that hope, overall, features prominently in human agency, especially in relation to both academic and non-academic outcomes. As educators and parents, in particular, we need to recognize that hope may serve to enhance and nurture children's long-term well-being. Drawing from previous research evidence, for example, it can be said that **hope instills confidence, heightens self-efficacy beliefs, and motivates individuals to realize they have the potential to succeed in life.** One important element of well-being, of course, arising from hope, entails the ability for one to flourish and succeed in life.

Narratives

Apart from the theoretical framework of hope, and its corresponding empirical research, it can be said that throughout the course of time, both men and women have undertaken and experienced the two major characteristics of hope—that is, the agency and pathway of hope. We often hear of powerful men and women who started out as ordinary individuals. Some have very little to offer, other than their hopes and dreams. The then-senator Barack Obama wrote his book, titled *The Audacity of Hope*, to reflect and encourage the need for hope and optimism. **Hope, in the face of uncertainty and difficulty, is a powerful resolve that transforms individuals' pessimism into positive outlooks and optimism.** It is hope, as Obama describes, that propels immigrants and refugees to seek for the distant shores. It is hope, similarly, that enables a skinny kid with a funny name to one day become the President of the United States.

I believe it is important for educators, stakeholders, and policymakers to continue with the study of hope. One avenue of inquiry, which I strongly encourage, entails an *in situ* documentation of hope in situations of hardship. Narratives that document the trajectories of one's own agency and pathway may yield fruitful information for us to consider. Some of us have it quite hard in life. How does hope explain why some choose to travel to distant shores, despite potential obstacles, difficulties, and uncertainties? To what extent does hope assist those who contemplate escaping from war-torn situations, risking their lives in the process, in order to experience that sense of freedom? These questions, I contend, offer a basis for powerful reflections and narratives that may shed personal insights into the importance of hope.

Decision making

Another inquiry, which may have merits, entails the positive impact of hope on individuals' academic long-term well-being in educational settings. Hope, as we have researched and discovered, intertwines intricately with a number of achievement-related attributes, for example decision making, academic flourishing, active citizenship, and social relationship. In the contexts of schooling, for example, introducing students to the concept of hope may enhance their personal well-being (e.g. enjoy attending school) and assist them in their anticipation of accomplishments. Training students to consider their sense of hope (e.g. what is it that I want to strive for?) and, similarly, their reflective thoughts on this concept (e.g. I have never been ambitious in my schoolwork), in particular, may motivate and facilitate other school-related outcomes.

In summation, as a concept for advancing, hope is an important element that features centrally in human agency. Hope, in this sense, is more than just a catchphrase that reflects a particular moment in time. Hope serves to motivate us, as individuals and as a collective society. It enables us to dream, contemplate, persist, and to set in motion a set of goals for personal accomplishment. It is more unique than we realize, and hope, I believe, forms the basis of one's striving for personal satisfaction.

The keys

→ **Hope is a dynamic motivational system that allows us to aspire and work hard toward our goals in life.**

→ **Hope associates positively with self-esteem, perceptions of control, optimism, positive affectivity, and outcome expectancies.**

→ **Hope may serve to enhance and nurture children's long-term well-being and their ability to flourish and succeed in life.**

Huy P. Phan is an associate professor in educational psychology and teaches in the School of Education, University of New England (Australia). His research interests are related to cognition, motivation, and non-cognitive processes in sociocultural settings. His current research focuses on theoretical and empirical multilevel examinations of individuals' learning processes and personal well-being. "I hope that this chapter on hope, from an academic point of view, will provide the reader with the inspiration and desire to dream and hope for the future."

"The higher levels of religiosity and spirituality, the lower levels of depression."

Spirituality as source of hope

"Hope is what allows us to keep moving forward. It enables us to keep our chin high and believe situations *will* get better, goals *will* be reached, and life *will* improve. Hope comes from various sources, like family and friends. But one source that may be of particular importance is religion and the spiritual nature that accompanies religion," state **Emma Khale** and **Edward C. Chang**.

In a broad sense, religion has been defined as a "system of beliefs and practices relative to sacred things... beliefs and practices which unite into a single moral community... and all those who adhere to them" (Durkheim, 1915). This practice of religion and a sense of spirituality are important to many individuals as they provide a moral code to live by, a system of beliefs and values, and a close community rooted in common principles. Thus, the shared sense of vision found in religious and spiritual beliefs can give individuals a sense of purpose and a sense of hope—whether it is the existence of an after-life or the ability to become an all-knowing Buddha. It gives them goals to continually work toward that are vitally important to their life and happiness.

Faith

Importantly, goals are intrinsic to hopeful attitudes. According to the research of pioneer in hope psychology Rick Snyder, *hope* represents a multifaceted cognitive set composed of *hope agency*, the belief that one has the ability to reach a desired goal, and *hope pathway*, the belief that one can reach that goal successfully in a number of different ways. Given that often the most highly valued goals of religious and spiritual individuals involve their faith beliefs (i.e. achieving entry into heaven, converting non-believers to the faith), it would seem that this sense of purpose and goal pursuit could be a source of optimistic and hopeful attitudes for religious individuals. As a result, these attitudes that develop from religiosity and spirituality could contribute greatly to the positive adjustment and mental health often associated with religious and spiritual individuals (Abdel-Khalek & Lester, 2012).

Mental health

Our research has examined the relationship between religiosity, spirituality, hope agency, hope pathway, negative affectivity, and depressive symptoms. Based on what has been discussed, we predicted that hope agency and hope pathway would be important in determining the relationship of religiosity with negative affectivity and depressive symptoms. As hypothesized, our results showed that hope was responsible for determining the relationship between hope and negative adjustment, particularly that higher levels of religiosity are related to lower levels of both negative affectivity and depressive symptoms. Likewise, we found that hope was fully responsible for determining the relationship of spirituality with negative adjustment, particularly that higher levels of spirituality are related to lower levels of both negative affectivity and depressive symptoms. Taken together, our findings are the first to offer promising support for the idea that greater religiosity and spirituality are associated with increases in hope, which in turn may reduce negative psychological experiences, like negative affectivity and depressive symptoms.

Positive adjustment

Accordingly, our findings suggest that efforts to reduce negative mood experiences in adults may be more directly impacted by efforts to increase hope. Taken in conjunction with the previous literature on the importance of religion in fostering hope, our findings give support to continue examining the relationship between religion and hope to discover what components of religious practice may help generate hopeful attitudes in individuals. Religion is a cultural practice that has an incredible impact on society and the lives of individuals, and therefore it is a very important variable to understand in relation to mental health. And given that hope is a psychological construct shown to be an integral factor in positive adjustment, better understanding the relationship between religiosity, spirituality, and hope seems like a good place to start in an effort to learn more about the influence of religion on mental health. We are hopeful that future research will help us understand how religiosity, spirituality, and hope may work together to create happy, positive individuals that have an outlook of great potential and the promise of a better life ahead.

The keys

→ **The shared sense of vision found in religious and spiritual beliefs can give individuals a sense of purpose and a sense of hope.**

→ **Greater religiosity and spirituality are associated with increases in hope, which in turn may reduce negative psychological experiences, like negative affectivity and depressive symptoms.**

→ **Religion is a cultural practice that has an incredible impact on society and the lives of individuals, and therefore it is a very important variable to understand in relation to mental health.**

Edward C. Chang is Professor of Psychology and Social Work at the University of Michigan (USA). He is Associate Editor of the *American Psychologist* and Fellow of the Asian American Psychological Association. **Emma Kahle** focuses on her doctoral studies in social welfare at the University of Michigan (USA). She hopes to continue researching areas related to psychological and physical health and is looking forward to better understanding the role of hope in her life and others. Coauthors are **Hannah McCabe, Paige Porter** and **Elizabeth Yu**.

"Hope gives us purpose. It keeps us alive."

Hope and faith

"Hope enlivens our present and designs our future and thus in turn is the great life force. It should not be lost or destroyed. But it sometimes gets annihilated due to circumstances that seem beyond our control," says Dr. **Anita Sharma**. She focuses on the relationship between hope and faith.

Hope keeps the last breath intact even if one is lying on his deathbed. This happened in our family when my father was taken seriously ill and was diagnosed with myocardial infarction. He was just surviving on one artery and the others (including the major ones) were near completely blocked. He was advised to have immediate surgery otherwise it could have been fatal. Keeping all hopes high we did as was advised. My father was weak and old but his hopes were also strong. And staring hard at the face of death, he came out of the operation theater victoriously.

Driving force

Hope holds prime importance in our lives. A life devoid of hope is without any direction, stability, and peace. **The ugliest thing about hopelessness is that it leads to an addictive cycle of negative feelings**, which leads one to indulge in wrong doings. It ultimately creates a perpetual lifestyle of guilt and shame.

Hope is something that we all must inculcate within ourselves. More importantly, we should know what it means and how it affects us and our ability to create and live the life of our dreams. All of us might have seen huge mountains being displaced to carve roads, cancer patients in their last stage convalescing, poor people getting affluent, and many such evidences are there to prove that hope is the driving force of life.

Mature decision

Faith is a term that complements hope. In my honest opinion, we should never have blind faith while following something simply because someone else tells us to or simply because something or someone believes it's best for us. Instead, we must learn to gather as much information as possible about what we are to have faith in. Then, and only then, are we able to place faith in something. **Faith is placing trust in that which we cannot see.** It does not mean that we must blindly trust, and we never should. Because, if faith is lacking, hope will not be sustained. Faith is simply taking the time to gather the information and start moving forward and paying attention to the results, then making a mature, educated decision based on the information gathered.

In order to have faith and start looking for a path to follow we must first have hope. Hope is a driving force that empowers us to understand that things can be better and that things will be better. Hope gives us purpose. It keeps us alive. It drives us, inspires us, and moves us to do and have more.

Aspiration

The reason so many people climb the ladder of success and end up killing themselves through the use of drugs and alcohol is simple. They end up with everything we are told to have and be, and yet they feel lost and empty. They lose their hope for something bigger, better, more valuable and important. One should aspire big but should at the same time have contentment coupled with hope. Then and then only can one achieve big and live peacefully.

One must have hope and faith in life and develop a personal relationship with these. These powerful words move everyone forward. They lift all and give them the drive to do more, be more, and have more for themselves. Therefore it would not be an exaggeration to say that by developing hope and faith within oneself, one can have faith in one's ability to improve one's life, and the hope for doing something better.

The keys

→ **We should all know what hope means and how it affects us and our ability to create and live the life of our dreams.**

→ **If faith is lacking, hope will not be sustained.**

→ **One should aspire big but should at the same time have contentment coupled with hope.**

Anita Sharma, PhD, is Assistant Professor of Psychology at Himachal Pradesh University, Shimla (India), and Assistant Director, UGC (ASC). She is the author of the book *Personality and Social Norms*. She has presented 25 papers in international and national conferences and has over 80 papers to her credit published in international and national journals. Anita likes reading books and gardening. She has a flair for teaching and is also a social worker helping the elderly by giving them counseling.

"People often completely adapt to many hopeless situations."

The "focusing illusion"

When someone we love dies, it is easy to believe that our sadness will never end no matter how long it takes. Prof. Nick Powdthavee investigates the impact of so-called hopeless situations and unveils the power of the "focusing illusion."

Perhaps the single most important piece of knowledge about human happiness can be summed up in just a few words, and that is "Nothing in life is quite as important as you think it is while you are thinking about it." The maxim, which was first stated by psychologists Daniel Kahneman and David Schkade in 1998, describes how we tend to over-exaggerate how much something—anything—matters to our happiness when we are thinking about it.

So, for example, students in California and the Midwest in America were asked the following question in one of the studies by Kahneman and Schkade: "Who do you think are happier with their life? People in California, or people in the Midwest of America?" Both groups gave an unequivocal answer that people in California were significantly happier with life than those living in the Midwest. However, when these same groups of individuals were asked to rate on a scale how satisfied they were with their own life, the researchers found that students in California were actually no happier with their lives than students in the Midwest. And the researchers' reason for their paradoxical findings? California and the Midwest differ mostly in terms of their weather, which is salient when we are trying to compare both places at the same time. However, weather between two places becomes a lot less salient to us when we are prompted to think about how happy we are with our lives overall. Here, other things—like income, marriage, employment, and friendships— matter a lot more.

Recover

You'll be forgiven for wondering, "What's this got to do with the story of hope?" Well, this particular cognitive bias, known to psychologists as the "focusing illusion," explains why people often completely adapt to many hopeless situations even when, at the exact point when that hopelessness feeling begins, many of us may feel that we will never be able to recover from it. Bereavement is one example of this. When someone we love dies, it is easy to believe that our sadness will never end no matter how long it takes. All we could probably think about in those first few months of grief is how we will never be able to think about anything else but that life-shattering event, that life can never be the same for us again.

However, many recent longitudinal studies—which are studies that followed the same individuals over a long period of time—have shown that people only took an average of two years to completely adapt to the death of loved ones. In other words, **their life satisfaction bounces back to the level they were before** becoming, say, a widow or a widower. People even adapt almost completely to having become seriously disabled in only just a few years.

So my message is this: Even when it might seem to us that all hope is gone, that we may not be able to get out of such hopeless situations, time will eventually heal almost all wounds. Whether you like it or not, your attention will soon shift from almost all adverse life events to other things that life has to offer. Humans are incredibly more resilient than we'd like to give ourselves credit for.

The keys

→ **We tend to over-exaggerate how much something—anything—matters to our happiness when we are thinking about it.**

→ **The "focusing illusion" explains why people often completely adapt to many hopeless situations.**

→ **Time will eventually heal almost all wounds. Humans are incredibly more resilient than we'd like to give ourselves credit for.**

Nick Powdthavee is a Research Professor in the field of Economics of Happiness. He holds a joint position as a Professorial Research Fellow at the University of Melbourne (Australia) and a Principal Research Fellow at the London School of Economics (United Kingdom). He obtained his PhD in Economics from the University of Warwick in 2006 and has held positions at the University of London, University of York, and Nanyang Technological University in Singapore. He is the author of the popular economics book *The Happiness Equation: The Surprising Economics of Our Most Valuable Asset*.

"To have a friend, you have to be a friend."

Hope and friendship

"The best way to find yourself is to lose yourself in the service of others." This quote of Mahatma Gandhi has inspired Dr. Nathaniel Lambert to investigate the role of friendship in the process of hope: "Focusing on others lightens your burdens and cultivates friendships."

I remember feeling so awkward in high school. Here I was: short, fat, with braces and a back brace, and it was often easy to feel like nobody understood me or what I was going through. I knew how difficult it was to be different, and it occurred to me that other people were likely going through the same thing I was. I knew how much it meant to me when people would take the trouble to learn my name or ask me how I was doing. When people shared some level of care or concern for me, it made a world of difference. I decided to be that person for others and proceeded to learn the names and the situations of others who were different or who had felt excluded for some reason. I think it made a world of difference to them, and it sure helped me to make a lot of friends, which made me feel even better about myself.

Focus on others

As I began doing this, I no longer felt misunderstood by others. As I sought to get to know others and help them to feel better about their own problems, I discovered that they struggled with many of the same feelings I did. No longer did my own problems seem

to be as large or as daunting. In fact, I often found that focusing on helping others seemed to make many of my challenges disappear from my awareness altogether.

Dale Carnegie, author of *How to Win Friends and Influence People,* suggested that people *love* to talk about themselves more than anything. If you can direct the conversation to focus on the person with whom you are talking, you give them a chance to talk about their favorite subject and they will love you for it. Carnegie said: "You can make more friends in two months by becoming interested in other people than you can in two years by trying to get other people interested in you." Let others talk about themselves and listen. **A good listener is a rare thing, indeed, so when someone finds a listener in you, it will be greatly appreciated.** As you give the gift of a listening ear, not only will you do a great service to someone else, but doing so shifts your focus from your own troubles to the needs of others. Hearing about the challenges of others makes your own problems seem less intense.

Better friends

One of the greatest benefits you will reap as you focus on others is friendship. As the old saying goes, "To have a friend, you have to be a friend." By showing genuine concern and offering a listening ear to those around you, you are being a friend, thus allowing you to build friendships. Those who make the decision to reach out and help those with fewer friends can become very well liked by those they reach out to.

"The best antidote I know for worry is work. The best cure for weariness is the challenge of helping someone who is even more tired. One of the great ironies of life is this: **He or she who serves, almost always benefits more than he or she who is served**" (Gordon B. Hinckley).

One of the best ways to alleviate any challenges you are having is to focus on helping others with the challenges they are facing. Giving the gift of a listening ear will be a huge benefit for them. Focusing on others helps lighten your burden while developing strong friendships. The best way to gain hope and to deal with your problems is to help others with theirs.

The keys

→ **Shift the focus away from yourself; give the gift of listening.**
→ **Focusing on others lightens your burdens and cultivates friendships.**
→ **The best way to gain hope and to deal with your problems is to help others with theirs.**

Nathaniel Mark Lambert, PhD, is a psychologist, professor, author, and public speaker (United States). He is the author of over 60 research articles and book chapters on the topic of thriving in life and served as an editor of *The Journal of Positive Psychology*. He has presented his research across the world and is the founder of an online happiness analysis and consulting company. Nathaniel loves hiking and playing sports. When does he feel hopeful about life? "When I am helping others around me. Another huge source of hope for me is gratitude. When you approach life with an abundant mentality you are imbued with hope."

*"The goal achievement is celebrated
with a contagious dance called 'We Did It.'"*

Promoting hope in youth

"When thinking about children and hope, the memories registered in Anne Frank's diary come to mind. Decades ago, hope was associated with the belief that something good is going to happen," say Dr. **Manuel Pulido Martos** and Dr. **Jonatan R. Ruiz**. They are looking for some concrete ways to promote hope in young children and adolescents.

Every single human behavior has a concrete goal. Therefore, when assessing levels of hope it is important to know the extent to which we believe that we are able to find successful ways to achieve these goals—and if we are motivated enough to start up the necessary actions to reach these goals.

Children's Hope Scale

This information is collected and used in tools such as the Children's Hope Scale. It includes six questions related to the hopes and goals of children and adolescents, who answer how they identify with the statements. There are statements related to the energy or motivation they use to achieve the goal(agency thinking), such as "I think I am doing pretty well"; and statements related to their capacity to find ways to reach the goal (pathways thinking), such as "When I have a problem, I can come up with lots of ways to solve it." Youth with high levels of hope according to the Children's Hope Scale are psychologically stronger. Several studies show that hope is associated with higher levels of well-being and a higher frequency of healthy behaviors. Regarding performance in academic contexts, children with high levels of hope seem to have higher academic performance.

The development of tools to assess hope in children and adolescents is only a first step in determining the chances of success, present and future, we have as a society. Achieving goals is the basis of that success. However, how does hope help us achieve our goals and, more importantly, how can we make children and adolescents more hopeful? As mentioned before, the explanation rests on the energy we exert to the achievement of our goals or how motivated we are to achieve them and, also, to the ability we have to establish ways that lead us to our objectives. Programs to promote hope in educational contexts often include stories or examples as a way to identify our goals, the possible

obstacles, and the pathways to reach our goals. The protagonists of these stories are often children with very high levels of hope.

Dora and Boots

As parents, how can we use the lessons learned from the implementation of programs to promote hope in the classroom? How do we take home the research about hope? Or, how can we include hope in the activities that our children and young people do in their free time?

Our proposal for youth is to use *modeling*, a key process of social learning. Modeling allows children to observe and imitate the actions of others—obviously, other hopeful children. Time spent watching television can be used to enhance hope. *Dora the Explorer* is a cartoon series based on the adventures of a Latina girl named Dora and her friends. Each episode revolves around the achievement of a concrete goal. Dora and her best friend, a monkey named Boots, are always highly motivated to achieve a certain goal and try to spread their agency to the audience. Additionally, Map, Dora's travel companion, is responsible for setting the path (pathways) to follow to reach the goal. Despite the obstacles and problems that arise, many of them prompted by Swiper the Fox, Dora and Boots always find alternative routes and ways to solve the problems that lead them to reach their ultimate goal. The goal achievement is celebrated with a contagious dance called "We Did It." We think that, for parents, seeing this series with their children is an opportunity to discuss with them each component of hope and thus to help them see their world in a positive and hopeful vision.

Soccer

For teens and older children, we propose an "active" way to promote hope: practicing a sport. Let's talk about the most practiced sport in the world: soccer. In this sport, along with having the players serve as "models," hope plays a key role in achieving goals. Practicing soccer outside of a formal competition environment, such as in leisure time, constantly raises small goals such as touching the ball a number of times, participating in team play, and ultimately scoring the goal. The constant feedback the child receives about achieving that goal or not makes them constantly re-orient the energy to achieve their goal. Furthermore, this situation promotes the exploration of new ways to achieve more and better goals, i.e. touching the ball more times or scoring more goals.

If we decide to enroll our children in a sports club or something similar, but in a competitive environment, the educator—such as the coach of the team—may promote the hope of children and adolescents in many ways. Under these circumstances, a goal might be to play some minutes in the team, to play as a starter, to play the entire game, to touch the ball as many times as possible, to score goals, or to increase the number of defenses (as if playing as a goalkeeper). The coach must be able to enhance their hopes, encourage players, contribute to the increase of motivation (agency), and teach different game strategies to achieve the goal (pathways). In this sense, professional soccer players, idols for many children, give lessons of hope when they persist in their attempts and show motivation even if they do not achieve their goals (or do not score a goal). They keep looking for ways to accomplish their goals.

The keys

→ **Youth with high levels of hope are psychologically stronger, have higher levels of well-being, a higher frequency of healthy behaviors, and higher academic performance.**

→ **Programs to promote hope in educational contexts often include stories or examples as a way to identify goals, the possible obstacles, and pathways (agency) to achieve those goals.**

→ **Hope is best promoted by modeling, a key process of social learning. Some TV programs or sport activities can inspire us.**

Manuel Pulido Martos, PhD, is a Lecturer in Social Psychology in the University of Jaen (Spain). His research is focused on the study of positive psychology and its application to organizations as well as the interaction between positive psychology and physical activity. Together with Dr. Ruiz, he is coauthor of the Spanish adaptation of the Children's Hope Scale. What are his hobbies, vocations, and sources of hope? "My two little children, Marcos and Amalia. I see them playing, laughing, and enjoying, and this makes me believe in this society's future. They reinforce my hope."

Jonatan R. Ruiz, PhD, is a Ramon y Cajal Research Fellow at the School of Sport Sciences at the University of Granada (Spain). He has a PhD in Exercise Physiology from the University of Granada, and a second PhD in Medical Sciences from the Karolinska Institutet (Sweden). His research combines physical activity epidemiology with clinical physiology. Running is part of his life and his source of energy. "Running keeps my hope alive. My daughter is the star that empowers my hope of being a better person and the best father ever."

"Hopeful teachers believe in their students."

Hopeful teachers

"Can you imagine a better place for inspiring young individuals than a classroom?" asks **Polona Gradišek**. "Teachers have a powerful influence on their students' development, so I wanted to investigate which characteristics of teachers contribute most to students' well-being. Based on my research, I observed that one of them is hope."

During my PhD studies, I examined the relationship between teachers and students in the view of teachers' personalities. People sometimes forget that teachers not only impact the learning of their students, but they also influence the level of students' satisfaction, their personal and social development, and also their happiness. Teachers' competency for teaching is important, but so is their personality, as they represent role models for their students. Can you believe that some students learn because of their teachers? They recognize their teachers' commitment to teaching and their sincere wish to help them optimize the learning process and to become happy individuals of good character. This is why positive relationships between teachers and students matter so much. And **teachers' hope plays an important role in this relationship.** Some researchers even argue that teachers' hope stems from positive relationships with their students.

Strengths

In positive psychology, character strengths represent positive personality traits that are morally valued and are supposed to be universal in both place and time. The VIA classification of character strengths, introduced by Christopher Peterson and Martin Seligman in 2004, consists of 24 strengths such as kindness, love, creativity, humor, and, of course, hope. Strengths are grouped under six broader virtues (wisdom and knowledge, courage, humanity, justice, temperance, and transcendence). All character strengths contribute to the good life, but the strength of hope is the one that contributes most to feelings of satisfaction with one's life—in the general population and, as I have shown in my research, in the population of teachers as well.

Interaction

Why do we want to have hopeful teachers? An important aspect of hope is that it can be learned and developed. Following this premise, teachers play a substantial role in fostering hope in children. However, it is apparent that children learn from example, so they can only develop hope from interaction with hopeful teachers. According to previous research findings, high-hope teachers are self-confident, optimistic, less depressed, report higher levels of well-being, and experience more positive and less negative emotions in comparison to low-hope teachers. They set challenging goals for themselves and find different alternative ways to achieve them. They use good problem-solving strategies and are effective at work. As such, **they represent positive role models for students.** In my research, teachers who expressed higher levels of hope were more satisfied with their lives and work. They reported that teaching was their calling, meaning that they valued teaching strongly, found a sense of meaning in their work, and felt that they contributed importantly to the society and made positive changes in their students' lives. Even students perceived teachers with higher levels of hope more positively: students were more satisfied with such teachers and they assessed their teaching as effective and positive. Furthermore, there was also a link between the hope of teachers and student academic achievement.

Trust

Why do students perceive hopeful teachers so positively and why is the hope of teachers even related to their students' academic achievement? I speculate that this is because hopeful teachers believe in their students. They trust that students will learn and try their best to engage actively in learning activities. Such **positive expectations and trust of teachers definitely motivate students.** Besides, hopeful teachers are optimistic about the future, set challenging goals, and try to achieve them in alternative ways. They represent important role models to their students, so if they teach students all this, students are likely to develop into hopeful and optimistic adults, capable of mastering the processes of goal-setting and problem solving as well as persevering in trying to reach their goals. Students of hopeful teachers will thus develop positive expectations about their future and learn how to find suitable pathways to make them real.

The keys

→ **For teachers and students, the strength of hope is the one that contributes most to the feelings of satisfaction with one's life.**

→ **Children learn from example, so they can only develop hope from interaction with hopeful teachers.**

→ **Hopeful teachers believe in their students and are more satisfied with their own lives and work. Their students feel better and have better results.**

Polona Gradišek, PhD, works as a teacher of future teachers at the Faculty of Education, University of Ljubljana (Slovenia), where she puts the emphasis on the importance of positive teacher-student relationships. She is researching positive and educational psychology and is specifically interested in teachers' character strengths and well-being. Her own strengths? "Trying to be kind, optimistic, zestful and curious."

*"Turn your face to the sun
and the shadows fall behind you."*

Hope in nature

A walk in the park might make us feel good, but is it also connected to our level of hope? **Holli-Anne Pasmore** and **Andrew J. Howell** tested this possibility among hundreds of participants in Canada. Under the seemingly "dead" snows of winter, hope is alive.

Fostering strength from the earth, spring always comes, bringing with it new life—fresh, green, and vital. Full of color. Full of hope. The struggle for existence, the flourishing of life even in harsh conditions, and the cycle of life–death–life-born-anew are salient features of the natural environment that provide us with symbols of transcendent immortality and hope which we can identity with and find solace in. **Feeling connected with, and appreciating, the natural world is an important source of hope.** Indeed, trees, flowers, and other forms of vegetation are often planted or shared by people as celebrations and symbols of hope at times of both joy and sorrow.

Blossoms

Numerous writers and scholars have espoused a crucial role for experiences in nature in the cultivation of hope. In an allegorical story by Jean Giono, a despondent World War I veteran regains hope in a forest rejuvenated by a shepherd who planted acorn trees in a barren Provencal valley. Similarly, Robert Jay Lifton described how, seven months subsequent to the bombing of Hiroshima, it was the appearance and flowering of the March cherry blossoms that evoked a strong sense of hope among Japanese people.

Beyond these insights, there are additional, theoretical reasons for expecting an association between affiliating with nature and experiencing hope. Positive psychologists Chris Peterson and Martin Seligman referred to hope and appreciation of beauty (including the beauty of the natural world) as transcendent strengths of character. Both hope and appreciation of nature foster feelings of connectedness with things beyond our current or immediate experience, to future possibilities and to the greater living world around us. Experiences in nature give rise to increased hope.

Our research supports these ideas of a connection between nature and hope. We found that **the more connected to nature people feel, the more hopeful they feel.** We also found that people who took photos of nearby nature were more likely to report feeling hopeful and rejuvenated, while people who took photos of nearby human-built objects and settings were more likely to report feeling tired and stressed.

Boost of hope

His Holiness the Dalai Lama once said "the very purpose of life is happiness, which is sustained by hope." Experiences in nature appear to not only cause an increase in hope directly, they may also cause an increase in hope by boosting our emotions and our sense of meaning in life. Feeling good and feeling that there is meaning or purpose in our lives are attributes that C. R. (Rick) Snyder identified as being central to the hope process. In studies involving a total of over 1,000 participants, we have consistently found that those who report a higher sense of connectedness to nature also report a higher sense of meaning in life. Our research has also demonstrated that people can boost their overall positive emotions, feelings of elevation, and sense of meaning merely by incorporating into their daily routines simple nature activities such as reading or eating in one's backyard, or walking in a neighborhood park. **Nature affects hope directly and indirectly.** Indeed, there is now a solid platform of evidence supporting associations between positive emotions and affiliating with nature, and between the transcendent strengths of character of meaning, elevation, hope, and appreciation of nature.

Fresh rain

We encourage readers to spend more time in nature on an ongoing, daily basis by enjoying close-to-home nature settings such as backyards and neighborhood parks and, when possible, to venture out to more remote nature settings to engage in activities such as wilderness camping, canoeing, or hiking. **Nature involvement has the potential to cultivate a renewed sense of life, vitality, and hope in each of us.** You can enhance the beneficial effects of nature involvement by approaching your nature activities in a highly mindful fashion. Truly be in the present moment—feel the warmth of the sun on your back, smell the freshness of fresh rain, look for the tiniest of flowers blooming in unusual places, listen to the birds chirping their mellifluous songs. And when you return home, savor your experiences in nature by revisiting your memories and photographs or recounting your outing with others.

A natural world of wonder, joy, and meaning is waiting to share its message of hope with you. For as the Maori proverb says, "Turn your face to the sun and the shadows fall behind you."

The keys

→ **There is an important connection between affiliating with nature and feeling hopeful.**

→ **Nature involvement can increase your levels of hope by boosting your positive emotions and sense of meaning in life.**

→ **Spend time in nearby nature on an ongoing, daily basis through simple activities such as reading in your backyard or walking in a neighborhood park.**

Holli-Anne Passmore is pursuing her PhD in Psychological Science at the University of British Columbia in Canada. **Andrew J. Howell**, PhD is an associate professor of psychology at MacEwan University in Alberta, Canada. Holli-Anne and Andrew have collaborated on many studies concerning nature affiliation and various aspects of well-being. They are immersed in positive psychology and highly value their time in nature.

Mobile schools for street children

Under the motto "If a child cannot come to school, we will bring the school to the child," Arnoud Raskin developed a mobile school for street children. **This moving blackboard with hundreds of educational games makes it possible for street workers to organize educational activities. Presently there are 36 mobile schools in 21 countries, spread across Latin America, Asia, Africa, and Europe. They are catalysts of hope.**

showers and freezing temperatures present no problem. Moreover it is resistant to theft: all materials are attached to the board and cannot be removed. One "school" offers more than 300 educational games, which makes it possible to offer street children of all ages a wide-ranging basic education: from literacy, mathematics, creative therapy, and health education to drugs and AIDS prevention. Fully extended, the mobile school cart is six meters long.

Mobile School focuses on two target groups: street children and the street workers who engage with them in informal educational activities. The mobile school is a cart on wheels, with extendable blackboards. Arnoud Raskin was educated as a designer but he wanted to use his skills for people who will seldom get the benefits of good design. Due to its unique design, the mobile school can be used on sidewalks and slums. It is fully weather resistant: tropical

The mobile schools are produced in a secondary school in Belgium. For the young students, it is an excellent cross-border project that involves aspects of social global education, technical education, and entrepreneurship. They are very proud of their work.

Empowerment

Mobile School offers support and solutions in setting up sustainable processes for people who have sometimes lost all hope.

Arnoud Raskin: "A street child is often labeled 'a homeless child, suffering from hunger and forced to sleep in a cardboard box on the sidewalk.' Many misconceptions about the problems of street children are due to oversimplification. These are fed by lack of insight into the psychological-educational profile of a street child. Traditional outreach work focuses on the problems of the child. We look for the positive in a child: What are you good at and what are you proud of? We aim to allow the child to reflect and communicate more openly about his or her situation. By doing this consciously, the child can more easily form a better self-image and gain a better understanding of the environment, possibilities, and his or her identity. Street children are most of the time very good entrepreneurs and have an incredible hopeful attitude that makes them survive."

Because the school is not a building, it asks for different attitudes from the workers using the materials to reach and teach the children.

Arnoud Raskin: "We make it possible for children to trust their own unique skills, and we allow them to exert influence on their entire process of growth. In

Streetwize

"Those with money study at the university. Those who are smart learn from the street." This is Mobile School's conclusion after 16 years of working in the world's slums. They may not be able to read or to write, but street children do use their talents. They are flexible, creative, and enterprising. The highly innovative program Streetwize translates these street skills into unorthodox training programs for companies. The result? Greater effectiveness and flexibility for companies in an economy that is changing more quickly than the streets of a big city. All profits are re-invested in the street children.

More information: **www.streetwize.be**

this way, the child becomes an active player in his of her own life. We support the kids in their development into potential change-makers. They are empowered to build a future for themselves and society. Our methods are inspired by the kids themselves: their skills of building and acting based on hope, opportunities, and faith in advancement."

More information: **www.mobileschool.org**

"The path less traveled by makes all the difference."

How hope develops global leaders

"There are two types of goals that are relevant to global leaders and explain why hope is so important when it comes to leading in a multicultural environment: operational goals and leader development goals," says Prof. **Rachel Clapp-Smith**, whose research focuses on global leadership development in companies.

The first type, operational goals, deals with the outcomes that the company strives to achieve. For global leaders, this goal needs to be packaged and communicated in a way that is motivating and inspiring for individuals with a wide range of cultural values. Leaders energize our sense of hope by providing a compelling vision. What makes us feel inspired by a vision is the appeal it makes to our deeply held values and whether it sparks an emotional commitment to the goal. Deeply held values are influenced by cultural upbringing, and this is where I see one of the largest challenges for global leaders. My research, work experiences, interactions with global leaders, and observations of students have uncovered time and time again that global leaders struggle to understand the cultural contingencies of inspiring culturally diverse followers.

Followers

But there is hope for global leaders. Several research studies have provided evidence that hope, defined as the will to pursue goals and the pathways to reach them, is experienced in different cultures around the world and that it predicts performance in a number of different samples. In other words, if a leader needs to inspire goal commitment among outsourcing employees in India, we know that hope operates similarly in India as in other cultures. The challenge for leaders, therefore, is not whether a diverse group of followers are capable of experiencing hope, it is truly a question of how to inspire hope, or the will to achieve a goal, when values are so diverse and leaders who have high hope use alternative messages to gain commitment for one goal.

Inspiring hope through a compelling vision is not the only challenge for global leaders. Because hope also deals with the pathways to goal attainment, the second struggle global leaders have is accepting that followers may see very different pathways than the leader. The pathways of hope are often overlooked, but it is equally as important as the willpower of hope. Global leaders with high hope recognize that the joy of leading a culturally diverse group is learning multiple unique pathways. This, then, opens leaders to recognize that leading a group does not mean they must have all the answers or illuminate all the pathways. They simply must create the conditions for followers to pursue the pathways that allow them to thrive.

Unfamiliar paths

The second type of goal that is relevant to global leadership deals with the leader's personal development. The "path" less traveled by makes all the difference. I hope the poet Robert Frost will forgive me for adjusting his words. If we have learned anything about hope, it is that while goals are important, pathways to achieving goals are equally important. Global leadership development has many paths, all of which are exciting and new, but potential leaders need to have the will to try the new, explore the unfamiliar, or to take the path less traveled by.

As an example, in one of my studies, students who have traveled abroad reported that leaving the familiar behind and embarking on unfamiliar paths influenced their development as leaders more substantially than if they had stayed home or embarked on the unfamiliar path with the comfort of a familiar companion. Stepping outside one's comfort zone allows leaders to reflect on who they truly are and to become more aware of how

they lead, including how their own cultural upbringing influences their leadership style. Given this, if hope is about seeing multiple paths but leadership development is about pursuing the least familiar path, how can one truly attain the important goals that give him or her hope in the first place?

Balance

One might expect experience to give individuals a series of tried and true pathways that are generally effective. However, the most effective leaders will continue to try new paths to expand their alternative avenues to successfully reaching goals. The key differentiator, therefore, hangs in the balance of which goals to pursue. Every organization has operational goals, but if I am hopeful that I can leave my mark on this world in some positive and meaningful way, then an absolute must is that I also strive to build my leadership capacity. When we accept the amazing returns on pursuing goals that develop leadership styles and choosing the path least traveled by, I am hopeful that we will see more global leaders emerge who can inspire diverse followers to achieve amazing goals.

The keys

→ **Leaders energize our sense of hope by providing a compelling vision.**
→ **Global leaders with high hope recognize that the joy of leading a culturally diverse group is learning multiple unique pathways.**
→ **The most effective leaders will continue to try new paths to expand their alternative avenues to successfully reaching goals.**

Rachel Clapp-Smith, PhD, is an Assistant Professor of Leadership in the College of Business and codirector of the Leadership Center at Purdue University Calumet (USA). Her research focuses on global leadership development, global mindset, and cultural self-awareness. She also serves as a coordinator of the Network of Leadership Scholars. Rachel is a native of New Hampshire, USA, but has lived and worked in Germany and the Netherlands. Her most inspiring embodiment of hope is watching her children learn empathy, kindness, and love. "There is something liberating from the stresses of an adult's life to see the fascination and joy of simply being. My 7- and 5-year-olds seem to remind me when I've taken myself too seriously. In reality, the true impact of my leadership is not what I accomplish at work or in my community, but the values I demonstrate to my children."

"Even more hopeless people
can increase their starting level of hope."

Personality of hope

Some people seem to be much more hopeful in life than others, regardless of what happens to them. Prof. **Peter Halama** studies the role of our personality traits related to hope. Some traits explain a broad range of our behavior. But it's good to know that they don't determine our whole behavior. They only set up the starting point of individual development and growth.

My research interest in hope arose from my fascination with this human phenomenon. Human ability to hope simply means that a person is able to anticipate future positive outcomes of his or her activity and be motivated by this anticipation to carry out an action. This ability becomes captivating in the situation when a person maintains his or her hope despite the fact that circumstances do not suggest a high probability of success and this hope leads to success. In this case, **hope can be a strong tool to overcome difficulties of life and reach the desired state.** I believe that hope of the individual persons is a driving force of progress at different levels of human functioning ranging from ordinary personal life up to cultural and societal development.

Inherited

However, my fascination for hope arises not only from the strength that hope gives to a person to deal with life's obstacles, but also from the differences in individual ability to hope. On the one hand, there are people who are able to develop and maintain hope in very difficult situations and are even able to inspire other people with their hope. On the other hand, some people have difficulties in hoping in the situation when only small obstacles appear and they do not even start an activity aimed at goal fulfillment, because they do not believe that their action will lead to the goal.

The question is where these differences come from and what the reasons are that lead to them. Until now, psychological research has been focusing on different factors of hope, especially on the role of learning and life experiences which can encourage or discourage hope in individual persons. However, psychology research shows that many human phenomena at the level of beliefs and behavior are extensively influenced not only by learned patterns but also by stable psychological characteristics such as temperament and personality traits, which are, to a great extent, inherited and biologically determined.

Characteristics

In my research, I focused on the personality sources of individual differences in hope. For the purpose of operationalization, I adopted the definition of hope by C. Snyder, which is based on the cognitive understanding of hope, that says hope is perceived capabilities to produce routes to desired goals along with perceived motivation to use these routes. From the existing approaches to personality traits, I chose the big-five personality theory, which defines five general and culturally consistent personality traits: neuroticism, extraversion, openness to experience, agreeableness, and conscientiousness. These traits explain a broad range of human behavior and are considered relatively stable and constant, some of them with a substantial hereditary element. As several research studies of mine suggest, individual levels of hope are substantially and consistently related to three of these traits: neuroticism, extraversion, and conscientiousness.

1. Neuroticism shows a negative relationship with hope. People with high levels of neuroticism showed lower levels of hope and vice-versa. Neuroticism is characterized as a tendency to experience negative emotion in higher measure as anxiety or unhappiness in life situations. These negative emotions are a reason for lower hope, because they are blocking positive thinking related to expectations of success.

2. On the other hand, extraversion is in a positive relationship with hope. This trait is characterized by a higher tendency to experience positive emotions including those related to goal-oriented behavior. Extraverted people feel more energy and are more enthusiastic, sociable, and action-oriented. These characteristics help enhance hope because they contribute to motivation for goal fulfillment and perception of a goal as available.

3. Conscientiousness is also positively related to hope. This trait involves the ability to organize and plan individual behavior as well as the ability to control and regulate actions toward a goal, which leads to experience of competence and skillfulness. This experience helps to enhance hope because it builds up beliefs in future success.

Despite the fact that these traits have a partial hereditary origin, it does not mean that individual levels of hope are constant and unchangeable. It is very helpful to know all sources of hope include personality, but it is good to know that personality traits do not determine all our behavior but only set up the starting point of individual development and growth. Even people with the configuration of traits not supporting hope can increase their starting level of hope through engagement in meaningful goals and activities, positive life experiences, feedback from success, learning ways to reach the goal, etc.

The keys

→ **There are individual differences among people in their ability to hope for the fulfillment of personal goals.**

→ **Hope is higher in people with low levels of neuroticism and high levels of extraversion and conscientiousness.**

→ **Although personality traits have partial hereditary origins, levels of personal hope are not constant and unchangeable as every person can increase his or her starting level of hope, especially through successful engagement in meaningful goals.**

Peter Halama is a research psychologist at the Institute of Experimental Psychology, Slovak Academy of Sciences in Bratislava (Slovakia). He is also associate professor at Trnava University, Slovakia, where he lectures on psychology of personality. His research and publications focus mainly on the question of how personality is related to optimal human functioning with special focus on the specific human phenomena as hope, meaning in life, religiosity, etc. Being aware of his personality limits; he puts his personal hope in two things: his belief that the world is not random but rather it has higher meaning that is worth looking for and fulfilling, and his continuing experience that some people involve him in close, deep, and mutually satisfying relationships.

"Hope comes through meaningful connections with others."

Opening horizons

"Hope certainly exists in a positive relationship between the present and the future. But there is more," says Prof. Pamela R. McCarroll. She describes a new definition of hope that offers a specific lens to interpret the presence of hope as it exists in life: the opening of horizons.

What gives you hope? More often than not, responses to this question include names of specific people, experiences of wonder and awe, or a spiritual connection with the transcendent. Such responses call into question the most common understanding of hope in the modern era that focuses on time—the experience of the present in relation to the desired expectation for the future. In this case, hope exists according to the degree of alignment of the present with a desired future. While research certainly supports the affirmation that hope exists in a positive relationship between the present and future, there are many other relationships that embody, manifest, and precipitate hope.

Research shows that a descriptive rather than a prescriptive definition of hope is most appropriate given the multiple and varied experiences of hope in human life. Hope is the experience of the opening of horizons of meaning and participation in relation to other human and non-human beings, time, and/or the transcendent.

Shift

Let us further explore the meaning of this definition. First, hope as the "opening of horizons of meaning and participation" points to a perceived enlarging of a context of interpretation, within which we read phenomena, including the experience of ourselves in relation. The term suggests an opening up of space, a broadening of perspective. Further, the "opening" reflects a shift through which we are relocated into a broader context; a vista opens up that had not been perceived previously. This relocation, this shift, this change and opening of perception, is a central element in the experience of hope.

Second, the definition emphasizes "meaning and participation." How we read the data of life and how we interpret ourselves in relation to the data and to the larger whole are elemental questions related to hope. The emphasis on "meaning" in the definition does not privilege a cognitive process, though it can include this. Rather, the focus on meaning as a horizon reflects the extent to which our location shapes the perception and interpretation of life. Our location affects the horizon of meaning available to perception. The emphasis on "participation" is related to meaning and could be included in its purview. However, "horizon of participation" draws attention to the ways meaning is embodied in the diverse relationships we participate in. This emphasis on participation describes how hope is related to discovering ourselves to be participating in a larger whole, connected to, engaged by, and in relationship with the things we are already part of, but are now seeing with new eyes.

Third, the descriptive definition includes the common modern understanding of hope as the relationship of the present to the future but is not limited to this. Further, it suggests that the experience of hope may, in fact, transform the relationship with the future as a consequence of hope but not necessarily as its source.

A lens

It may be most accurate to say that this descriptive definition offers a lens by which to interpret the presence of hope as it exists in life and potentially a lens by which to discern ways to facilitate and practice hope. Hope comes through people's increased sense of agency and empowerment to achieve future goals. It comes through meaningful connections with others and in communities where trust, understanding, and mutuality are present. It emerges when a sense of belonging in community is experienced through shared narratives and visions. Hope comes when stories of past trauma are shared through speech, when meaning is cathartically opened up and a future appears. It comes in relationship to creation when we are awakened by awe to our participation within the interconnectivity of all things. It emerges in experiences of being met by transcendence in spiritual practices, in acts of justice and mercy, when eyes are opened and the world is seen with eyes of compassion. All of these examples of hope's emergence point to different ways horizons of meaning and participation are opened up in relation to time, to other humans and creatures, and to the transcendent.

Research is uncovering the multiplicity of ways hope is experienced in human life. It challenges us to pay greater attention to hope's presence and possibility in the everyday. It invites us to develop intentional practices that feed and nurture hope—opening us to our interconnectivity and to the larger whole in which we live, move, and have our being.

The keys

→ **Hope certainly exists in a positive relationship between the present and future, but there are many other relationships that embody, manifest, and precipitate hope.**

→ **Hope is the experience of the opening of horizons of meaning and participation in relation to other human and non-human beings, time, and/or the transcendent.**

→ **This descriptive definition offers a lens by which to interpret the presence of hope as it exists in life and potentially a lens by which to discern ways to facilitate and practice hope.**

Pamela R. McCarroll is Associate Professor of Pastoral Theology and Director of Field Education at Knox College in the University of Toronto, Canada. She is a certified teaching supervisor in the Canadian Association of Spiritual Care (CASC). Her recent work on hope includes "At the End of Hope—The Beginning: Narratives of Hope in the Face of Trauma and Death." Pamela has a special interest in discovering the gifts of nature and culture in and around Toronto. At this time in her life, she finds that hope erupts in moments of awe and gratitude in the face of beauty through music, creation, and other people, and in stories of resilience and hope hidden amidst adversity.

"Hope nudges people into a happier place."

Hope and happiness: fraternal twins

"I am convinced that the greatest achievements in my life and why many dreams come true can be attributed to that inner and stubborn little voice called 'Hope' that whispers 'You can do it, give it one more try,'" says Prof. **Nicole Fuentes**. "Hope is my appointed nudger and has a nice side effect called 'Happiness.'"

Through my research on happiness in Mexico I have learned that happiness and hope are like fraternal twins: they come together and share many common traits. In the field of Positive Psychology, happiness is defined as the degree to which a person evaluates the overall quality of his present life as a whole positively. In other words, how much someone likes the life he lives. Hope, on the other hand, is a desire of some good or goal accompanied by a confident expectation of obtaining it as well as a route map. Happiness and hope are both positive outlooks on life: our life today, and our life in the future.

Studies around the world show that individuals with high hopes are happier and report higher levels of overall well-being; like fraternal twins, hope and happiness come together. High-hope people confidently believe they are going to get what they want, and are going to be in a better relative place or position; they visualize positive scenarios, and problems

or difficult situations being resolved. We are happier when we enjoy the life we have, and have a confident expectation in our ability to create a better future. Hope and happiness have many things in common. To wit:

1. **Happiness and hope are connected to powerful positive outcomes.** Happy and high-hope people have better health, stronger immune systems, endure pain better, and are less prone to depression and anxiety. Happiness and hope have been linked to better performance in school and at work, particularly in challenging jobs. Happy and high-hope people are better athletes, have more successful relationships, have goals and find the tools and motivation to achieve them. They actively engage in life. Higher-hope individuals are happier than lower-hope individuals.

2. **Hope and happiness are contagious.** Happiness and hope have a positive spillover effect. We are all interconnected, and according to research, our odds of being happy increase up to 15% when someone in our network is happy. Having frequent social contact

with happy and high-hope individuals improves our chances of feeling happier and being hopeful. Happiness is like a benign virus that spreads easily from one happy person to the next. The same can be said for hope. We feel happier and more hopeful when we share space with happy and high-hope individuals.

3. Hope and happiness can be learned. Studies in the field of positive psychology have come to the conclusion that up to 40% of our happiness is within our ability to control. We can improve our happiness with our intentional daily actions. According to *Martin E.P. Seligman*, just like optimism, hope is a thinking style than can be learned. Hope includes behaviors and thought processes that we acquire through socialization. We can learn from people around us that even when things are out of our control, and the scenario is not optimistic, there is still hope.

4. Hope and happiness lead to goal achievement. One of the key ingredients to happiness is having a clear purpose in life and the commitment to achieve personal goals. Happy people have the ability to visualize goals and the drive to fulfill them. Hope is their main tool. Hope is at the core of every dream, every desire, every longing, and new adventure. Hope is where it all begins; it gently encourages us to take the first step, and it is what keeps us going, for hope is tenacious. And it is along the road to achievement of dreams where happiness is to be found. Hope nudges people into a happier place.

The keys

→ **Hope and happiness are both powerful positive outlooks on life.**
→ **Since we are all interconnected, they both have a contagious, positive spillover effect.**
→ **We can learn to be more happy and hopeful, to set goals in life and to achieve them.**

Nicole Fuentes is an assistant professor in the Department of Economics at the Universidad de Monterrey (Mexico). Her research work has revolved around the study of the relationship between economic welfare, psychological well-being, and happiness. She has developed a program called "Tools for Happiness" and currently works with children to help them develop habits and carry out simple actions to increase their everyday happiness. It is her hope that she will be able to share her knowledge on happiness to positively contribute to the lives of those around her. She has a passion for photography and hopes to live up to a hundred because there is so much to do.

"Hopeful minds are happy minds."

Fear for the future

"How we think about the future—good or bad—has a substantial effect on our life satisfaction now," says Dr. **Alan Piper**. He published on what Germans call "Zukunfsangst / Fear for the future." Fearful people are less satisfied with the life they live.

Our life satisfaction now is affected by our thoughts about the future. Having hope for the future is an important contributor to current life satisfaction. Recent research presents evidence that the size of this effect is substantial: not as large as having very good physical health, but **about two to three times larger than the life satisfaction of being married.** This is a sizeable effect. Being hopeful, or optimistic, with respect to the future should be an aim for anyone looking to be satisfied with their life.

In contrast, having fears or being pessimistic about the future is associated with low levels of current life satisfaction. **Unemployment is well-known to contribute negatively to life satisfaction, and the effect on life satisfaction of being pessimistic about the future is even greater.** We must be very careful regarding our thoughts about the future: being hopeful generates increased satisfaction with life whereas being fearful reduces current life satisfaction.

Ignoring the future

Approximately two thousand years ago Seneca, the Stoic philosopher, claimed that "the mind that is anxious about the future is miserable." This recent research, using modern quantitative techniques, has provided evidence that Seneca was correct. Importantly, there is quantitative evidence for the opposite too: the mind that is hopeful about the future is happy. If life satisfaction is a goal, we should try to find or cultivate hope for the future no matter what our personality is like and what our circumstances are. This evidence is obtained by methods that can account for the different personalities and dispositions of people. Furthermore, the modern methods employed are also able to take into account the possibility that how someone perceives the future and their life satisfaction may be interdependent (endogenous being the technical term) and difficult to calculate with slightly older methods.

Related research demonstrates that our current situation (marriage, employment status, health) contributes much to our current life satisfaction, that life satisfaction is largely contemporaneous. Likewise, our current thoughts about the future matter for our life satisfaction now. **For personal life satisfaction, we should try to focus on positive aspects of the future as well as trying to create them, for ourselves and for others.** Our current life is important, and this thinking about the future is not simply to be seen as avoiding the present. A central point is that our hopes and fears regarding the future are important for our current life. This research does not suggest that we should try to ignore the future. Ignoring the future, and trying not to think about it, if successfully achieved, is better for current life satisfaction than being pessimistic about the future. Better still is thinking about the future with hope.

Thought process

This finding regarding the importance of our current thoughts about the future for our life satisfaction offers support for arguments that call for greater resources to better understand mental health, and to help more people enjoy better mental health. Aspects of mental health research and practice, for example cognitive behavioral therapy, try to understand thoughts and the thought process and **help people better control their responses to their thoughts and not get trapped in spirals of negative thinking.** Meditation, it has similarly been argued, is also helpful for an enhanced understanding of our thoughts and the increase in control this understanding and awareness can provide. What can help to enhance our thought patterns can help us to think more hopefully about the future and thus enjoy more life satisfaction now.

The keys

→ **Being hopeful generates increased satisfaction with life whereas being fearful reduces current life satisfaction.**

→ **If life satisfaction is a goal, we should try to find or cultivate hope for the future no matter what our personality is like and what our circumstances are.**

→ **Ignoring the future, and trying not to think about it, if successfully achieved, is better for current life satisfaction than being pessimistic about the future. Better still is thinking about the future with hope.**

Alan Piper, PhD, is a British academic in the North of Germany, having previously worked as an academic in the middle of the UK for over a decade. His main area of research is within the economics of life satisfaction. He is interested in the brain, creativity, happiness, immigration, mental health, poker, sport, and travel. Being aware of the importance of hope for the future for our current life satisfaction, he is really looking forward to reading the other entries in this book along with the related science.

"Hope is hearing the melody of the future."

Learning to be hopeful

"It is desirable and possible to learn hope," says Prof. **Ahmed M. Abdel-Khalek**. "Of importance is to learn the central role of control, mastery, autonomy, and hopeful orientation in our lives. To develop hope, we have to learn adaptive ways to think about our efficacy, and our control over our destinies."

Psychology is the scientific study of behavior and mental processes. Psychology has a long past (more than two millennia) but a short history (since 1879). During much of its first century, psychology has focused exclusively on pathology, pathos, and negative emotions. It has been concerned with identifying human weakness—and relieving, treating, or ameliorating it. Psychologists in the first century of their important scientific discipline have concentrated on repairing damage within a disease model. Before a few decades ago, psychologists had scant knowledge of what makes people happy, normal, and flourish under everyday conditions with their ups and downs.

Strong people

Before the turn of the twentieth century, a strong positive psychology movement had begun. Its objective was to begin to catalyze a change in the focus of psychology from preoccupation only with treating disorders and relieving symptoms and syndromes, to also building positive qualities. Positive psychology is the study of the conditions and processes that contribute to the flourishing or optimal functioning of people, groups, and institutions. It is the scientific study of ordinary human character strengths and virtues. As Seligman pointed out, the domain of **positive psychology is about valued subjective experiences: well-being, contentment, and satisfaction (in the past), hope and optimism (for the future), and flow and happiness (in the present).** It also deals with gratitude, forgiveness, religiosity, and spirituality, among others. By and large, positive psychology is able to tell us how to nurture strong and resilient people.

Hope is one of the main constructs in positive psychology. It represents a relatively stable general expectation about the future. It involves goal-based cognitive processes that operate in the face of a valued perceived outcome. Hope is largely a cognitive trait. It may be a state, a trait, or a generic approach to life events.

Motives

The late Professor Snyder and his colleagues introduced a theory of hope that received widespread attention in psychological literature. They operationally defined hope as a goal-directed, cognitive set involving two interrelated components: pathway and agency thinking. Pathway thinking is the perceived ability to generate successful routes to reach one's desired goals. Agency thinking taps the perceived motivation to use those pathways so as to initiate and sustain movement toward the desired goals. Therefore, they defined hope as a positive motivational state that is based on an interactively derived sense of successful (a) agency (goal-directed energy), and (b) pathways (planning to meet goals). These pathways and agency thoughts interact, reinforcing each other all along the goal pursuit sequence. These two components of hopeful thinking are distinct constructs. Both of them are necessary but neither is sufficient alone.

Professor Scioli and his colleagues have developed an integrative approach to hope, emphasizing the motives of mastery, attachment, and survival as well as spiritual beliefs. In a cross-cultural study based on this approach, it was found that Arabic participants reported greater spiritualized hope, whereas Americans reported greater non-spiritualized hope.

Resilience

Several correlates of hope have been detected. To enumerate some examples, hope and optimism are related constructs, but they are not redundant. Optimism has been defined as the stable tendency to believe that good rather than bad things will happen. Self-efficacy is also related to hope. Self-efficacy describes beliefs in one's ability to carry out specific behaviors. Hope is a separate but related construct in satisfaction with life. Other correlates of hope are as follows: psychological adjustment, self-worth, social acceptance, and physical appearance. In sum, hope fuels subjective well-being and builds psychological resiliency.

Religiosity is a key factor of well-being and hope in the lives of many people, particularly the old and the very old. Religious faith offers a hope that in the end, all shall be well. As professor Myers stated, religious and spiritual commitment offer answers to some of the deepest questions, encourage a more optimistic appraisal of life events, and, in addition, a sense of hope emerges when confronting the terror resulting from our awareness of vulnerability and death. As Rubem Alves stated, "Hope is hearing the melody of the future. Faith is to dance to it." For many of the world's populations, hope is largely derived from their religious and/or spiritual beliefs.

Orientation

It is desirable and possible to learn hope. Of importance is to learn the central role of control, mastery, autonomy, and hopeful orientation in our lives. A lack of control may create a pessimistic style of explanation, thus leading to depression and other maladies. To develop hope, we have to learn adaptive ways to think about our efficacy, and our control over destinies. Learned hope is based on shifting our emphasis from negative to positive. **This is the royal road to engendering hope in children, and to inculcating hope in every one.** It is crucial in this respect—to know that we can not change the world in several occasions. It is certainly easier to change our way of thinking about the world: promoting hope, particularly in the two central features of human life: work and love.

The keys

- → **Positive psychology is able to tell us how to nurture strong and resilient people. Hope is one of the main constructs in positive psychology.**
- → **Hope fuels subjective well-being and builds psychological resiliency.**
- → **It is desirable and possible to learn hope. Of importance is to learn the central role of control, mastery, autonomy, and hopeful orientation in our lives.**

Ahmed M. Abdel-Khalek is an Egyptian citizen, working at Alexandria University as Professor of Psychology. He has published more than 23 books in Arabic and more than 300 research papers in Arabic or English. His research interest is focused on personality structure and assessment, cross-cultural comparisons, attitudes to death, childhood depression, and sleep disorders. In the last few decades he became interested in optimism, love of life, religiosity, happiness, and hope.

"The instillation of hope
is a universal goal in any therapy."

Recapturing hope

Approximately 20% of the 2.6 million U.S. veterans who have
served in Iraq, etc. have been diagnosed with post-traumatic
stress disorder, representing a 656% (!) increase since 2001.
Prof. **Rich Gilman** and his team carry out one of the first
longitudinal analyses that examine the role of hope in symptom
recovery. When hope appears lost, recapturing hope is essential
for positive adaptation and health.

My work with individuals suffering from the most adverse experiences has illuminated
the key reason for their coming to therapy: a sincere hope that their lives will improve.
Their progress through therapy underscores the importance of hope as a vital factor
toward personal growth and recovery.

Stories are legion of individuals who experience the most horrible circumstances
(e.g. being held hostage, prisoners of war) and survive. Follow-up interviews with these
individuals often find that their hope for a successful outcome was a main reason for their
survival. Conversely, there are numerous historical accounts of individuals in similar
situations who lost hope in their future, which rapidly led to deterioration of their health
and ultimate demise. Beyond these most extreme circumstances, **there are millions of
individuals who, for myriad reasons, experience a profound sense of hopelessness
in their future**, and this realization is a main catalyst for their seeking therapy.

Veterans

Decades of research has shown that therapy can effectively treat presenting symptoms. However, what has been less clear is how hope plays a role in therapeutic outcomes. For example, most therapy outcome studies focus on the presenting symptoms without understanding the dynamic processes that explain this improvement. Investigating the processes that explain why and how therapies work are considered to be the next step in therapy research.

Recently, we have examined the role of hope as a key facilitator in treatment outcomes among combat veterans diagnosed with post-traumatic stress disorder (PTSD). We chose this specific group because approximately 20% of the 2.6 million U.S. veterans who have served in Operations Enduring Freedom and Iraqi Freedom (OEF/OIF) have been diagnosed with PTSD, representing a 656% increase since 2001. Further, PTSD rates in veterans are four times higher than is found in the general U.S. population. Finally, veterans with PTSD often report that they are immobilized in their attempts to attain life goals (careers, relationships, etc.) and consider their hope for their future to be bleak at best, nonexistent at worst.

Recovery

Although studies are ongoing, to date we have collected data from hundreds of participants who have entered either outpatient or inpatient services at their local Veterans Administration. Our studies are based on treatments that adopt cognitive-behavior techniques, which focus on having veterans generate alternate explanations for their trauma in order to create more healthy and accurate perceptions of the events. Once these perceptions are modified, the veteran then develops more appropriate coping behaviors that would alleviate their internal distress. It is important to note that none of these treatments directly target hope per se, and thus hope would be considered as a non-specific mechanism of change to explain how therapies work. Our studies include both self- and clinician-reported scales of mental distress (including PTSD), as well as the oft-cited *Hope Scale* to assess veterans' hope as they progress through therapy.

Collectively, our findings have shown the following:
1. There were no changes in hope levels between baseline and mid-therapy. However, levels of hope began to sharply increase after mid-therapy. The changes occurred presumably as the veteran developed compensatory coping strategies to address their difficulties and to develop the confidence to overcome them.

2. Change in levels of hope (from mid-therapy to the end of therapy) predicted PTSD symptom/depression reduction from mid- to post-treatment, not the converse; hope is a necessary factor in **PTSD** symptom reduction and not merely a byproduct of the process. In other words, symptom improvement did not occur until the veteran regained their sense of hope in the future.

3. These findings held regardless of gender, cultural background, socioeconomic status, or initial severity of PTSD symptoms.

Our studies represent some of the first longitudinal analyses that examine the role of hope in symptom recovery. Our findings echo eminent clinical scholars such as Irvin Yalom, who asserted that the instillation of hope is a universal goal in any therapy. Although much work remains in this area (including how our findings extend to other health conditions), our research conducted thus far illustrates how recapturing hope, when hope appears lost, is essential for positive adaptation and health.

The keys

→ **In therapy, changes occur as the person develops compensatory coping strategies to address his difficulties and to develop the confidence to overcome them.**

→ **Hope is a necessary factor in post-traumatic stress disorder symptom reduction and not merely a byproduct of the process.**

→ **When hope appears lost, recapturing hope is essential for positive adaptation and health.**

Rich Gilman is Professor in the Department of General Pediatrics at the University of Cincinnati Medical School (USA). He is also the Director of Clinical Services and Training at the University of Cincinnati Stress Center and a licensed psychologist at Cincinnati Children's Hospital Medical Center. His research examining quality of life issues across the developmental lifespan has been recognized by the American Psychological Association and the International Society of Quality of Life Studies. "What symbolizes hope for me is the recovery people make in the face of extreme adversity. The idea that one can regain their sense of self—and indeed flourish—after a traumatic event is a reminder of the power of the human spirit."

"Hope reflects trust in the Other."

The passage of time

We all know the expression "hope springs eternal."
"This particularly banal expression is more essential than you
might think," says prof. **Dirk De Wachter**. "Beyond banal
optimism, hope forms the basis of our collective existence.
There can only be hope through the passage of time."

Human beings are probably the only creatures that are fully aware of their mortality, so that
their sense of existence is one of inevitable fatality. Because we live with death constantly
in view we are forced to find meaning in life, and hope is an unavoidable characteristic of
human existence.

This hope shows itself in daily life as a banal given, by definition "small" and trivial. We look
forward to the following day full of confidence or fear or desire; we hope it will be better
than today or that our situation will stay the same. **This attitude determines our existence
and even seems to be our existence. In this sense, life without hope is impossible.**

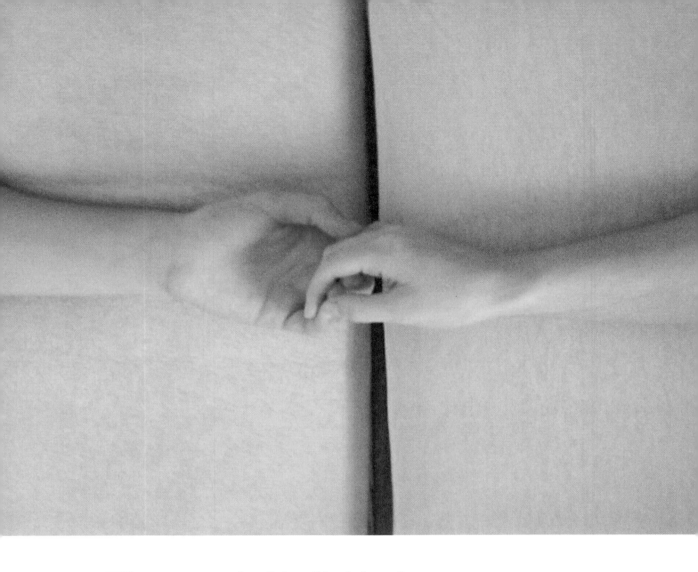

The wounded individual

Nevertheless, the concept of "hope" is tarnished, polluted with utopian desires that can translate into religious and political impossibilities. Hope then becomes a potential catastrophe and paradoxically opens up the way to destruction and death.

Here paradox enters in as one of the essential characteristics of the human condition. The wounded individual whose trust has been damaged, whose hope in the future has darkened, clings to the exaggerated, insatiable salvation of totalitarian ideas.

Hope is psychologically rooted in basic trust, in the parent that is there for the child and will always be there, in an internalized, womb-like obviousness that to a certain extent is capable of resisting the fatalities of the world.

New discovery

The belief that there is always someone there to support you is reflected later in life in love. Hope as such is not an individual quality, but a fundamental relational given: someone else who can and will be there for you. Hope reflects trust in the Other.

This hope goes beyond imaginable desires, beyond predictable paths, breaks through the prescribed order of things. This hope, in the gaze of the Other, in what is different and alien, drives us to engagement, to concrete action, to creative activities. **Hope embodies our desire for change**, for improvement, for making new discoveries and forming new thoughts about the world and the cosmos.

Beyond banal optimism, beyond goal-oriented efficiency, in a form of hopeless acceptance or tragic love, in a fundamental and mysterious un-knowing, hope forms the basis of our collective existence.

There can only be hope through the passage of time.

The keys

→ **Because we live with death constantly in view we are forced to find meaning in life, and hope is an unavoidable characteristic of human existence.**

→ **Hope as such is not an individual quality, but a fundamental relational given: someone else who can and will be there for you.**

→ **This hope, in the gaze of the Other, in what is different and alien, drives us to engagement, to concrete action, to creative activities.**

Dirk De Wachter is a professor, psychiatrist, psychotherapist, and head of the department of Systems and Family Therapy at the Universitair Psychiatrisch Centrum of the Universiteit Leuven (Belgium). He is a trainer and family therapy supervisor at various centers in Belgium and abroad. Dirk is the author of the successful books *Borderline Times* and *Liefde, een onmogelijk verlangen*. He finds hope in his fellow human beings, in an ongoing history of caring for one another in spite of grief, adversity, deprivation, and homicidal tendencies.

"People with little hope for the future tend to live day by day, with higher levels of stress."

Hope is the key

"Hope is a key dimension of well-being and life course outcomes," says Prof. Carol Graham, who is a leading authority in research of happiness and quality of life. "Hope and optimism about the future are related to higher levels of well-being and to long-term outcomes."

The new "science" of well-being measurement has provided us with a tool to better understand and enhance human welfare. Well-being has two distinct well-being dimensions. *Evaluative well-being* encompasses how people think of their lives as a whole, including over the life course and the ability to lead meaningful and purposeful lives. *Hedonic well-being* captures how people experience their daily lives and their mental states, such as happiness at the moment, stress, and anxiety, as they do so. Individuals with higher levels of evaluative well-being tend to have more of a sense of what their futures look like and more capacity to craft those futures; they also tend to be more likely to postpone positive daily experiences to invest in those futures. Individuals with less agency and capacity to craft their futures focus more on the daily experience dimension of well-being, both because their future outlooks are far less certain and because simply getting through each day can be a struggle.

Craft your life

Hope is an important dimension of well-being and of these different long and short-term time horizons. Hope and optimism about the future are related to higher levels of well-being and to long-term outcomes. New research, including my own, shows that people with more positive attitudes about the future have higher levels of well-being in the present and better outcomes in the labor market, health, and social behavior arenas in the future. This is in part because of intrinsic motivation and in part because of the capacity to have longer time horizons and preferences. **People with limited opportunities discount the future more**, both because they have less capacity to set aside their limited means to invest in their futures, and because they have less confidence that those investments will pay off.

Those individuals who have little hope for the future, either because of innate character traits and/or because of challenging circumstances, tend to live day by day, with higher levels of stress, and with very little capacity to make choices about their futures and to craft the kinds of lives they may want to lead. Those with the capacity to make those choices and invest in their futures tend to do so, and tend to have more fulfilling lives and also facilitate their children doing so.

Rich and poor

There are large gaps in the opportunities and kinds of lives led by the rich and poor in many countries in the world. The U.S. is providing an increasingly stark example. The gaps in levels of stress between the rich and poor (stress is much higher for the poor), and in attitudes about life as a whole (scores are much lower for the poor) are greater in the U.S. than they are between the rich and poor in Latin America, a region long known for its high levels of inequality. Our research on well-being suggests that these gaps are likely to result in major differences in the futures of these distinct cohorts—and of their children. Well-being research, including on hope and optimism about the future, is one way to address the collective challenge of providing citizens of the globe—and not just the privileged ones—the opportunity to seek and lead meaningful, purposeful lives.

The keys

→ **Individuals with higher levels of evaluative well-being tend to have more of a sense of what their futures look like and more capacity to craft those futures.**

→ **People with more positive attitudes about the future have higher levels of well-being in the present and better outcomes in the labor market, health, and social behavior arenas in the future.**

→ **Well-being research, including on hope and optimism about the future, is one way to address the collective challenge of providing citizens of the globe—and not just the privileged ones—the opportunity to seek and lead meaningful, purposeful lives.**

Carol Graham has a PhD from Oxford University. She is Leo Pasvolsky Senior Fellow at the Brookings Institution and College Park Professor at the University of Maryland (USA). She has been a Vice President at Brookings and a Special Advisor to the Vice President of the Inter-American Development Bank. Graham is the author of numerous articles and books—most recently *The Pursuit of Happiness: An Economy of Well-Being* and *Happiness Around the World: The Paradox of Happy Peasants and Miserable Millionaires*. In 2014 she received the award for substantial contribution to the field from the International Society of Quality of Life Studies. Her three children provide her with much hope and happiness, as does distance running.

"One door closes… and another door opens."

Hopeful interventions

At the University of Zurich **René Proyer** and his colleagues test the impact of positive interventions on small and huge groups of people. These interventions focus on uncovering and fostering strengths of individuals rather than targeting weaknesses. Hope is one of them.

While being a senior teaching and research associate at the Psychology Department at the University of Zurich, still the first thing that comes to my mind thinking about *hope* is… soccer. I love my work and enjoy what I am doing for a living (seeing my work as a calling) but, at the same time, find myself caught in an almost whimsically exaggerated hope that my club wins its next game, qualifies for playing internationally in the next season, and—most importantly—finishes the season ahead of the "other" club of my hometown. Unfortunately, the players of my team are (mostly) not really blessed with great playing skills, so my impression is that hope is one of the few things that we can rely on. Hope, however, has greater potential than calming down overly excited soccer aficionados.

24 strengths

In my academic work, I was involved in several studies on the effectiveness of so-called *positive psychology interventions*. These interventions focus on uncovering and fostering strengths of individuals rather than targeting weaknesses. Evidence is growing (e.g., from meta-analyses) that the interventions are effective in increasing subjective well-being and ameliorating depression. In some studies these effects seem to be sustainable even over longer time periods.

Hope seems to play an important role here as well. Together with my colleagues (Willibald Ruch, Fabian Gander, and Sara Wellenzohn) I am responsible for a large project on positive interventions (funded by the Swiss National Science Foundation). In one of our studies we were interested in testing whether a program that addresses specific strengths of Peterson and Seligman's *Values-in-Action* (via) classification of strengths and virtues are effective in increasing our participants' life satisfaction—i.e., the cognitive component of subjective well-being. Work using a questionnaire for the assessment of the twenty-four character strengths of the via classification has consistently shown that all strengths are positively related with life satisfaction but also that the strengths of gratitude, curiosity, love, zest, and *hope* are those most related to life satisfaction. This has been shown in numerous studies using different assessment methods and samples.

Shift

In one of our recent studies we were interested in seeing whether a program that was targeting these five most correlated strengths (with the exception of using a *humor*- instead of a *love*-intervention) would lead to greater effects on life satisfaction than a program that addresses strengths-based interventions that target strengths that typically yield low (or lower) correlations (i.e., appreciation of beauty and excellence, creativity, kindness, love of learning, and perspective). The findings show that there was an increase in life satisfaction in the group that trained the most correlated strengths, but also that participants perceived a benefit from working with the other strengths. The interesting thing in this study was that hope (in pre- and post-measures) increased in the group that trained the low correlating strengths. One might argue that this could be a side-effect of participating in an intervention or that one working mechanism for the other interventions was to activate hope in the participants—e.g., by shifting their own attention to more positive aspects of the future or the past. In another study we used a self-administered online setting and participants wrote about a negative event in their life ("one door closes…")

that unexpectedly led to a positive consequence ("...and another door opens"). Findings show that their happiness increased for up to three months after completing the intervention.

Serious-cheerfulness

Work in the realm of positive psychology in general and on positive psychology interventions in particular have further increased the awareness of seeing hope as an important contributor to people's well-being. **Developing hope as a habit—as a positive view of the world—indeed seems to be a good path to sustainable well-being.** This also seems to converge well with what the Austrian theologian Karl Rahner had in mind when he suggested the German-language neologism *Ernstheiterkeit* (serious-cheerfulness) as a preferable view of the world—i.e. being able to smile through tears but also recognizing the gravity in all earthly cheerfulness. At least this stance also helps us to cope with losses in soccer...

The keys

→ **Positive interventions, focusing on uncovering and fostering strengths, are effective in increasing subjective well-being and ameliorating depression. Hope is an important contributor to people's well-being.**

→ **Writing about a negative event in our life that unexpectedly led to a positive consequence can increase our happiness for up to three months.**

→ **Serious-cheerfulness is a preferable view of the world: being able to smile through tears but also recognizing the gravity in all earthly cheerfulness.**

René Proyer is a senior teaching and research associate at the division of personality and assessment at the department of psychology at Zurich University (Switzerland). He got his master's in psychology at the University of Vienna (Austria) and received his PhD from the University of Zurich. His main research interests are adult playfulness, positive psychology interventions, humor research, and test development. He is the author of more than 100 scholarly publications in these areas. In his leisure time he collects Soul, Jazz, and Beat records from the 1960s and enjoys watching soccer rather than doing any type of sport himself.

"Fortunately, optimism is a trainable muscle."

Ten minutes a day

"Web-based courses, trainings, and coaches are mushrooming in the increasingly online world," says Dr. **Katja Uglanova**. "There are numerous interventions to promote healthy behaviors, prevent burnout, deal with stress, and boost general well-being. But where do such interventions really help and how substantial can their effect be? What about, for example, training optimism —one of the most important prerequisites of being happy?" Do ten minutes (online) a day keep the doctor away?

We are able to influence our level of well-being. Although our happiness is partly genetically determined, as it has been shown in twin studies, and objective life circumstances that are difficult for us to change also do play a role, a part of how well we feel about our life is under our control—and the entire field of positive psychology is investigating scientifically grounded strategies of enhancing our own well-being. Fostering an optimistic outlook on life is one of the strategies of increasing happiness that seems to pay off.

Simple strategies

Optimism and hope—which are the main themes of this book—are two central constructs of positive psychology; these are closely related, albeit not identical concepts. **What is common for high-hope and optimistic people is their way of framing the future**, with a focus on opportunity-seeking and a belief that a desirable outcome can be achieved.

Optimism means being lenient in evaluations of past events, appreciating positive aspects of the current situation, and emphasizing positive opportunities for the future. Besides its potential of enhancing well-being, optimism increases performance in study, work, and sport activities; facilitates social contacts to make one more popular among peers or increases one's chances on the relationship market; and it helps maintain good health. **Optimistic people are steady in pursuing their goals.** Be aware, however, of *unrealistic optimism*, which is self-deceptive and distorts reality, as it may result in unjustified risky behavior, neglecting measures of health care, and making negligent plans for the future.

An optimistic outlook on things is a valuable psychological asset. But what if you haven't got one? Fortunately, optimism is a trainable "muscle," and there are some effective, albeit simple, strategies one might consider worth trying. One technique is *identification of dysfunctional optimism-suppressing beliefs*, such as "envisioning positive outcomes might be harmful and deluding because they never come true." Instead, while recognizing that we might not get the desired outcome, it is worthsearching for a *silver lining* in every situation. Contrary to a common belief that expecting too much usually leads to disappointment, practicing *positive thinking*, for example, in a form of *visualization of a desired outcome,* has proven to be another effective way to train optimism.

Training

As simple as it sounds, many of us still need guidance in putting these strategies into practice. The Internet seems to be a very promising medium for delivery of such support. Self-administered web-based tools are easily accessible day and night, and their cost-effectiveness is quite high. On the other hand, personal contact with a coach is missing, and one needs to be quite self-disciplined in order to pursue the goals of the online training on one's own. This is a challenge, which leads to high drop-out rates when it comes to web-based programs. That's why much debate is going on regarding whether online instruction is effective at all and if it can possibly compete with traditional face-to-face coaching. From up-to-date literature, we know that web-based optimism training tools can be as effective as traditional face-to-face coaching. It would be naïve, however, to expect that a web-based training of a few weeks would induce long-term changes in optimism and, consequently, in well-being. But what it can do is give a chance to systematically practice the above-mentioned activities and develop some routine in practicing them.

Online coach

How do you choose an online-coach that is likely to help? We can, of course, as usual, rely on peer recommendation. There is, however, a growing body of research on the design factors that affect the effectiveness of the program (although there are still many questions to answer). Here are a few hints.

1. First, choose programs that promise a realistic outcome. A short-term intervention will not boost your optimism forever anyway. What you can learn is how to practice an optimistic outlook and how to implement simple activities that help pump optimism into everyday routines. If this is what an online-program announces as a goal, that's a good sign.

2. Second, web-based training is especially helpful when it's tailored to a person's particular needs. As difficult as it seems to develop a tailored online program, there are good examples of computer-tailored interventions out there. Advanced programs usually offer an opportunity to develop a flexible action plan, which one can adjust to individual preferences.

3. Finally, interactive programs with many entertaining or game-like elements might be fun, but always ask yourself: are you actually learning something? In my view, the best online programs are those that don't give you a fish but instead teach you how to fish; the goal should not be to make one dependent on an app but rather to transfer skills, which one can successfully use on one's own after having completed the online course.

In short, even a short intervention can make a difference. But stay realistic: a two-week online training will not make an eternal optimist out of a chronic pessimist. The goal is to *learn how* to practice optimism. As with all kinds of psychological help, the key to success is one's own proactivity. Try to stay disciplined and don't give up too easily.

The keys

→ **Fostering an optimistic outlook on life is one of the strategies for increasing happiness that seems to pay off.**

→ **Web-based optimism training tools can be as effective as traditional face-to-face coaching. Especially when they promise a realistic outcome, are tailored to a person's particular needs, and the goal is to transfer skills.**

→ **Even a short intervention can make a difference. But stay realistic. The key to success is one's own proactivity.**

Katja Uglanova, PhD, used to work as a lecturer at the Higher School of Economics in St. Petersburg (Russia). Her main research interests are subjective well-being, life-span psychology, and plasticity of human development. In her doctoral dissertation, titled "Rethinking the Hedonic Treadmill: Differences in Adaptation Patterns across Events, People and Nations," she analyzed the process of hedonic adaptation to major life events, such as marriage, divorce, birth of a child, widowhood, and long-term unemployment. Her current work at the University of Hamburg (Germany) for the EngAGE project gives her the opportunity to explore the potential of psychological interventions for improving well-being at work. In her free time she enjoys spending time with her loved ones and her hobby—historical dance. As for her personal definition of hope, she has chosen a line from Star Trek: "To hope is to recognize a possibility."

"It is almost impossible for one to be too hopeful."

Hope for the better, no need for the best!

"Largely speaking, being optimistic is good for happiness. However, one may lose in happiness and in money by being too optimistic," says Prof. **Yew-Kwang Ng**. "Being a born optimist, I found this out painfully over the height of the global financial crisis in 2008 when my net worth decreased by over 50%."

Yes, at that moment I did laugh, though somewhat bitterly, even after some loss of sleep. Moreover, I went through that year still very happy, partly because I knew that, above survival level, money is not very important for happiness, and partly because I remained hopeful.

Exercising

An important piece of advice on how to be happy is on the importance of sufficient exercise in both physical and mental relaxation. Everybody knows this. However, many make the most important mistake in thinking "I know that exercise is important, but I have no time!" The important part of my advice is that if you have too much time, you may not have to do exercise; if you do not have enough time, you must do exercise! By exercising, say, half an hour a day, you may sleep half an hour a day less and yet feel and work better the next day. In the long run, you also live longer. **Exercise helps you gain time almost all the time.**

While those not having enough time must exercise, *all* people must have hope—that is, all people who want to achieve happiness, and that is virtually everyone. Whether already

successful or not, all of us must not give up hope or have low hope. Hope is very important for both achievement and happiness.

The top

Renowned hope researchers all over the world have shown that "higher hope" is consistently related to better outcomes in academics, athletics, physical health, psychological adjustment, and psychotherapy.

It is almost impossible for one to be too hopeful. **Being too hopeful is different from hoping for too much.** One may be too greedy and hope for too much. However, one cannot be too hopeful for the right outcomes. This is consistent not just with my own life experience of over seven decades, but also with the studies of hope researchers. They also find that hope is a better predictor of life satisfaction than optimism. Thus, do not be too wary of having false hopes or being too hopeful. Let us all hope for the better. No need to have the best. The urge to go to the top is an evolutionary legacy that, at least if pursued without appropriate limits, is actually detrimental to happiness in net terms. To most of us, the top is a will-o'-the-wisp. Many advise people just to try for their personal best, no need for the global best (beating all others). My advice is to go just for the "good enough". The last few millimeters are not worth the high costs involved. By all means, be positive, but not excessively. This is consistent with the Confucius principle of moderation.

Long term

Researchers (David Feldman and Dianne Drecher in 2012) show that even a single 90-minute goal-pursuit session "can increase hope in the short term as well as lead to greater levels of goal progress as much as a month later." If a short research-conducted session can have such remarkable effects, I am confident that, **if a person decides to be more hopeful, many more positive effects will ensue.**

Especially for those with not enough time to do things, let us start by hoping to have more time to achieve more things and increase happiness by doing our daily exercise. We will then achieve more, be healthier, and feel happier!

The keys

→ **To increase your well-being, do enough exercise in both physical and mental relaxation. Especially when you think you don't have enough time for it.**

→ **One cannot be too hopeful for the right outcomes. Let us all hope for the better. No need to have the best.**

→ **Even a single 90-minute goal-pursuit session can increase hope in the long and the short term. So we can all decide to be more hopeful, and positive effects will ensue.**

Yew-Kwang Ng is professor in economics at Nanyang Technological University (Singapore). He was a professor of economics at Monash University from 1985–2012 (and an emeritus professor since 2013) and has been a fellow of the Academy of Social Sciences in Australia since 1980. In 2007, he received the highest award (Distinguished Fellow) of the Economic Society of Australia. He has published over two hundred referenced papers in leading journals in economics, philosophy, psychology, and sociology. His most recent books are *Common Mistakes in Economics by the Public, Students, Economists and Nobel Laureates* (2011) and *The Road to Happiness* (2013). He likes poetry.

"Failure being seen as so negative comes from an inbuilt reactionary response that we no longer need."

Positive failure

We do our best to avoid failures, as they seem to be the opposite of success. Dr. **Alastair Arnott** has a different point of view: "We can often think that success fosters hope. Indeed, in some ways it can. Failure, however, with the right preconditions, is a recipe for resilience, hope, happiness, and positivity. Positive failure works like a psychological vaccine."

Perhaps our greatest achievement as a species has been to get it wrong. If we think back to all the ideas and schemes that we have conjured up that have been mistaken, but we have used as a platform for progression, we try to erase them from the history books. In the abstract we know that no one is perfect—so why do we act externally like this is the case and, indeed, like this is the goal?

The very language of perfection and success is counterproductive. Who really wants to hear from the perfectionist? She/he who knows it and has got it right time and time again, those who could be described as flawless? **There is something inhuman about perfectionism.** Indeed, perfectionism is perfectionism's undoing. No one is flawless, no one is perfect, and there is something incredibly human about being imperfect and flawed and about failing. What would happen if we were to use failure as a psychological catalyst as opposed to something to be avoided at all costs? If we punish experimentation and creativity—thus restricting failure—then I argue that we will reduce our successes.

Embrace imperfection

What happens when you get it right? When you win? When you are a total success? Nothing. It stops you in your tracks. I ask the reader to think back to times in their life when they have failed, then to ask themselves the honest question: Was there a positive outcome in the end? If you use positive failure to fuel progress and give people permission to get it wrong then this provides an extremely fertile environment for learning, growth, progression, light, and passion. In contrast, success can often immobilize, halt growth, and enforce an overly optimistic hallucinogenic outlook on life, especially if one has very little "real world" adult experience. Far too often we seem to place human beings in mechanical or artificial environments and then expect success. In the worst-case scenario, we get it. Why worst-case? Because the psychological cost to success "at all costs" is that it costs a lot. Success can come with a large unseen psychological cost.

So, what is positive failure? Surely that in itself is an oxymoron? My theory is that failure comes in two categories: positive and negative. To evoke these, one must put resources into creating the preconditions.

> *Preconditions for positive failure: acceptance of one's own vulnerability, having a growth mindset, and embracing imperfection.*
> *Preconditions for negative failure: defiance of one's own vulnerability, having a fixed mindset, and embracing perfectionism.*

Then one is able to clearly distinguish between the two types.

> *Positive failure: failure after appropriate investment that leads to further learning or development.*
> *Negative failure: failure after inappropriate investment that stunts further progress or development.*

The issue with failure being seen as so negative comes from an inbuilt reactionary response that I argue we no longer need. To counter this, positive failure works like a psychological vaccine.

Failing hurts

The ideal place to foster skills in adaptability and psychological efficiency is school. Often, in too many countries across the world, success and in particular exam success is prioritized above learning. Surely, to immunize and almost create a relative failure immunity ready for the real world is desirable? Nobody knows what the world will be like by 2100, however, we seem sure that by advocating exam success, we are fully preparing our children for the future...

There seems to be a stereotypical view on the relation between ability and effort, this is, that there isn't one. Therefore, someone who exerts more effort is only doing so in order to make up for his or her lack of ability. Could failure carry the same stigma? Failing hurts. In essence, the metaphorical jab of the immunization needle is never going to be pleasant. **That slightly embarrassing and dawning realization that we have got it wrong can be re-programmed as a fuel for progression.** We look at those who have failed within the growth of individualism in western culture and perhaps judge too harshly. I urge readers to embrace positive failure and invest resources into the organizations, environments, and preconditions where positive failure can take place. Let's get it wrong... then giggle about it.

The keys

→ **If you use positive failure to fuel progress and give people permission to get it wrong then this provides an extremely fertile environment for learning, growth, progression, light, and passion.**

→ **Accept your own vulnerability, develop a growth mindset, and embrace imperfection.**

→ **Positive failure is failure after appropriate investment that leads to further learning or development.**

Alastair Arnott is an education lecturer at the University of Wolverhampton (United Kingdom). He has written extensively on positive psychology in education. He is the author of the successful book *Positive Failure*. His most recent book *Demanufacturing Education* aims to introduce positive psychology into the mainstream of teaching and learning. Alastair is passionate about working with children from disadvantaged backgrounds. His personal idea about hope? "Hope can be created as well as found. For me, I have found it in compassion. From colleagues, students, and, on occasion, the random person on the street. It is everywhere, if you know where to look."

"We can inspire our hope when we might feel it least but need it the most."

Hope in the darkest of days

It seems to be easy to live a hopeful life when things go well.
But what about our very dark moments, when things go wrong?
How do we find strength in hope after a dramatic experience?
Dr. **Alex Linley** shows five positive effects of post-traumatic growth.

Hope is our sense of positivity for the future. It is drawn primarily from our beliefs about our motivation and our capability to bring that future about. In hope, we set our face against the world, determined and believing that we will achieve—perhaps against the odds, perhaps with the odds in our favor. But no matter, for hope is calculus, not probability. Hope is about the realization of an outcome, not the weighted chances of achieving that outcome. The more we believe in ourselves and our chances of success, the greater the hope we have.

But **maintaining hope when everything is stacked against us can be hard.** At least, that is, until we realize that hope is often tested and forged in the crucible of bitter experience. We need hope most when we are suffering. There is a pleasing symmetry that, by looking at the outcomes of suffering, we can find hope for hope even in the midst of suffering itself.

Across the great philosophies, religions, and literatures of the world, the evidence for the value of the struggle through suffering is shown time and again. In the last twenty years or so, psychologists have started to catch up with this, labeling the phenomenon as post-traumatic growth.

Growth

Broadly speaking, there are five good things that can come about through our struggle with suffering, known as post-traumatic growth.

1. We may **improve in our relationships** with others, valuing and appreciating people more, perhaps recognizing that they are there for us, and understanding more gratefully what they do for us.

2. We may **see new possibilities** for our lives and our future, exploring new hobbies, careers, or even changes to our lifestyle as a result.

3. We may **discover new sources of personal strength**, finding that there are things we can do that we would never have dreamed, or that we have deeper reserves than we had ever suspected.

4. We may **change spiritually**, developing a deeper connection with something that is bigger than we are, finding or strengthening a belief in a higher power.

5. We may **shift up a notch in our appreciation of life**, noticing things like the changing seasons, the warm words of a friend, or the fact that our bus is running on time. When we see that we could have lost all of this, its presence is now appreciated, no longer taken for granted as it was before.

Freedom

When we recognize that good things can come—and do come—from our struggle with suffering, we are able to see hope blossom anew. In the midst of the darkest hours of our struggle, knowing that there is a brighter future on the other side. Thus, we can inspire our hope when we might feel it least but need it the most.

When hope takes hold, it changes the trajectory of our thinking and our progress. Rather than seeing everything wrong and getting worse, we now see what's right and how we can make it better. **Rather than feeling helpless and impotent, we start to remember and realize our own power.** As we re-awaken our power, we rediscover our *will*, the same will that helps us find our new *ways*.

This hope is internal to us, our beacon but also our responsibility. And yet, sometimes, we will face situations where no matter what we do, the outcome is beyond our influence, let alone our control. At times like this, our hope changes. From a belief that starts within ourselves, it becomes a belief in the beneficence of our God, however we may define Him or Her, or even a belief just in the power of a benign universe. And it is here that hope meets its close cousin, faith. **Hope is for when we can influence and control the outcome, faith is for when we can't.**

Viktor Frankl famously wrote that the last freedom that can never be taken away from us is the freedom to choose our attitude to our circumstances. Embracing this, we can choose hope. And in hope, we can choose a better future. So even in the worst of times, when everything else seems lost, we can always choose hope. Even in the darkest of days.

The keys

→ **Hope is about the realization of an outcome, not the weighted chances of achieving that outcome.**

→ **Post-traumatic growth may include improved relationships, seeing new possibilities, discovering personal strength, changing spiritually, or shifting a notch in our appreciation of life.**

→ **The last freedom that can never be taken away from us is the freedom to choose our attitude to our circumstances. Even in the darkest of days we can always choose hope.**

Alex Linley, PhD, is the Chief Executive Officer of Capp, a leading strengths-based assessment provider. He holds a first class psychology degree from the University of Leicester (United Kingdom), where he has been a Visiting Professor in Psychology, and a PhD from the University of Warwick. He is recognized internationally as a leading expert on positive psychology and its applications. He is the author of seven books including the Human Resources bestseller *The Strengths book*.

One moment of hope

Chido Govera grew up as an orphan in Zimbabwe. Now she is a social entrepreneur, the founder of **The Future of Hope Foundation**, an expert in edible and medicinal mushrooms, and a pioneer of the popular innovation of farming mushrooms on coffee grounds. This innovation has ignited dozens of entrepreneurs in different parts of the world to take inner-city mushroom farming to a whole new level. This is her story.

Mushrooms

At age 11, I experienced my first moment of hope. I had the unique opportunity to learn about mushrooms, enabling me to feed my family and a chance to reach out to other orphans in my community. That moment of hope brought me the fortune to be mentored by great individuals who recognized my potential and supported me in perfecting my art of farming.

At an early age I committed myself to ending poverty, abuse, self-pity, and victimhood at grassroots level in Africa—giving hope—through food security.

With 17 years of experience, I have reached over 1,000 women from communities in Zimbabwe, Congo, Ghana, Cameroon, Tanzania, and South Africa. I have impacted schools, communities, and entrepreneurs all over the world. Now I mentor other young women

My name is Chido Govera. In my native language Shona, my name means passion or love. I was born on April 6, 1986, in Zimbabwe. I grew up as an orphan after my mother succumbed to HIV/AIDS when I was only 7 years old. Immediately, I turned into a parent, mothering my brother and caring for my nearly blind grandmother. By age 8, I had already experienced the worst possible abuse, inflicted by close family. As early as 10 years old, I was offered to marry a man who was 30 years my senior so I could have food on my plate. When I refused to marry, I turned away the best help I had been offered and, henceforth, I was on my own. **Distressed by my situation then, I vowed to myself that I would grow to be a woman who empowers, saves, and protects other orphans from experiencing what I, and so many others, had suffered.**

and girls, teach people how to convert agricultural waste into healthy food in the form of mushrooms, and how to utilize the waste to produce more food. **From just one moment of hope as a little girl, my life turned around and I set out on a journey to go beyond anything I had imagined.** I am no longer bound in the chains of what happened to me as a little girl.

The future of hope

When I was 20 years old I wrote an autobiography as a way to deal with the traumas I had experienced growing up. The title, *The Future of Hope*, was inspired by the epochal conference organized by Nobel Peace Laureate Elie Wiesel and my adoptive father (Gunter Pauli). Elie Wiesel concluded that this meeting had to focus on The Future of Hope, calling upon young people to fill the gaps that the present leadership has failed to respond to.

Following my biography emerged the idea to entitle my foundation "The Future of Hope Foundation." Through this foundation I continue **to give hope to disadvantaged**

women and girls through skills training and mentoring processes, empowering them to own their food security, take care of their health, and convert their hardships into opportunities: the basis to end poverty and abuse and more.

Inside fire

Looking at my story, hope for me means **harmonizing** with my past and its pains, acknowledging all that happened, and still choosing to **open up** to a future of possibilities and the continued effort of more harmonizing work. My moment of hope offered me a chance to be **purposeful** in

rewriting my narrative; redefining my goals, hopes, and dreams; and choosing my **engagement**. I have learned that one moment that instills hope in any human being can change their life forever. **Hope sparks an inside fire and a learning experience that changes the vision of generations**, young and old, rich or poor. Hope converts victims into change agents and leaders in local communities. Hope facilitates life processes that are vital in today's world such as forgiveness and love.

More information:
www.thefutureofhope.org

> *"Homo sapiens has seen his changeless savanna transmuted to an ever-changing modernity."*

Hopeful evolution?

For more than half a century he has been one of the most respected, thoughtful, and creative political scientists in the United States. Now **Robert E. Lane** (1917) is still working on a 1,000-page volume on the process whereby the big-brained primate that evolution produced takes over the job of managing his own destiny. Is this a hopeful evolution?

Across the globe most people have a positive emotional set point. Income and poverty make a difference, but the positivity bias persists across almost all circumstances. But evolution was not aimed at human happiness. Positive moods are by-products of the genetic fitness tests: breeding to preserve the gene pool. Why, then, is almost 7 percent of the world's population depressed? And why do another 4 percent suffer from anxiety disorder?

I suggest some systematic strain in the way we live causes this misery. Most of the neurological equipment guiding our behavior, our hormones, and the structure of our brains were laid down by evolution five million years ago to adapt the hominid genus to survival on the African savanna. Changes in cranial capacity as recent as 1.9 million years ago prompted anthropologists to change the species' classification from *Homo habilis* to *Homo erectus*. Only about 200,000 years ago did we merit "sapiens." But the cognitive and emotional structures of the brain are basically those adapted to survival under Paleolithic and Neolithic circumstances.

Cosmic puzzle

It is a tribute to both evolution and its big-brained products that they do as well as they have done in a complex, information-age, urban society. But the strain and stress of these achievements has been great. Given that both the neural equipment and the ever-changing circumstances of society appear to be normal, diagnosis of the source of our *malaise* is exceptionally difficult. Nor can it be assumed that the problem lies in a maladaptive human nature, for many have diagnosed modern society, itself, as "sick."

There is a cosmic puzzle in this diagnosis. Is the current prevalence of depression and anxiety mostly the product of an erratic, double-bind society, the "sick society" to which Freud and his followers referred? Alternatively, is our unhappiness and chronic worry the product of failed adaptation by a creature created to adapt to the African savanna 5 million years ago and forced to respond to the stimuli of a modern, urban society, as Edward Wilson suggests: "The human species can change its own nature. What will it choose? Will it remain the same, teetering on the jerrybuilt foundation of partly obsolete Ice-Age adaptations? Or will it press on toward a still higher intelligence and creativity...?" Our judgments presume the norms of a "normal person," but that standard fails when the normal person originates from a gene pool that is, itself, the source of the problem.

Four ways

I think of four ways the society may systematically distress the big-brained primate whose welfare we care about.

1. The first is the erosion of the *communities* we have adjusted to. Like other primates, we evolved as social animals living in small groups and adapted to families and companions known personally and in their multiple roles of brother, hunter, and community member. Traditional society did not break this pattern, but modern metropolitan society did. The trip from living with friends and family members to living with collections of strangers is a journey the big-brained primate in the gray-flannel suit was not ready to take.

2. Second, these strangers were important to each other in a pair of single, flat roles: they were merchants. *Human relations were absorbed by market relations*—the "cash nexus." What had once been a matter of affiliation and trust became a matter of economic advantage, wary lest one had not received the "best deal." *Homo* sapiens changed from social man to economic man. His pursuit was utility or happiness, but his official character, rational and greedy, prevented him from achieving his goal.

3. The big-brained primate had survived to see his changeless savanna transmuted to an *ever-changing modernity*. Modernization itself required a total change in perspectives, values, even of ethical codes as "neighborliness" dropped from the etiquette of daily concerns and "productivity" took its place. **The society that worships progress is an anxious, stressed society.** Everywhere you look, the immigrant, the pioneer, the multi-tasking executive, the adolescent facing career choices, the trans-gender experimenter, yesterday's information specialist—they are all in process. None are really "at home," *chez soi*.

4. Finally, there is the *pace of events*, information, number of stimuli-per-minute, of bits or bytes per second. All physiological studies show high payoff for relaxation, for occasional focus away from task performance, even for distraction (but not while driving). **This density of stimuli is pernicious for modern man,** partly because his unconscious is paced to savanna-style events and partly because of the physiology of the average brain—itself a product of more leisurely eons in the dim, Paleolithic past.

Which is it? Have we created a stressful society where any set of "human natures" would have a relatively high rate of misery? Or is modern society a healthy one to which our Paleolithic natures cannot adapt?

The keys

→ **The cognitive and emotional structures of our brain are basically those adapted to survival under Paleolithic and Neolithic circumstances.**

→ **Homo sapiens changed from social man to economic man, living with strangers instead of companions, in ever-changing modernity with a density of stimuli.**

→ **Our judgments presume the norms of a "normal person," but that standard fails when the normal person originates from a gene pool that is, itself, the source of the problem.**

Robert E. Lane is Emeritus Professor of Political Science at Yale University (USA). He is a fellow of the British Academy, a past president of the American Political Science Association, and a past president of the International Society of Political Psychology. He is currently working on a new volume of which the focus is on the juncture of evolution and civilization. He thinks of this as a natural extension of political science.

"It turns out that change does happen in prison."

Hope in prison

"Hope often emerges from paradox. This is why I am repeatedly delighted and not a bit surprised to find the expansive experience of hope in the limited setting of prison," says Dr. **Phil Magaletta**. He is the Chief of Clinical Education of the Federal Bureau of Prisons, Department of Justice, USA. "Hope is the guiding principle of reentry."

For two decades I have been fortunate to study among correctional workers and the public they serve. More specifically, I have been recruiting and training psychologists to practice in correctional settings. The psychologists who begin this work and remain employed seem to share several common traits. I've discovered that these traits are not just found among those providing psychological services. Rather, it is found among all ranks of successful correctional workers—from the student trainee all the way up to executive leaders. And these traits all rest upon one common, foundational principle: hope.

Two worlds

Correctional workers offer both inmates and our communities radial acts of public service and self-giving. Often unrecognized by those outside the prison, they faithfully and with hope provide custody of and care for inmates. To achieve this, the successful correctional worker lives in two worlds. And they are not the two you might suspect (i.e., "in here" and "out there," separated by walls and barbed wire). Rather, they are (1) the world of recognizing and being aware of an inmate as she or he is now and what the inmate has done that resulted in incarceration, and (2) the world of how this inmate could be. They work among inmates as the inmate is now while simultaneously envisioning them as they could be. For this is the only place where the reasons for inner change are found, the now. However, they must also envision the future as it could be for each individual inmate.

In contemporary corrections, the philosophy of this correctional process and approach is called reentry.

Barriers

Reentry is a natural evolution of the unit management philosophy that established active listening as the center of gravity for effective correctional management. Interviewing, measuring, listening to, and understanding inmate needs became central concepts of unit management as it developed in the 1970s. As these principles evolve within a reentry services framework, staff and inmates can refine their understanding of what exactly they need to be hopeful for and about. Contemporary correctional workers have a better grasp and understanding of the barriers to successful reentry and also the evidence-based solutions these barriers may require. **They assist inmates in learning and practicing these solutions.** Sometimes this means helping remove internal barriers such as substance abuse, deviant peer networks, and criminal cognitions; sometime the barriers are external such as housing and health-care needs.

Tomorrow

Perhaps most importantly it means helping inmates achieve an internal sense of agency to seek multiple, legitimate ways of achieving successful outcomes once released from prison. Despite what may appear to be an environment not conducive to growth and development, it turns out that change does happen in prison. And it is not the architecture of a facility or its location that fuels this process, although these can help. No, hope emerges from the tuned hearts of human resources. It is the prison staff that creates and sustains hope. While numerous program evaluations provide evidence for changing behavior, it remains true that these programs and services are enlivened by the staff that operates them.

Because of hope, correctional workers became my favorite people. They are ordinary people asked to envision the possible with some very difficult individuals, often in very challenging circumstances. To top it off, they are rarely discouraged when the vision of what might be possible is not yet realized. Instead, they choose to remember that the possible part of the process, to keep the inmate behind the wall, safely, one more day, actually was achieved. This alone gives both inmate and the staff another chance, tomorrow.

The keys

→ **Correctional workers live in two worlds. They work among inmates as the inmate is now while simultaneously envisioning them as they could be.**

→ **Within a reentry services framework, staff and inmates can refine their understanding of what exactly they need to be hopeful for and about.**

→ **It means helping inmates achieve an internal sense of agency to seek multiple, legitimate ways of achieving successful outcomes once released from prison.**

Phil Magaletta, PhD, is the Chief of Clinical Education and Workforce Development for the Psychology Services Branch, Federal Bureau of Prisons (USA). He has administered and practiced correctional psychology for nearly two decades. A graduate of University of Scranton, Magaletta earned his MA from Loyola College in Maryland and his PhD in Clinical Psychology from St. Louis University. In addition to prisons, he has practiced in several hope-centric communities "such as his family, Jesuits, Sufis, and others."

"Even in truly hopeless cases,
it is still better to hope
than to fall prey to despair."

The best context for hope

"I grew up in Singapore, which is among the world's wealthiest countries," says Professor **Eddie M. W. Tong**. He tries to understand the hopeful attitude of his neighbors. Singapore has the third-highest per-capita income in the world but one of the world's highest income inequalities. "I examine how people behave when they are in certain emotional states, and discover that emotions can lead to positive or negative consequences, depending on the context." What is the best context for hope?

In my research, I examine emotion, studying the factors that lead people to feel certain emotions, such as hope, gratitude, joy, love, anger, and fear, focusing on their thought patterns.

Singapore is internationally esteemed for numerous achievements in areas such as finance, education, health-care services, legal services, social harmony, cleanliness, aviation, security, water management, and so on. Its development is considered miraculous by many because just about 50 years ago, Singapore, then a new nation, lacked the infrastructure to make these achievements possible. Many factors contribute to its success, but I would also like to believe that Singapore would not have developed so well if the pioneers who built this nation felt hopeless about it. This historical perspective makes it even more meaningful to reflect on hope and its nature.

A better future

Among the many ways that make humans unique as a species is the ability to imagine. This ability underlies the ability to hope because hope is about envisioning a better future than what the situation suggests. Hope is unique because it could very well be *the* emotion that enables people to focus on their hopes and dreams despite what others perceive to be crippling obstacles. It is a critical emotion that sustains people when they feel helpless, having exhausted every possible means to cope, against odds that appear (or in actual fact are) insurmountable. But the danger of hope is that one may slip into false hope. In such cases, it could be better for the person to pursue a different goal.

However, an argument can be made that even in truly hopeless cases, it is still better to hope than to fall prey to despair. Even when nothing can be done, hope rejuvenates lives. Indeed, research has shown that hope predicts many positive outcomes, including well-being, academic excellence, athletic achievement, and better physical health. Hope also counteracts the effects of daily stressors, reduces depression and anxiety, and helps in psychotherapy. Hence, hope can free one from the shacklers of setbacks and misfortunes and enable the person to live with vigor and dignity. But the challenge is in sustaining hope. It is one thing to feel hopeful for the moment, but another to remain hopeful over a long period of adversity.

Keeping hope alive

How does hope come about? Expertise, good planning, confidence, intelligence, teamwork, resources (e.g. money), and supportive institutions can make a person feel hopeful that problems can be solved. But hope is in its most enigmatic form when one is stripped of such competences. People can also feel hopeful when they feel that there is little that they can do. In such cases, some remain hopeful that someone or something, from somewhere, will come to their aid. Some keep their hope alive for others, pressing on because certain people in their lives want them to hold on. There are also others whose hope rests simply but firmly on the faith that things will be better. These people might also be visionaries of sorts, envisioning and enlivened by realistic possibilities that escape those who have given up. **Remembering stories of hope, whether real or fictional, helps too.** Hope can be contagious too, spreading from one person to another (but so can despair). Finally, hope often taps into a spiritual element. Many persevere because of their religious convictions, such as beliefs in a good God or in karma. The non-religious, not subscribing to any particular faith, may also have core beliefs that are hope-sustaining, such as the belief that there is a reason for everything or that justice will be done.

Therefore, **there are many pathways to hope, which could be a reason for humanity's ability to adapt and thrive over calamities.** However, the ability to hope should also be accompanied by the ability to act and the ability to learn, so that one can act when the opportune time comes and learn so as to avoid the same calamity. Likewise, I believe that the individuals who built Singapore did not just hope, but also took prudent and decisive actions to solve their problems and ensure that important lessons are passed down for future generations to keep in mind.

The keys

- → **The ability to imagine and envision a better future than the situation suggests makes humans unique and predicts many positive outcomes.**
- → **The challenge is in sustaining hope. It is one thing to feel hopeful for the moment but another to remain hopeful over a long period of adversity.**
- → **The ability to hope should also be accompanied by the ability to act and the ability to learn.**

Eddie M. W. Tong is an Associate Professor in the Department of Psychology at the National University of Singapore. He has published numerous articles on the cognitive processes associated with specific emotions (including hope). The insights into people's emotional experiences that his research give him, make his work very satisfying. As for hope, when things are hard going? "I remain hopeful in many ways, such as counting my blessings, remembering my personal heroes, or simply keeping the faith that my efforts will be rewarded. And I enjoy good music, which I suspect (a potential research question here!) is capable of evoking and enhancing hope."

"High-hope individuals tend to divide their final goals into smaller sub-goals."

Adapting goals

In 2000, he established the first Positive Psychology Laboratory in China. Since then, Prof. Samuel Ho has been examining the properties, measurements, outcomes, and applications of hope among children and adults in school and medical settings and in times of good and bad. He completes the traditional hope model with three important elements on the capacity of adapting goals. They improve our resilience.

I was first introduced to the psychological concept of hope by the late Charles Richard Snyder, the founding father of the Psychology of Hope, in 2002 when he came to Hong Kong to conduct a workshop on the topic, and I happened to be the facilitator of his workshop. Rick died in 2006. I still feel deep gratitude to him for being a good friend and mentor. He has given hope to me and many people all around the world.

Rick taught us his cognitive model of hope, which consists of three components: goal, agency, and pathway. He told us that in his conceptualization, high-hope individuals tend to set more goals for themselves and possess goals that are slightly more challenging than their prior achieved goals. More still, high-hope individuals, as compared to their low-hope counterparts, are more inclined to plan alternative routes to achieve their goals (pathway) as well as being more capable of summoning resources to increase self-motivation to achieve goals despite obstacles (agency).

Protection

I have learned from my clinical psychology training that there exists a negative cognitive triad, including negative view of self, future, and world, among individuals with depression and other psychopathology (see publications by Aaron Beck, Judith Beck, and colleagues). Reducinging severity of the negative cognitive triad can alleviate psychological symptoms. Rick's 2002 workshop was the first time in my life to hear that clinical psychologists can help to facilitate a positive cognition to prevent psychological symptoms and to enhance well-being. I, therefore, reacted with skepticism, thinking that Rick just re-labeled some old concepts in positive terms to come up with a new model. But in the years following 2002, Rick and I happened to come across each other quite often in psychology meetings and conferences. We talked, became friends, and I learned more about what Rick was doing. Out of curiosity, I started conducting empirical studies to examine the role of hope in helping people cope with trauma, including cancer, traumatic medical procedures, and other life adversities.

In all my research, hope as a positive cognition and psychological strength turns out to be a key (and perhaps the most important) factor in protecting people from psychological distress while promoting resilience and growth. We have shown that **high-hope individuals**, when compared to their low-hope counterparts, tend to

1. **show more resilience** after traumatic encounters;
2. **exhibit less depressive and anxiety symptoms** in difficult situations;
3. **think less about suicide** when situations become hopeless; and
4. **perceive more positive changes** under adversities.

More resilience

Recently, I have been focusing on dissecting different components of goals in the hope model, and discovered that the following characteristics of goal setting should play an important role in the overall hope model.

1. **Goal dis-engagement.** High-hope people do not hold onto their previous goals but have a general tendency to let go of them when circumstances change. For example, a father who had set a goal to be a successful businessman but had quit his job to look after his son after learning that his child had autism.

2. **Goal re-engagement.** After dis-engaging from their previous goals, high-hope people have a tendency to re-engage into other goals that are more suitable to their present circumstances. The father I mentioned earlier enrolled in a postgraduate program to further his studies as well as started to write a book in his field of expertise.

3. **Sub-goaling.** High-hope individuals also tend to divide their final goals into smaller sub-goals. More than that, they have the capability to sustain efforts to overcome present difficulties for a higher goal. In sum, they are future-oriented and are more capable of looking beyond present adversities.

The above tendency of goal dis-engagement, goal re-engagement, sub-goaling, and future orientation enable high-hope individuals to have higher resilience and less psychological symptoms in even "hopeless" situations like terminal cancer and life imprisonment. The following figure summarizes our present conceptualization of hope.

The above figure shows that hope consists of three inter-related cognitive components: Goals, Agency, and Pathway as proposed by Snyder and colleagues (also see Shane J. Lopez in this volume). On top of these three components, we propose that there are three elements of Goals related to resilience. They are Sub-goaling, Goal Dis-engagement, and Goal Re-engagement. For Goal Re-engagement, one can set higher goals (Upward Re-goaling) or lower goals (Downward Re-goaling), depending on circumstances. The above cognitive style can enable one to adapt successfully to challenging situations.

Interventions

Despite the relatively stable nature in one's dispositional hope, hope can also be enhanced through systematic intervention programs. We have been doing hope-based interventions as a stand-alone (hope-only) program or as an enhancement of existing psychological intervention programs. Most recently, we have published three sets of hope story books (all in Chinese)—one for parents of deprived children, one for parents of children with special needs, and one for children suffering from cancer—for hope education and training. All books have received overwhelmingly positive feedback from users. I do believe that cultivating positive cognition like hope earlier in life would help our next generation face challenges better. Let's hope for a better future.

The keys

→ **Hope as a positive cognition and psychological strength turns out to be a key (and perhaps the most important) factor in protecting people from psychological distress while promoting resilience and growth.**

→ **The tendency of goal dis-engagement, goal re-engagement, sub-goaling, and future orientation enable high-hope individuals to have higher resilience and less psychological symptoms in even "hopeless" situations.**

→ **Despite the relatively stable nature in one's dispositional hope, hope can be enhanced through systematic intervention programs.**

Samuel M. Y. Ho, PhD, is a professor of psychology in the Department of Applied Social Sciences at the City University of Hong Kong (China). His primary research interest is in clinical health psychology, in developing an in-depth knowledge about factors facilitating people's adjustment to life-threatening illnesses (e.g. cancer) and traumatic events (e.g. major disaster). Most recently, Samuel has been developing experimental paradigms to examine the underlying cognitive mechanisms for people's response after life-threatening illnesses and traumatic events.

"Hope is positive anticipation with its sleeves rolled up."

Expanding our horizon of hope

She began her career as an elementary teacher working with children from poor neighborhoods in an inner city school. During her doctoral training she worked in a large regional cancer hospital. "In both contexts, hope fueled my work and became an enduring passion," says Prof. **Denise Larsen**. Now she is Director of Hope Studies Central at her university. Trying to find hope in the face of struggle, she is broadening our horizon of hope.

Those who suffer often believe deeply in hope, and psychotherapy researchers are beginning to understand the vast benefits of hope when working with those who suffer. The experience of hope is often intimately linked to struggle. We most often hope when the future looks questionable, even bleak. Nevertheless, having hope means that we are willing to become engaged and involved even when we are not sure we can make a difference. Becoming involved means that we experience hope in the moment and it may even increase the likelihood of our desired outcome. Finally, the positive emotion of hope means that we can remain more open to and aware of novel possibilities.

Here I focus on four simple but profound aspects of hope that can expand our horizon when facing difficulties, offering ways to find hope when the future seems dim. Though I write specifically about the psychotherapeutic context, these four aspects of hope transcend psychotherapy and offer possibilities in many circumstances.

1. **You are more than what you hope for.** So often hope becomes tied to a particular personal goal or success. We hope to achieve a good grade on a test. We hope to be offered a good job. We hope for a cure. When a particular hope is not met, hopes can be dashed. We can feel like a failure or that the world is not fair. A more stable focus for hope can be one's values and personal identity. Consider who you hope to be. What kind of a person do you hope to be? How are you already living out these values? How can you put more of who you hope to be into practice?

2. **Get hope from your interpretation of the past.** Why is it that some people seem to "bounce back" from difficulty so quickly while others do not? Research suggests that our sense of hope is linked to our past. Perhaps even more importantly *how* we remember our past is associated with how hopeful we are likely to be. What has happened to us is very important. However, where hope is concerned, *how* we remember the past may be even more important. *How* we remember our past provides evidence for what we believe is possible in the future. Every story is an edited story. We tell stories to convey information and to persuade our listeners. Importantly, we are listeners to our own stories. Consider your own stories. What information is remembered, included, or not? How are you choosing to tell your story? What do you hear yourself saying? What story from the past can offer evidence of hope for the future—no matter how small that story might be right now? Who can help you remember your hopeful stories?

3. **We are also hoping for others.** Reflecting on our own experiences will remind us that we hope for others as well as for ourselves. Indeed, those working with even young children will know that children sometimes offer their hopes for others unsolicited and aloud. We hope for others in many different ways. We hope for those close to us. We hope for those in need. We even hope for others we may have never met. Research suggests that patients look to health professionals for evidence of hope—a reason to keep going. A simple phrase offered by a therapist to a struggling client, "I have hope for you because…" offers evidence of caring and belief in the possibility of a good future. Hope can be shared. How might we share our hope for others when they are struggling to see hope for themselves? What might change if we explicitly shared the hope we have for others with them?

4. **Possibility more than probability.** Notice how often circumstances turn out better than you expect—even small things. You find a parking spot you had not expected.

You see a friend you had not planned to meet. You finish a task faster than you thought you could. Hope is about the possibility of good. Hope is different from optimism. Optimism is based on our assessment or expectation of something good. Being optimistic is easy. We are optimistic when we believe our desired outcome is likely. We see the outcome as probable. Hope is harder work. Hope is positive anticipation "with its sleeves rolled up." It is not about anticipating the things we know are likely to happen. We hope when we are uncertain about the outcome, but the outcome is so important that we are willing to work toward that better future. The mountain climber stuck in a crevice doesn't give up because she thinks her likelihood of rescue is low. She works more carefully, smarter, harder. The outcome is too important not to. The effort may pay off. This is the power of hope. It is the power of recognizing possibilities and our willingness to engage in hoping and working toward the good for ourselves and for others.

The keys

→ **A stable focus for hope is not what you hope for but who you hope to be, based on your own values and personal identity.**

→ **Our sense of hope is linked to our past. *How* we remember our past provides evidence for what we believe is possible in the future.**

→ **Reflecting on our own experiences will remind us that we hope for others as well as for ourselves. Hope can be shared.**

→ **The real power of hope is the power of recognizing possibilities and our willingness to engage in hoping and working toward the good for ourselves and for others.**

Denise Larsen is Professor of Counseling Psychology at the University of Alberta (Canada). She is Director of Hope Studies Central, a research center dedicated to the study of hope and development of hope interventions in applied contexts. She has published extensively on hope in psychotherapeutic and educational contexts. Awards include the Canadian Mental Health Assocation Ron Lajeunesse Award and the Silver Duncan and Craig Non-Profit Sector award. She is convinced that research on the effective use of hope in real life situations is a cause most worthy of her life's work.

"Hope is sustainable only through joy and delight in life."

Five commitments for the future

"We are living through a time that is as challenging to our humanity as any in recent years, a time that taxes the values of human understanding, mutual respect, and compassion," says Prof. **Martha C. Nussbaum**. "I want to say just a little about living through times that test, in particular, our values of respect and toleration, surrounded by an ugly politics of xenophobia and hate. We need to face our difficult future with at least five commitments. Hope is one of them."

I should say that I prefer the word "respect" to the word "toleration," because "toleration" suggests a hierarchy, in which a majority condescends to live with people whom it does not necessarily like; for that reason the first President of the United States, George Washington, rejected it. Writing to the Jewish congregation of Newport, Rhode Island, and assuring them that they had a respected place in the new nation, he said, "It is now no more that toleration is spoken of, as if it were by the indulgence of one class of people that another derived the enjoyment of their equal natural rights." So: respect, and equal natural rights. How to preserve all this, in these trying times?

I suggest that we need to face our difficult future with five commitments, all of which are very hard to maintain in a time of fear. It is the most solemn duty of our systems of education, at both school and university levels, to foster these values and the duty of journalists as well: Intelligence, Principled consistency, Imagination, Teamwork, and Hope.

1. Intelligence

We must look for the facts, and judge by the facts. We must not be stampeded by irresponsible voices into disregarding evidence or judging by crude stereotypes. One thing I mean by this is that we should all be learning a lot about the varieties of Islam in our world, so that we understand clearly how diseased and anomalous the version purveyed by terrorists is, and so that we know how we may treat our Muslim fellow citizens with respect. The majority needs to study its own history too: for example, we should become aware, when we talk about idolatry, that prohibitions against idolatry are prominent in Judaism and in Protestant Christianity, as well as in Islam, and that in both Judaism and Christianity these prohibitions have led to terrible acts of violence—for example, during the English civil war, when the Puritans destroyed representational art in churches and killed those who made it. We should also study Muslim nations in which Islam has undergone a liberal Enlightenment transformation; I mean in particular India and Indonesia, the two largest Muslim populations in the world.

But there are many other things to learn: the history of colonialism and the many-sided struggle against it; threats to the natural environment and the causes of global warming; the obstacles that nations face in trying to achieve a decent living standard. **These are just some of the topics that an informed "citizen of the world" will study,** and these studies must be offered to all students, in both schools and universities, not only to those who select history or environmental studies as their major subject.

As we learn all these things we must also learn to think critically and to test what we hear or learn for accuracy, for good reasoning, and so forth. We must, as Socrates said, lead the "examined life," not being bewitched by rhetoric, but looking for cogent arguments.

2. Principled consistency

We should judge others just exactly as we judge ourselves, and hold ourselves to the same rules that we impose on others. If we ban a form of Muslim dress on the grounds that it is long and bulky and therefore a security risk, then we should be equally concerned about Martha Nussbaum, who walks down Michigan Avenue in Chicago in her usual deep winter attire, which covers not only the whole body but the whole face except for the eyes— and even these are covered by special wind-protecting sunglasses. Terrorists typically seek to blend into the crowd; the Boston Marathon bombers wore baseball caps and carried backpacks. So the thought that we are safer if we demonize those who look different is not only offensive, it is stupid.

But in our pursuit of consistency we should move beyond the protection of our own security to decency and respect. Let me give a somewhat lighthearted example—but not so lighthearted, since sports are a huge influence on cultures and a central site in which moral values either are or are not enacted. The National Football League in the U.S. recently announced it was going to impose a fine on a Muslim player because he prayed after an especially good play, by kneeling on the ground. There is a rule against going on the ground after a play, I have no idea why, and they said he had violated that rule. But players and fans immediately pointed out that pious Christian players had always been exempt from that rule, being permitted to kneel on the ground in prayer; and they rightly demanded that the same treatment be given the Muslim player. I'm happy to say that the league backed down. So that's what I mean by principled consistency, and the need for it is everywhere we look in our plural societies, but it is not always honored.

3. Imagination

We are all born with the ability to see the world from points of view other than our own, but typically this ability is cultivated very unevenly and narrowly. We learn how the world looks from the point of view of our own family or local group, but we are ignorant of more distant viewpoints. To become good citizens of our complicated world, we should try to see the world from many different positions. Informed by our knowledge of history, we must ask how choices we make as voters and citizens affect the lives of many different sorts of people, and we can't do this well without seeing the world from their viewpoint. The cultivation of the imagination is one of the most important tasks of the educational system, which is why we need to strengthen, and not cut, programs in history, and literature, and philosophy (for I hope you will permit me to insist that philosophy is an imaginative discipline).

4. Teamwork

We live with others, but we often merely exist side by side, or, still worse, view others as competitors to be defeated. Humane values cannot prevail in our dangerous time unless people join together to address humanity's problems. And they must join together in ways that involve non-hierarchy, respect, and reciprocity. In fact, teamwork involves all of my first three values, for real reciprocity with others requires intelligent deliberation, it requires holding ourselves to norms of principled consistency, and it requires a constantly searching imagination. There is very little teamwork at the level of the modern nation.

Politics has become an activity in which each group tries to block or defeat the other, with no sense of common purpose. In my country, politicians who cooperate across party lines are attacked by their own party and often lose their jobs. This must stop if humanity's problems are to move closer to a solution.

5. Hope

This last value will sound odd to many. Where could hope come from in such a bleak time? And why indeed should we hope? Well, Immanuel Kant said that even when we see no grounds for hope we have a moral duty to cultivate hope in ourselves, so that we will maximize our efforts on behalf of humanity, and take any opportunity of advancing good values that the world may offer us. He did not say much, however, about where hope would and could come from, and he made the duty to hope sound like a grim business. I, however, would like to suggest that hope is sustainable only through joy and delight in life. So we need to remember to take pleasure in our friends and our community, to play as well as to work, indeed to enjoy the values of "rustic life" that have always mingled joy with effort, and commitment with fun. Hope is not about being grim and somber. It is about being playful and maybe rather silly. It is about dancing or painting. It is about pleasure and delight, and it is delight in life that sustains us, that makes us go on being loyal fans of respect and compassion and justice, as we try to overcome the obstacles we meet.

The keys

→ **We need to face our difficult future with five commitments, all of which are very hard to maintain in a time of fear.**

→ **These commitments are intelligence, principled consistency, imagination, teamwork, and hope.**

→ **Hope is not about being grim and somber. It is about pleasure and delight. It is delight in life that sustains us, as we try to overcome the obstacles we meet.**

Martha C. Nussbaum is Ernst Freud Distinguished Professor of Law and Ethics at the University of Chicago (USA). She is the author of numerous influential books, including *Upheavals of Thought: The Intelligence of Emotions*. She has forty honorary degrees from colleges and universities in North America, Europe, and Asia. The American magazine *Foreign Policy* named her one of the Top 100 Global Thinkers.